STRUCTURAL STITCHES

A MACHINE KNITTER'S GUIDE TO CREATING FORM AND TEXTURE

Victoria Salmon

STRUCTURAL STITCHES

A MACHINE KNITTER'S GUIDE TO CREATING FORM AND TEXTURE

THE CROWOOD PRESS

CONTENTS

INTRODUCTION

This book has been written with the intention of helping you to develop your machine knitting skills outside the stereotypical use of the knitting machine. To delve into textures, form and three-dimensional techniques that create intricate and geometric knits. It will be a comprehensive guide to several different techniques and structures to increase your knowledge, also including different yarns and their properties, and methods and tips to progress your knitting skills. You may not use all the techniques, but they should serve as inspiration to see what can be achieved on a domestic machine.

It has always fascinated me just how much texture we can develop through the manipulation of the stitches on the machine, and also the vast array of techniques. Having been a tutor, technician, teacher and everything in between, the idea of spreading knowledge of a skilled craft that is still very niche is something I feel strongly about. We should not harbour knowledge to keep techniques to ourselves because it is something we feel that we own since no one else is doing something similar; we need to spread the ideas and the skills not only to keep machine knitting alive, but to expand the knowledge of others who can elevate it further and push the boundaries continuously.

We will look at existing techniques that you may already know, but we will delve further into them, exploring methods and structures that will enable you to incorporate more texture and form into your knitted pieces. We will also cover different types of yarns that can elevate your knit, how to use them, and when it may be necessary to use them to achieve quality results that match the technique you are working with.

OPPOSITE: A self-supporting piece of knit which is made using a combination of techniques found in this book.

The techniques that are covered work really well for interiors and for those who are interested in texture incorporated within textiles. Development for garments is of course an option; however, it is not a focus within the book. The structures worked within this book will provide an introduction and a basic exploration into the methods. Once you have grasped the basics, you are encouraged to further develop your knowledge by continuing to experiment with the methods shown.

The very basics of machine knitting, such as casting on and off, are not covered within this book. Therefore it is advised that you know and understand the fundamentals of machine knitting before starting the methods presented. The basics of each technique are covered at the beginning of each chapter to ease you in slowly. From there on, the techniques will develop further and become more challenging.

EXPLORATION AND EXPERIMENTATION

My personal inspiration comes from geometry and symmetry, as you will see throughout the knitted samples – particularly with those that create three-dimensional elements. That does not necessarily mean that you need to follow suit with your ideas and patterns, and I fully encourage more organic shapes to be explored, considering this is something that my own mind struggles with. Exploration, experimentation and constant questioning of methods are key to the development of your own work. This development is also achieved by playing through a variety of yarn choices and accepting mistakes made, learning why the knit fell off the machine when it did – because, let's be honest, it happens to us all, including myself. Just sigh, swear loudly and cast back on again.

HOW TO USE THIS BOOK

In-depth descriptions for each technique and sample are written out for you to follow, along with charts for most samples. Variations of the techniques have been described and written to encourage you to explore and experiment with the basic samples, but also to show what is possible with the basic methods.

You do not need to work through the book from the first chapter to the last, as the chapters introduce individual form-making methods rather than work through a progression of techniques that build from the very first chapter. However, I would suggest starting at the beginning of a given chapter and working through the basic samples to progress. Whilst it might seem obvious to say this, I am someone who flicks through a book and settles on an inspiring technique then tries to knit it without reading up first how it was made – therefore creating complications and challenges for myself. I hope that within this book I have explained the basics well enough that you can begin to make your own decisions and design choices to develop the samples included and bring them into your own knitting world.

Each chapter is a method or technique in its own right, and starts with the basics then progresses further into more complex ideas and suggestions for the basic method. Start with whichever chapter you feel comfortable with and explore the different elements in your own way. There are a few rules that may need to be followed for some methods, but rules are also made to be broken, and I fully suggest pushing them to the limit of your machine's capacity to really see what is possible and where the techniques can go.

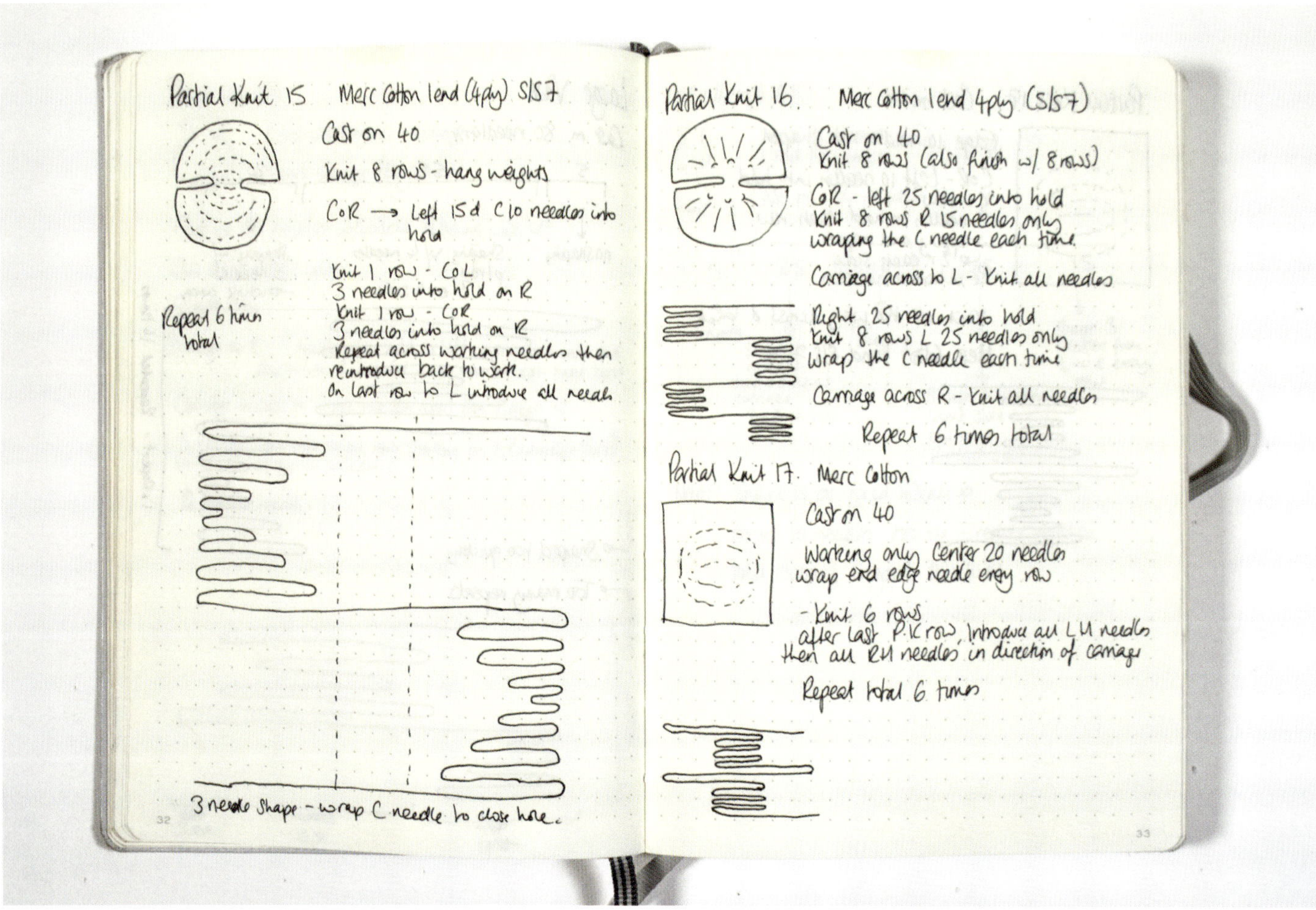

An image of the notebook that the author used in the process of writing this book. All thoughts, notes and techniques were written down and drawn out. A notebook is her most favoured tool when developing knitting techniques.

I would also suggest that a notebook becomes your go-to tool whilst developing techniques. I cannot live without mine. Whether it is to draw out pattern ideas, write down notes or problem-solve. I almost encourage you to turn this book into a notebook of your thoughts and alterations to the patterns, therefore keeping your ideas, concepts and notes in one place that you can refer back to later if you wish to revisit a particular technique or idea.

Lastly, I also advise you to keep things simple and to try not to over-complicate the design or method you are trying to learn. Many of the best knitted garments or pieces that I have seen are derived from a very simple technique using very simple yarns. Understated yet beautifully knitted items are more eye-catching than something that has every single technique and yarn under the sun thrown at it. Be selective yet explorative and the knit will speak for itself.

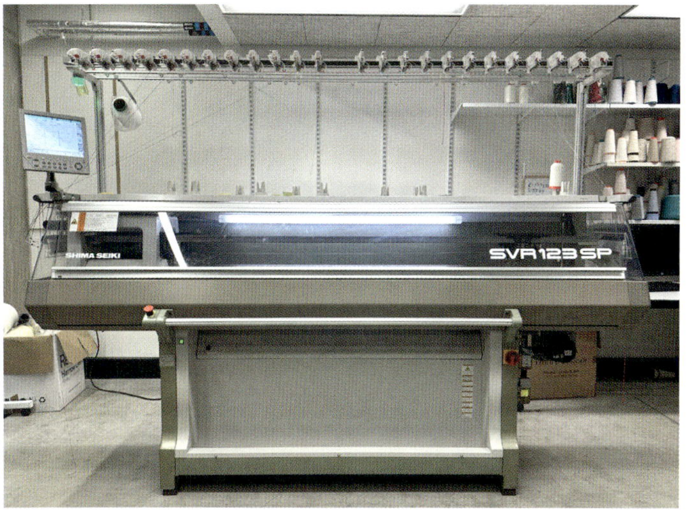

A Shima Seiki flatbed machine that is programmed and then knits out automatically. Every element of the knit needs to be confirmed and determined prior to knitting, compared to the hand machines where you can evolve and alter the knit as you go.

THE MODERN DEVELOPMENT OF KNIT

The potential for knit as a material is being explored more widely outside the typical use of creating garments on needles. Knitted structures are gaining momentum within medical and scientific fields with purposes such as knitted stents and garments with sensors to monitor a patient's vital signs; in the automotive industry with uses for car fittings; and in interiors for climate control, acoustics and temperature control.

The development of the knitting machine from the humble domestic machine, still loved and appreciated in today's craft world, has now progressed to much more complex and intricate industrial machines that are capable of knitting 24 hours a day, seven days a week, churning out garments for the fashion and textile industry.

The flatbed machines have been developed to accommodate knitting a whole garment in one process, ready to wear straight off the machine. Some machines no longer only have two beds but four, to allow for intricate stitch structures and shaping to be included within these whole garments. This means that no assembly after knitting is needed, yet the complex structures worked on a double bed can be integrated. The knitted whole-garment development cuts out waste and construction time, improving sustainable practice.

Simulating knitted material and garments cuts down on the sampling process within the fashion industry, which encourages it to become more sustainable. Simulation on Shima Seiki software APEXFiz.

Today's technology also allows us to simulate knitted material that was once problematic to imitate virtually due to its elasticity. Yarns of all qualities are also being simulated along with structures, which fundamentally allows designers to create vast ranges of garments in different yarns and colour schemes without knitting a single sample.

Aside from flatbed knitting machines, there are also the technologies to create circular knitted material formed by large spinning drums with thousands of individual needles knitting simultaneously and several cones of yarn, through to warp knitting machines that can very quickly build up high-density materials for sportswear. These machines are generally used for jersey material, or large knitted lengths for cutting and sewing, but some machines have been developed that can knit with metal yarns for electrically conductive material.

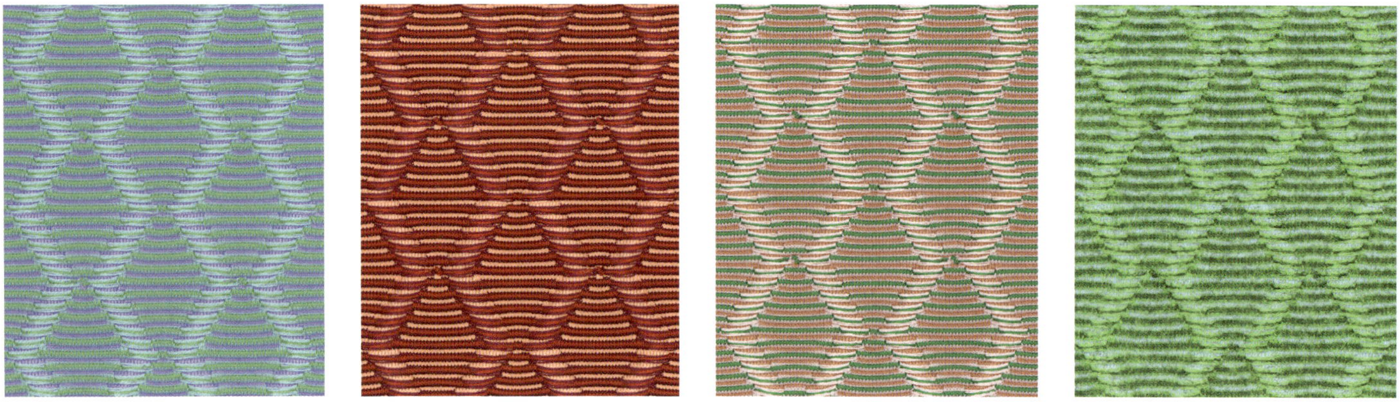

Knit simulation also allows you to simulate structures and textures for textiles and create a variety of colour schemes using different yarn qualities, as in these four samples. Here you can see variety in terms of colours but also in yarn qualities.

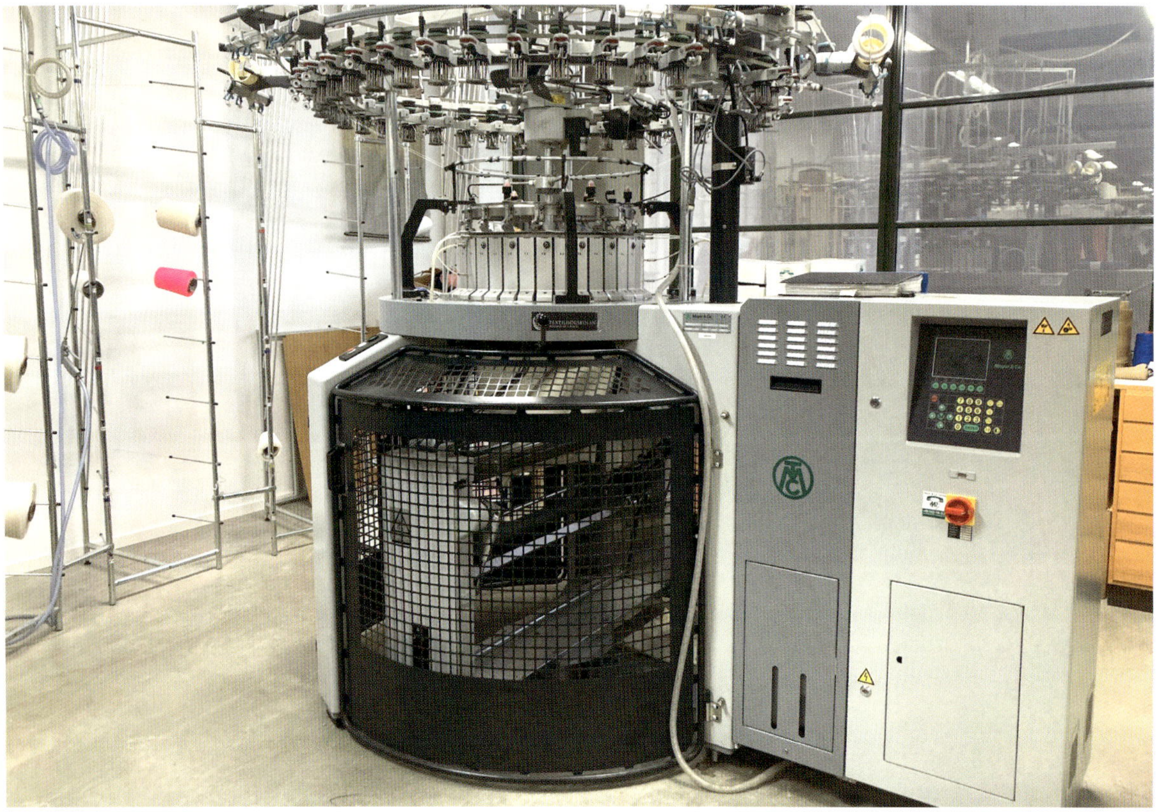

The metal Mayer & Cie circular knitting machine in the Swedish School of Textiles, Borås. It is one of only five in the world that have been adapted to handle stiff and wire yarns due to special Relanit sinkers that move in the opposite direction to the needle, lessening the strain on the yarn when the stitch is created.

MACHINE INFORMATION

Domestic Knitting Machines

For the majority of the techniques seen in this book I use a Silver Reed SK840 or SK280 along with the SRP60N ribber attachment for the double-bed techniques. This is a standard-gauge domestic knitting machine. All the techniques are transferable over to similar machines such as those by Brother, Knitmaster and Passap. If you are unsure at any point on the functions of your machine for techniques such as partial knit, or which parts of the carriage need to be engaged for that particular technique, it is suggested that you check your machine manual as these elements will not be covered in depth within the book. Not all techniques will need a ribber attachment, and some techniques, such as partial knit, are only being explored on the single bed. This allows you to work to your abilities and your machine's capability.

V-Bed Knitting Machines

Some of the techniques explored within this book will be worked on a semi-industrial V-bed knitting machine. This type of machine was used in industry to create a variety of materials in a much larger range of gauges, from 2.5gg through to 14gg, but the machines are no longer manufactured today. All of these machines that are currently being sold or in use are refurbished. The Dubied company is the most commonly known manufacturer; other makers include Universal and Stoll. Where the use of a V-bed machine is stated for the technique, this means either a Dubied, Universal or Stoll semi-industrial machine rather than the double-bed domestic machine.

All techniques shown on the V-bed machines are transferable to the domestic machines with a ribber attachment. However, not all techniques from the domestic machines are transferable to the V-bed machines. It will be stated where and how to transfer the techniques onto the V-bed machines. This is mainly due to the ability to needle-select with the domestic machines but not with the V-bed machines. Note that Passap machines come under domestic machines for their ability to work partial knit.

The Silver Reed domestic knitting machine is a machine suitable for home knitting for garment and textile construction. This is the set-up for the author's machine: raised up on a standing table rather than the standard knitting-machine table.

The carriage of the Dubied machine.

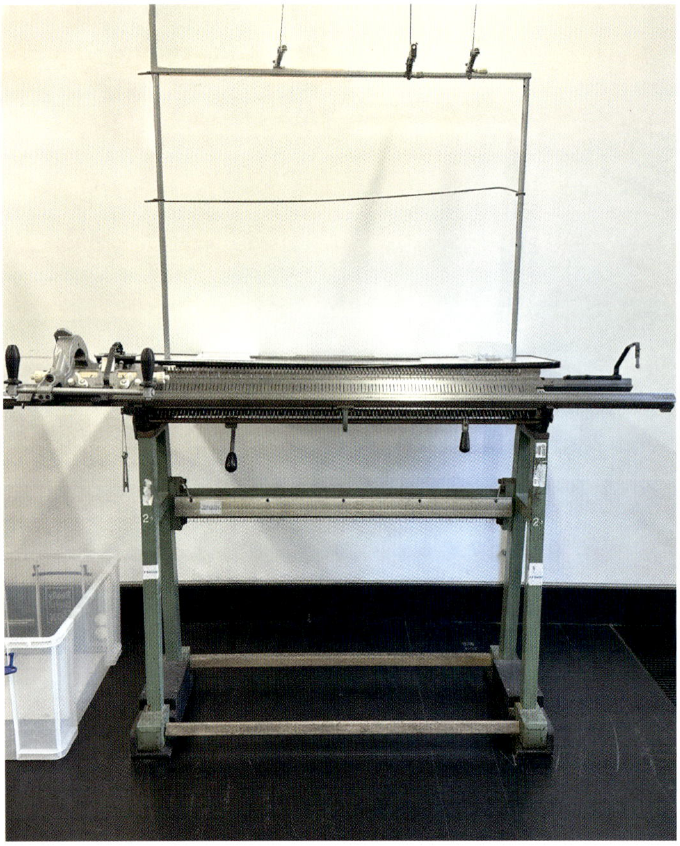

The Dubied knitting machine is a V-bed knitting machine that is used for industrial knitting of garments but it is also suitable for home knitting, for those lucky enough to have the space. It comes in a large variety of gauges and lengths of bed.

CHARTS

Charts have been used in this book to illustrate the technical drawings of the knit and to help you understand the instructions. They will show the needle placement for a particular sample, or the direction of the carriage. Where necessary, colour coding will be used to help clarify a change of yarn or needle position.

Keys within the charts will aid your understanding. There will be slight differences between the charts, depending on the chapter you are reading. Sometimes a change of colour within the chart will represent a change of yarn, but sometimes it represents a change of needle bed. Please refer to the individual chart that you are working with and its caption rather than assume that it is the same as a previous chart.

Each chart is made with a graph of squares. One square generally represents one stitch, with a bolder line every fifth row and column. This should make it easier to read and to count the stitches and rows as you progress through the charts.

Each chart will show a repeat of a pattern. For the smaller patterns this may already include a repeat or two, but for the larger patterns there will only be one repeat. Repeat the pattern across the horizontal and the vertical to create a larger piece.

It is important to note that the images of the samples will be mirrored to the charts in most cases. This is especially true for Chapter 1 as the single bed will be mainly used for all samples. As the material will come off the machine facing away from you, the positioning of the structure will therefore be on the opposite side to the side you have been working on. Be sure to recognise the difference and understand that the charts may look mirrored to the image.

YARNS

Yarn choice will become increasingly important throughout the chapters of this book to achieve the same results that I have demonstrated. That is not to say that we can only use specific yarns with specific techniques, but more to advise that some techniques work better with certain yarns. All techniques can be achieved with all yarns; however, the final result may vary.

Within a design, it is very often the yarn choice that creates the textile. The material can be one of the simplest knitted structures but, with the right yarn choice, the structure is elevated and made into something more enticing. It is good practice to work some basic samples in a waste yarn, or a yarn that is not important or expensive, until you are comfortable with the technique, therefore not wasting the yarn that you will use for the final piece.

Below I talk through a few yarns which are very common in my own practice and my own work as I feel these are the yarns that I get the best results with. They are not the only yarns I use, and I also suggest testing and trialling other yarns that may be more suited to your own work and practice.

Wool has been a fibre of choice for knitting for many hundreds of years, due to its natural insulative properties. This hand-knitted wool jumper is made in an Aran-weight wool.

Natural Yarns

There is a large group of natural yarns that are worked on knitting machines, from traditional wool, cashmere, silk and cotton yarns through to yarns which are becoming more commonplace, such as bamboo and flax, and on to more unusual yarns that are still being developed, for example seaweed yarn and paper yarn. I will highlight a few natural yarns that I use frequently within my own work, and that are the most easily obtainable for other machine knitters. This is to showcase the yarns' benefits and also their qualities on the knitting machine rather than each yarn's characteristics.

Wool

Wool is one of the (if not the) most traditional and sustainable yarns available for knitting. Wool has many characteristics that allow it to be breathable, insulating, warm, water-repellent, fire-resistant and self-cleaning. It can be spun for fine-gauge machines, for example merino for luxury garments, or left unspun for chunky hand-knitted pieces.

'Wool' is an umbrella term for most fibres that come from an animal (such as a sheep, alpaca or goat) that has to be annually shorn.

Wool can also be felted as a post-knit process. Felting wool enables it to become much more stable and thick. This process is used for materials for interior sound insulation and temperature control. Felted wool fabric can be produced without the need for it to be knitted or woven (non-woven material), and once felted the material will not fray or unravel. Similarly, a knitted piece that has been felted can be cut and the material will not unravel.

Wool is generally very easy to knit with. It has a very slight stretch, meaning the yarn can handle smaller stitch sizes and more tension placed upon it, making it an ideal first yarn to work with, or a great yarn to test out ideas. It is very accommodating.

Cotton

Cotton can be seen as a 'hard' yarn. With relatively little stretch and often quite a high twist, this yarn can prove quite difficult to work through the machine, and certainly works the arm muscles. You will find that you often need to increase the stitch size when working with this yarn. This is, however, also a very accommodating first yarn to work with. There are many finishes to the yarn that can also offer additional qualities. Combed cotton has the most stretch for cotton yarn and is a great basic yarn to use. Mercerised cotton has an additional sheen that adds a visual lustre to the final material which, for some techniques, can highlight the structure.

In this piece created with undyed cotton, Hedda Börresen used cotton to create undulating ripples and floats as part of a body of work. Plying up the yarn, the floats of cotton have become soft, giving movement to the knit, whilst the ripples incorporate a structured form.

Linen

A hard yarn with a lot of drape, this yarn is best for summer knits to help keep you cool in the warmer weather. It can also be blended with another yarn to increase the yarn properties or durability of the material, and is most commonly blended with cotton.

Synthetics

Often deemed as unsustainable and bad for the planet, this large umbrella of yarn types has gained a bad reputation. However, these yarns can be some of the best for knitting. Not only are they great for knitters on a budget, they also come in many types suitable for a variety of machines and techniques. They are easy to work with, strong and have a very subtle stretch that the knitting machine favours.

Yes, there is the sustainability factor that plays a large part in the discussion of synthetic materials and their impact on the environment and awareness of this; but considering that you have bought this book to develop your knitting skills, you are probably not going into mass production, so synthetic yarns can be a great choice to begin with. A few examples are explained below.

Acrylic

Acrylic is one of the most common synthetic yarns that is used for machine knitting. Often used for hand knitting and bought in balls, once spun into a cake from a yarn winder it is suitable for use on a machine. Also relatively cheap, the variety of available yarns for machine knitting can reduce the cost for those who like to experiment on a budget, or for those first tests to master a technique or become comfortable with your machine. Acrylic-mix yarns are often the ones I find on cones in charity or second-hand shops, which therefore are naturally the ones I use when trying out a new technique; this is often how I work out shapes and patterns before reworking again in the final yarns.

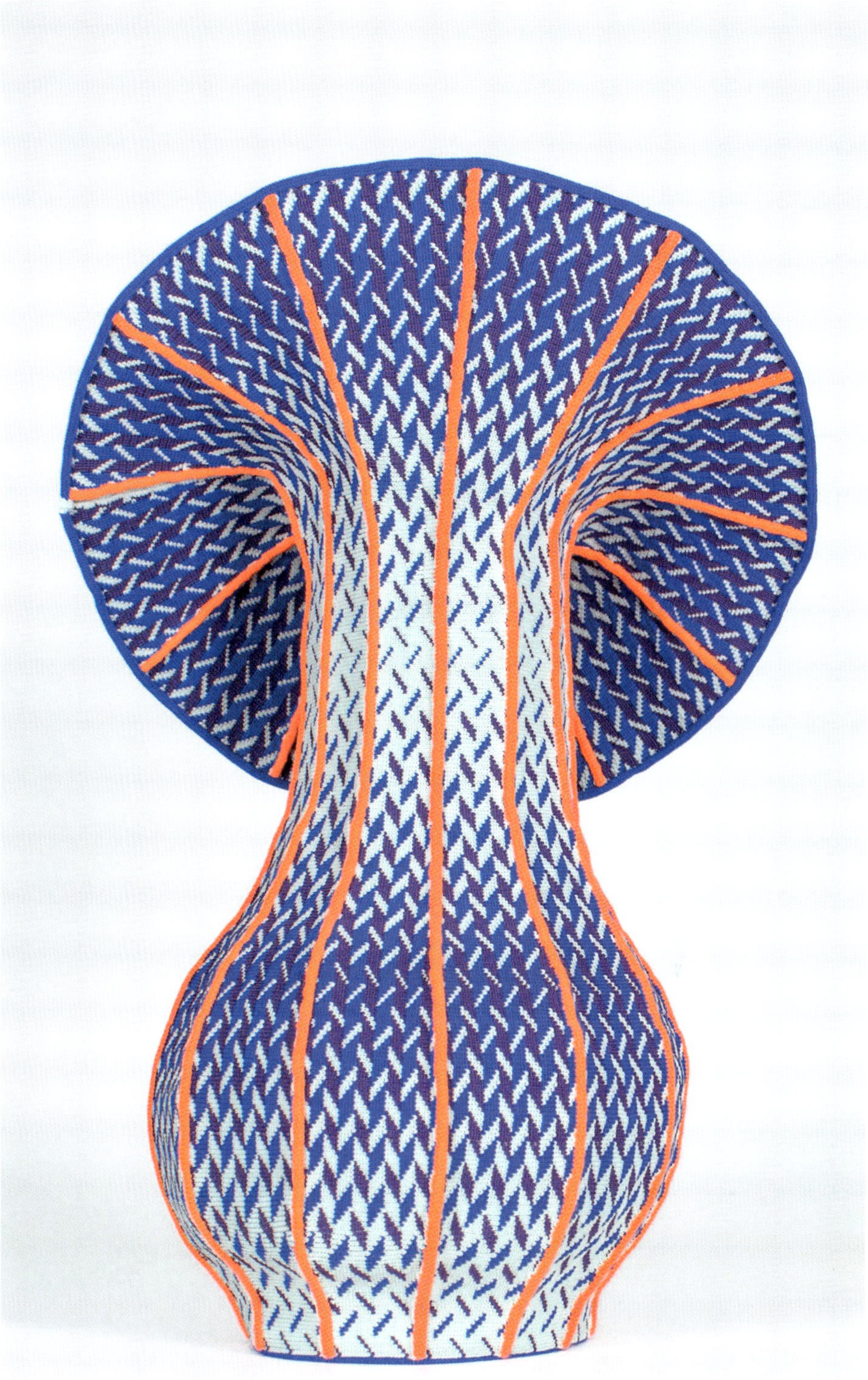

As his main yarn, Gaspard Fleury-Dugy works with polymide (discussed overleaf) with both partial knit and a Jacquard to create structural forms resulting in beautiful knitted vases. The polyamide can incorporate the necessary high density and tightness into the knit. The forms would not work so well with a natural yarn due to its lower density and tightness.

Polyamide (Nylon)

A polyamide or polyester is a yarn type that often silently graces our garments, especially socks, and it actually works wonders for the knit samples that need a little more density and strength. These yarns shrink slightly once steamed, aiding the density of the knitted material if one is knitting a structural piece, but they can also contribute to the overall expression due to their multifilament structure. You will see how they play more of a role in aesthetics in Chapter 2: Lifted Stitches and Ottoman.

Elastane

A great yarn to incorporate alongside your main yarn, or to use completely on its own, elastane adds strength to knit and increased elasticity, but also an additional density that I have yet to find replicated with another yarn. It is most often used as an additive to garments to give the textile structure, support and density. Sometimes it is used on its own to create restrictive garments or compression pieces, and it can also be used in a textile to create shape and form within the structure.

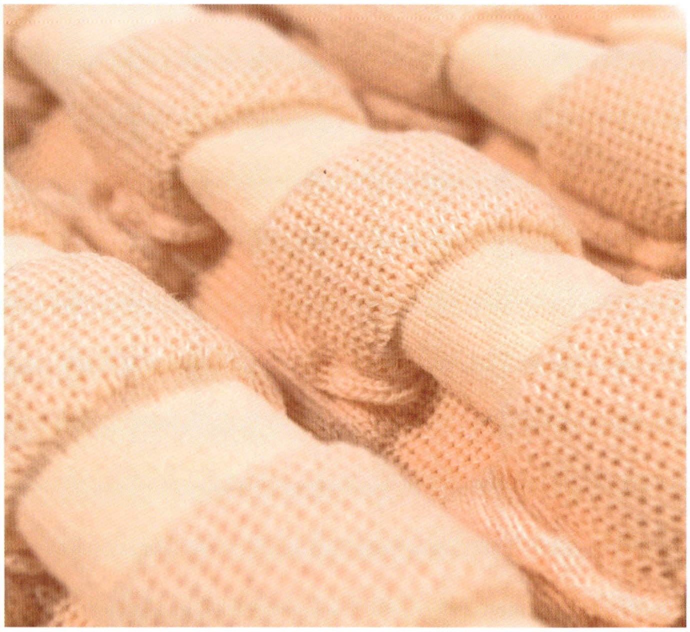

A tubular Jacquard knitted on the Shima Seiki machine with a wool–cotton blend and a Lycra shirring elastic. This very easily creates form and shape outside of the typical flat surface seen in a Jacquard. The Lycra constricts the material, shrinking the areas it has been knitted into and leaving the secondary yarn to bulge and form.

Although not an actual image of the thermoplastic, this shows an example of the properties that thermoplastic yarn can provide as an additive to natural yarns. Thermoplastic has been plated with the main yarns to help the structure support itself. This allows the knit to stand upright rather than drape like a conventional knitted material.

Thermoplastic

Finally, thermoplastic yarn. A relatively new yarn that, once heated to relatively low temperatures, will shrink to around 40 per cent of its original size. This yarn will essentially convert into a hard plastic once activated by steam, which allows for structure and strength to be included in more extreme knitted forms and shapes. It is used much more within industry for form-making and shape retention, but is now becoming more accessible within research and craft.

Yarn Counts

Throughout this book, where possible I have stated the counts of the yarn used in the samples to help you understand the weights of the yarns that I have used.

NM

'Numero Metric' yarn count. This states how many 1,000m of yarn there are per 1kg in weight. Therefore if the yarn states 1/16NM, it is one twisted strand of a yarn that has 16,000m to 1kg of yarn. If the count is 2/30NM, this means there are two strands of yarn twisted together with a weight of 30,000m to 1kg of yarn. The numerator within the yarn count is always the number of ends spun together, and the denominator is the yarn weight.

NE

'Number English' yarn count. This is generally a cotton count and comes from imperial measurements, hence its use in the UK and USA. Similar to the NM count, as the denominator increases, the size of the yarn (width) decreases, and the numerator signifies how many strands are spun together. The denominator is the number of times that the yardage in 1lb weight of yarn can be divided by 840 (the number of yards in one hank). If the count is 2/16NE, this means two strands of a yarn that each have 13,440yd in 1lb.

Therefore, a 1/16NE cotton yarn is a very similar weight to a 1/28NM yarn. Translating the 1/16NE to an NM count, there would be 13,440yd to 1lb of yarn (16 × 840 = 13,440). As 13,440yd is equal to 12,289m, and 1lb is 0.45kg, you multiply length in metres by 2.2 to calculate the yardage in 1kg, which is just over 29,500yd. If it were 2/16NE, this just means there are two strands twisted together and it does not affect the weight. Therefore 2/16NE is a very similar yarn weight to a 2/28NM; and 3/16NE is very similar to 3/28NM, and so on.

Decitex

Applied most often to synthetic yarns and yarns used within mass production, this indicates how many grams of yarn there are in 10km of length. This is due to these yarns being much finer and lighter in weight than the natural yarns.

Ply

Whilst this does not give the exact measurement of a yarn, it can tell you how many ends (or strands) of yarn have been plied together to make that yarn. For example, a 4-ply yarn has four ends spun together to create the yarn.

- 1-ply: equivalent to one end of yarn, around 2/30NM or higher.
- 2-ply: equivalent to one end of 2/16NM yarn or two ends of 2/30NM or higher.
- 3-ply: equivalent to one end of 2/12NM, two ends of 2/28NM or three ends of 2/30NM or higher.
- 4-ply: equivalent to one end of 2/8NM, two ends of 2/16NM, three ends of 2/28NM or four ends of 2/30NM or higher.

Please note that where yarns have been measured in ply in the samples featured in the book, this is either the ply given on the cone or from the yarn suppliers, or an approximate ply based on the number of ends within the yarn.

CHAPTER 1

PARTIAL KNIT

The process of partial knit is my go-to technique to create dimension and structure within a knit piece. It is simple, effective and has endless variations of techniques, usages and final results. It was the method that started my intrigue into dimensional knit samples, and is the technique I immediately jump to when developing three-dimensional structures.

'Partial knit', 'short rows' and 'holding' are different names for the same technique: the process of choosing directly which stitches you want to work over, whilst leaving the remaining stitches in hold or in rest. Working with domestic machines, this is achieved through needle selection. This process builds up material in specific areas, or where the needles are still working, to shape the fabric away from the standard rectangle, or to create three-dimensional textiles.

In this chapter we will quickly recap the basic workings and structures of partial knit before moving on to more complex shapes. We will look at taking the knit out of the basic flat rectangle shape to create a more fluid and structural piece. It is then suggested that you test and experiment with combinations of your favourite partial-knit techniques from this book along with other knitted techniques to make unique and creative pieces.

PARTIAL KNIT AND V-BED MACHINES

Partial knit cannot be achieved on a V-bed machine using the same method as a domestic machine. For domestic machines, the needles are moved up into a position away from the needle guides within the carriage, which means the needles are bypassed when the carriage is passed across the needle bed. V-bed machines do not have this position in the carriage, therefore if we were to move the needles into the forward working position similar to a domestic machine, they would only be brought back into the working position and the stitches dropped when the carriage is passed.

To knit partial knit on a Dubied machine, we can only work with a single jersey and techniques are limited. Stitches to be held would have to be transferred over to the opposite needle bed with that side of the carriage turned off, meaning only one bed is in action and the stitches to be held are transferred to the other bed that is not in work. The weight on the knit can prove problematic in keeping the stitches at the bottom of the stem of the needle when the needle moves, and it is harder to rescue dropped stitches. Therefore it is not recommended to work partial knit on these machines unless you are very familiar with the technique and the workings of V-bed machines.

OPPOSITE: Mirrored partial knit sections create an intricate surface pattern and knitted structure.

SUGGESTED YARNS

Yarn choice for partial knit relates to the type of yarn you prefer to work with and what you would like the resulting material to be made from. There will, of course, be some instances where a certain type of yarn might have a better effect, for example a shrinking yarn might exaggerate a three-dimensional shape; however, it is down to personal choice. If there is a specific yarn that I feel would give a technique a better result, it will be stated in the instructions; otherwise, use whichever yarn you feel most comfortable knitting with.

A QUICK RECAP OF THE BASICS

For the basics of partial knit, you will need to engage the hold position of the carriage. Once in position, any needle that is then pushed out into the forward working position (the 'D' position for Silver Reed machines, the 'E' position for Brother machines) or hold, will remain in that position when the carriage passes the working needles. This means that those needles will not knit, and only the needles in the normal working position, or the 'B' position, will be knitted. If you are unsure how your carriage is to be placed into hold, please consult your user manual. Generally, for Silver Reed machines this is done by using the Russel levers on each side of the carriage, and for Brother machines by using the button located on top of the carriage.

Partial knit is often used when shaping shoulders or necklines on garments, and godets in skirts. As there are no garment patterns within this book, we will focus on creating fabric shape and texture with partial knit, rather than garment detailing. However, any technique in this book can be implemented into garments or garment details.

Needles can be brought in and out of the hold position at any time during the knitting process. There are some rules that make for a cleaner knit, which are explained further on in this chapter, but generally speaking it is a very free and exploratory technique that quickly builds up form and shape.

Once the desired number of needles have been brought out into hold, the hold levers can be returned to the normal knitting setting, and with that last pass of the carriage all needles will be brought back into work. Alternatively, you can push each needle back into the upper working position (UWP), or 'C' position, and the carriage will automatically re-knit that needle, placing it back into work. To make clean knits, please read the box 'A General Rule for Partial Knit to Avoid Floats' later in this chapter, as this may be useful later on.

To select needles that are not to be knitted, therefore holding the stitches, bring the chosen needles out into the hold position. Here you can see that several needles on the right-hand side of the working area are in the FWP; therefore, when the carriage passes them, they will not knit and the carriage will only knit the needles on the left in the working position.

This shows that the number of needles in the hold position has increased by ten. The number of needles placed into hold or back in the working position can be as many or as few as desired, depending on the pattern that is being knitted. It is advised that the needles placed into hold are always adjacent to each other rather than randomly across the bed, to ensure that no unwanted floats are created.

If this is something you have yet to play with, then I suggest a quick experiment on the machine to test out the holding levers and watch what the needles do. You can practise this without yarn to avoid getting in a tangle if you are unsure.

Basic Shaping

We can work a couple of basic partial-knit shaping techniques to start with, to begin to explore how we can use partial knit not only to create shape within a piece, but also to introduce pattern and colour.

This first sample will begin to explore beyond the standard rectangle shape. We will work with partial knit to create a curved sample which is constructed by building up a series of triangles on one side of the working area.

Cast on 30 needles with yarn A and knit a few rows to establish some single jersey. With the carriage on the right-hand side, change to yarn B and place the carriage into hold. Starting on the left-hand side of the working area, bring 2 needles out into the hold position for every row knitted, until there are no needles left to bring out into the hold position, ending with the carriage on the right.

Bring the hold levers out of work and knit 2 rows with all needles knitting to reintroduce all the needles back into work. The carriage should finish on the right-hand side. Change back to yarn A and repeat the above.

A basic sample that alters the shape of the knit by building up material on one side of the working area through the use of partial knit. *Yarn A: Green 2/15NM wool. Yarn B: Lilac, three ends of 2/48NM wool–cotton blend. Tension: 6.*

The usual method to bring needles back into action is to simply move them back into the UWP, which is about 1cm (3⁄8in) back from the FWP. This will automatically reintroduce the needles as the carriage passes, knitting them.

A secondary method is to use a transfer tool to manually rehang the stitches back onto the needle hooks. This is more time-consuming but it ensures that the stitches do not drop. This method must be used when working with a punch card or patterning method when colourwork is involved.

Take note that, as the fabric builds up on the right-hand side through the rows, the weight will need to be adjusted to accommodate it. Ensure the weight is lifted up and rehung on the knit at least for every triangle knitted, otherwise work the weight manually by hand by holding the knit down out of the way of the needles in place of weights.

The change of colour will allow you to see the shaping area of the knit, and to see that the fabric built up is created on the areas where the needles are still in work. This build-up of material will form a triangular shape on the right-hand side.

Because we are taking needles out into hold with every row, we do not need to wrap the last working needles as no shaping hole will be made. Instead, there will be a very small float on the underside, every other shaping row, to show that the carriage missed two needles as they had been brought into hold.

Alternating Sides

To further explore this basic technique, we can work partial knit in exactly the same way but changing the side where the needles have been brought out into hold. You will still be able to see the shaping of the piece through partial knit, and the colour blocking through needle selection, but the build-up of stitches on opposite sides will even out the shape of the piece, returning it to a standard rectangle.

Again, cast on with 30 needles and establish the knit, finishing with the carriage on the right-hand side. Next, with yarn B and working from the left-hand side of the working needles, bring 2 needles out for every row knitted, in exactly the same method as the previous sample. Once you have reached the end and the carriage has finished on the right-hand side, knit 2 rows of all-needle knit to reintroduce all the needles that are in hold back into the working position.

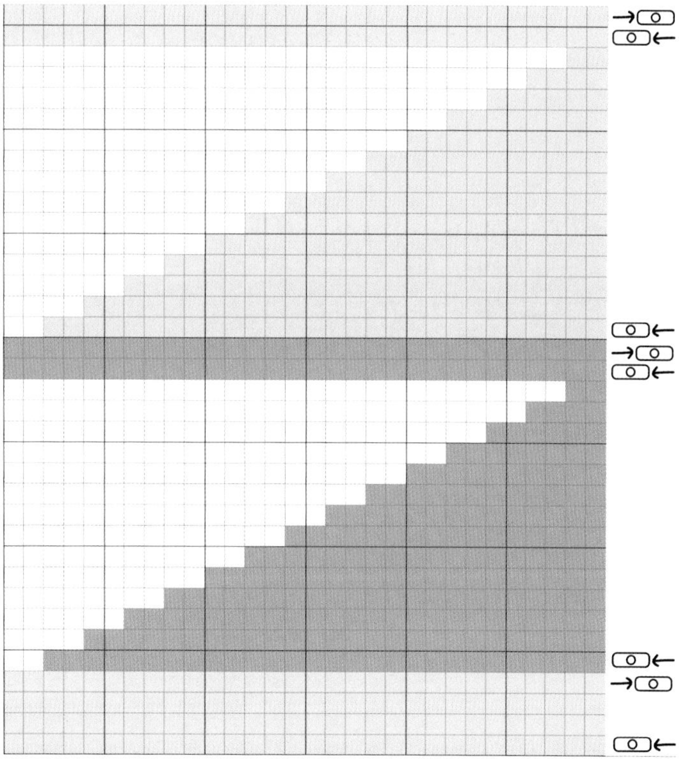

To illustrate the working area of the yarn over the needles that are used through the partial-knit shaping, we show the course of the yarn in this way. This graphic shows the course of the yarn over the needles through the squared grid, rather than the stitches that have been made. We will be using this type of graphic for most of the partial-knit samples to illustrate the working areas.

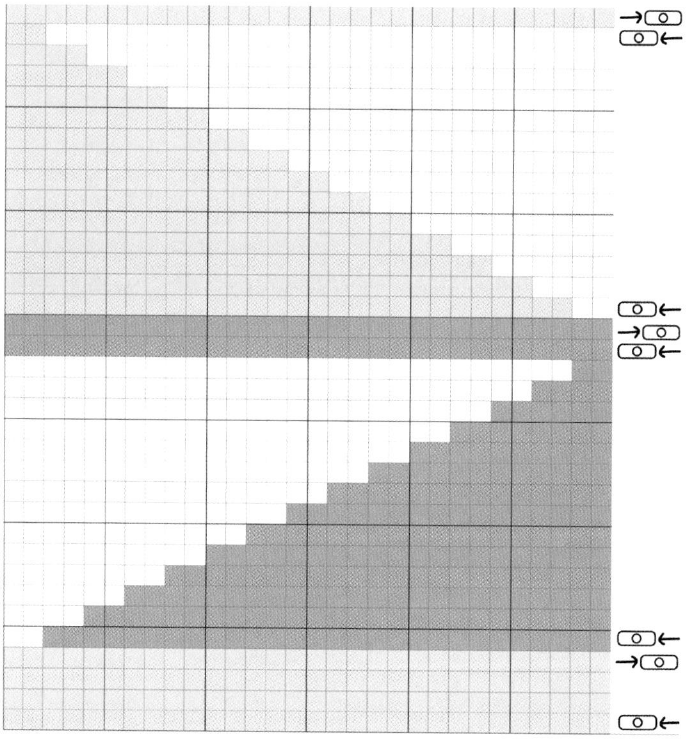

The direction of the yarn and carriage when the side the knit is shaped on is altered. The change of yarn is represented by the different shades. The knit evens itself out.

Altering the side of the shaping will alter the shape. In this instance, the triangle made through partial knit becomes evened out through the second triangle made on the opposite side. *Yarn A: Green 2/16NM wool. Yarn B: Lilac, three ends 2/48NM wool–cotton blend. Tension: 6.*

Change back to yarn A. For the next section, again place 2 needles into hold for every row knitted. This time, start from the right-hand side. Work across the working needles until the last needles have been brought into hold; this time, the carriage needs to finish on the left-hand side. If this means working one row that will not knit any needles but is purely to pass the carriage to the left, then this is okay. With the carriage on the left, work one row with all needles knitting to reintroduce them into the working position, finishing with the carriage back on the right-hand side.

Repeat these two steps as many times as needed. For each time the build-up of material begins to turn the knit, the following partial knit section, worked from the opposite side of the working area, will generally even the material back to a straight piece.

Carriage Direction and Hold Position

It is important to understand the direction of the carriage and the needles that are in the hold position. If, for example, we have the carriage on the right-hand side and our last working needles are on the left with a section of held needles in the middle, we need to work a row to get the carriage back to the left. We essentially move groups of needles on the opposite side of the carriage to avoid creating large floats.

A rule that I teach when covering the basics of partial knit is always: 'the last needle knitted should be the first needle to knit'. It is possible to skip a needle or two as a few needles off is of no concern and will only create a small float. However, if it looks like there will be a large jump of needles before the next working needle, it would be advisable to double-check the positioning of the carriage and the needles that are being brought back into work. An extra row knitted will have very little effect in the overall scheme of the technique, but will get the carriage to the correct side.

Please see the box 'A General Rule for Partial Knit to Avoid Floats' later in this chapter for more information.

Rate of Shaping

The rate at which the shaping is made is completely up to you, the knitter. The more needles that are brought out into the hold position for each row, the less material is built up, therefore a thinner partial-knit section is made. Countering that, the fewer needles that are brought out into the hold position, or the more rows knitted before bringing a needle into hold, the larger the partial-knit section tnat is made. Whilst it is completely your decision as to how you want the piece to be shaped, it should be noted that it will have an overall effect on the outer edge (*see* overleaf for examples).

Bringing one needle out for every pass of the needle will result in more rows being knitted over that area, fundamentally resulting in a longer straight edge than if four needles were brought out for every row knitted. Think of it as a geometric shape: the fewer sides there are within the curve, the less smooth the curve becomes; therefore, more partially knitted sections within a piece will result in a smoother edge as there are more sides incorporated into the knit.

The rate of shaping will determine the shape of the piece knitted. Here, one needle has been brought out with every row, which makes the shaping larger overall as more rows have been knitted per shaping area. *Yarn A: Green 2/16NM wool. Yarn B: Lilac, three ends 2/48NM wool–cotton blend. Tension: 5.*

In this sample, four needles have been brought out of every row, therefore fewer rows have been knitted per shaping area, which means that more shaping areas need to be knitted to create the same shape. *Yarn A: Green 2/16NM wool. Yarn B: Lilac, three ends 2/48NM wool–cotton blend. Tension: 5.*

Through this build-up of repetitions of partial-knitted areas, we can begin to build form. An easy example of this would be to continue repeating the partially knitted shaping triangle on the same side. This would create a spiral of material from the machine as one side is knitted up much more than the other. Opening this piece out, we could have the shaping for a peplum top, or the basic shape of a knitted spiral left as it is.

By altering which side the material is built up by repeating sections and then changing the shaping side, we can curve a piece of knit into a wave. This has been explored further on in the book and is explained in detail, and can be a relatively easy development in terms of material and texture by using the right yarns.

A knitted spiral has been made up from a repetition of shaping over the same area. When left to rest, this creates a spiral shape. *Yarn: Three ends 2/16NE mercerised cotton. Stitch size: 6.*

Worked with a needle placement and an elastane yarn, this shape and texture is built up from the repetitions of material shaping, through partial knit with an additional needle structure and yarn combination. *Yarn: Four ends 2/30NE cotton blend worked simultaneously with an elastane.*

COLOURWORK WITH PARTIAL KNIT

Striping and Partial Knit

To add interest to the shaping potential within partial knit, we can begin to play with colour at the same time as working needles in and out of the hold position. A basic introduction would be to work the shaping of the partial knit in one colour, and then the knitting of all needles with a secondary colour. Not only does this create a godet shape in one colour, but a striped effect with the secondary colour that runs the entire length of the knit sample. This is very similar to how we have approached the first basic techniques to understand the shaping properties, but is more developed and refined.

Cast on 40 needles with colour A. With the carriage on the right, change to colour B. We can start the shaping by bringing into the hold position 5 needles and knitting 2 rows. Repeat the shaping with 5 needles in hold on the left-hand side of the working area. Wrap the end needle in hold after the carriage has passed to the left to close up any shaping holes. (See the box 'Wrapping Needles with Partial Knit' later in this chapter).

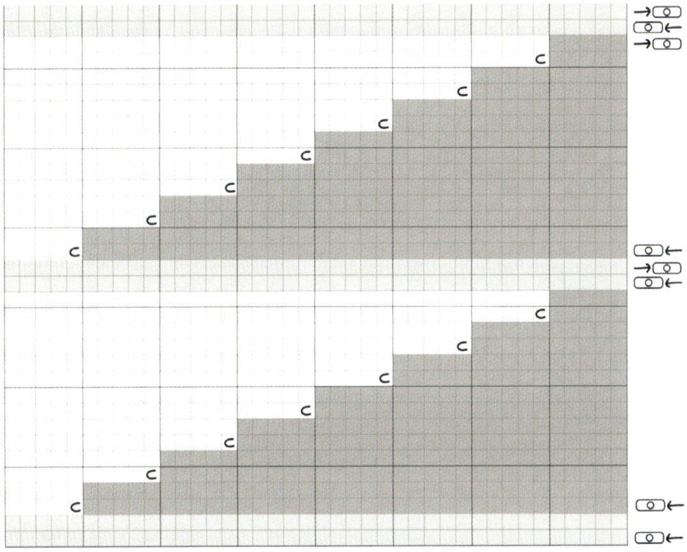

This graphic shows the colour change and the working needles as the shaping is worked. The C-shaped symbol in the chart represents a wrapped needle.

Working one colour over the all-needle areas and a separate colour over the shaping areas can build up some colourwork within the piece. *Yarn A: Green 4-ply mercerised cotton. Yarn B: Dark green 3-ply wool. Tension: 6.*

After all the shaping, the carriage should end on the right-hand side of the working area. Change back to colour A and knit 2 rows with all needles knitting to bring all the needles in the hold position back into the working position.

Ensure you check the weights of the knit whilst the material builds up on the one side.

Repeat these two sections to build up material on one side of the working area and to turn the work.

To begin turning the work in the opposite direction, an extra row will have to be knitted when working an all-needle knit row with colour A, to get the carriage across to the opposite side. Then the shaping can begin from the right-hand side, rather than shaping from the left-hand side, thus turning the knit in the opposite direction.

The shaping alternates between sides after six sections have been built up. This not only evens out the shaping, but gives more impact with the striping effect. In this sample, eight needles were brought into hold each time.
Yarn A: Green 4-ply mercerised cotton. Yarn B: Dark green 3-ply wool. Tension: 6.

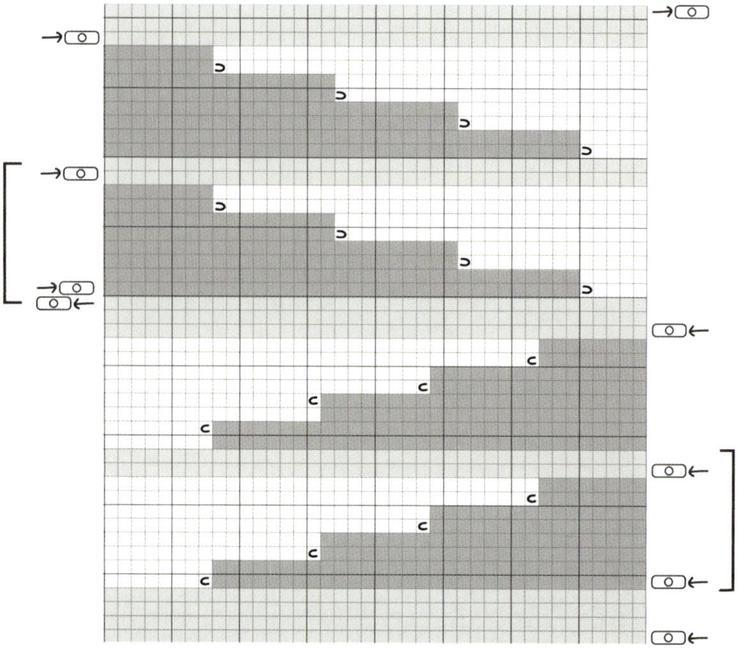

The shaping through the changes of yarn and needles brought into hold. This shows the sides the shaping is achieved on, and only two repeats of the shaping, rather than several that are knitted in the sample.

Striping and Shaping Simultaneously

Additionally, we can stripe whilst the shaping process is happening to give a striped effect within the knitted piece. Providing the colour change happens on the same side as the carriage, you can effectively change colour at any point during the process.

Cast on 40 needles with colour A and establish the knit to hang the weights. For each retraction of working needles, the colour of the yarn will be changed. For each change of colour the carriage should finish on the same side: in this instance, the right-hand side.

Begin by bringing the left-hand side's edge 5 needles into the hold position, knit 2 rows with colour B. Wrap the end right-hand side needle that is in the hold position when the carriage is on the left-hand side.

Introducing stripes and shaping to create pattern and colourwork within the knitted sample. *Yarn A: Purple 4-ply mercerised cotton. Yarn B: Blue 4-ply merino. Tension: 6.*

Change back to colour A when the carriage is on the right-hand side, and again bring out the next left-hand side 5 needles into the hold position and knit 2 rows, always wrapping the end needle when the carriage has been passed to the left.

Repeat these two steps of shaping with 5 needles on the left-hand side of the working area, alternating between colour A and colour B and knitting 2 rows until the last 5 working needles on the right-hand side are knitted. This should be in colour B.

To reintroduce the needles back into action, work still with groups of 5 needles and bring them back into the working position either by rehanging them or pushing them into the upper working position. The colour that should be knitted should match the colour of the stitches on the needles being brought back into work.

Knit 2 rows, again wrapping that end needle.

Repeat this reintroduction of all needles across the working area whilst changing colour, until all needles have been brought back into work and you are knitting across the full working area.

Again, ensure that the colour of yarn placed into the carriage matches the colour on the needles being reintroduced. By repeating this shaping, a shape that is very similar to the basic shaping pieces is created, but this now has a detail of stripes.

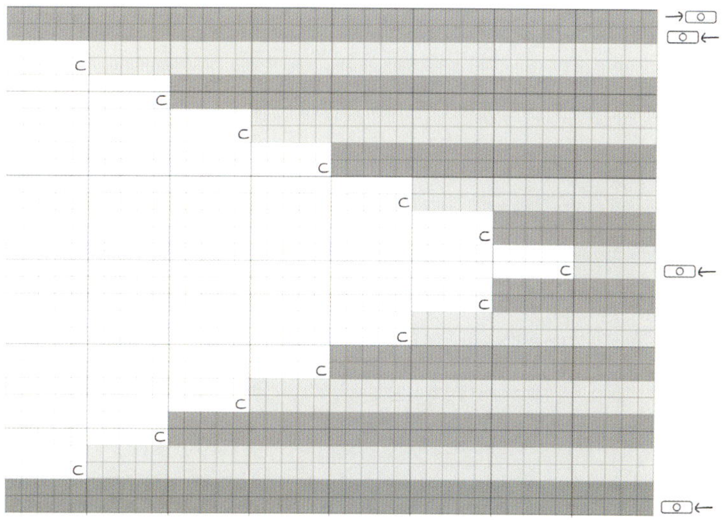

The base graphic incorporates stripes and partial knit to create a more complex striping effect. The different shades represent a colour change.

Balancing the Shape

To create a piece which is more balanced in shape, we can work the shaping on both sides of the knit, in exactly the same way we explored previously. Cast on 40 needles with yarn A, work to establish the knit and hang the weights, finishing with the carriage on the right-hand side. Shape the first part of the knit in the same way as the last sample, by bringing 5 needles out into the hold position for every 2 rows knitted, alternating between the colours and wrapping the end needle when the carriage is on the left-hand side.

For the last shaping row when the last set of needles is brought back into the working position, knit instead 3 rows with all needles knitting in yarn A. This will take the carriage over to the left-hand side where we can begin to shape on the opposite side of the working area to correct the shape of the knit. Begin shaping again in the same way as before, but this time bringing needles on the right-hand side of the working area into hold in groups of 5.

You will need to cut yarn B before reusing it with the next set of shaping, as it would naturally be sitting on the right-hand side and your carriage is now working from the left-hand side of the working area.

Repeat these two steps, with the final row for each section working an odd number of rows to take the carriage across to the opposite side. The zigzag patterning will build up yet create a generally straight piece of material from the shaping.

Alternating the side of the shaping and the colour striping, a chevron-patterned knitted piece can be built up. *Yarn A: Purple 4-ply mercerised cotton. Yarn B: Blue 4-ply merino wool. Tension: 6.*

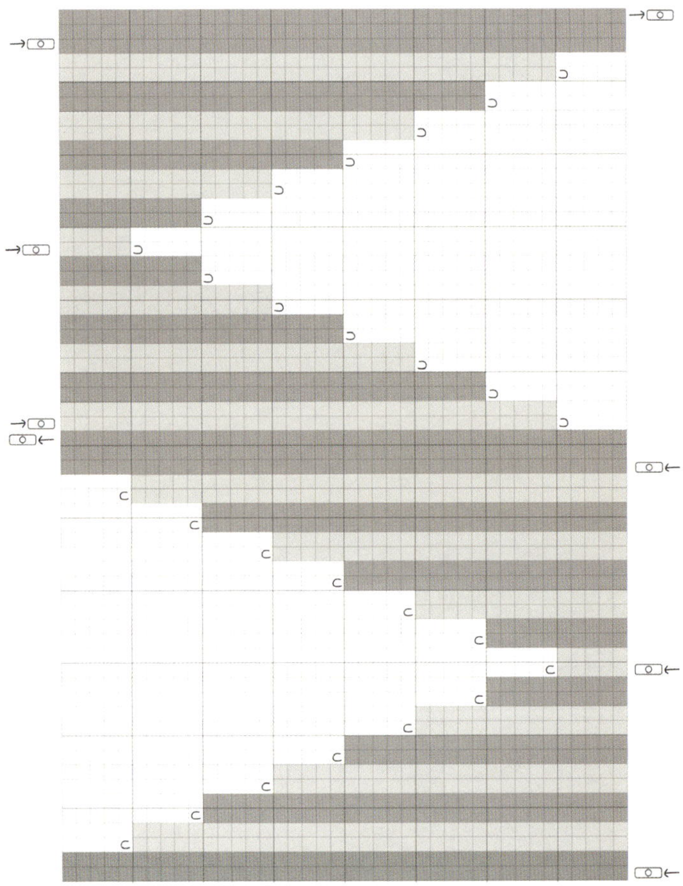

The shaping on both sides to reduce the knit area down to a couple of needles in the centre of the knit before the needles are then reintroduced.

Exaggerating the shaping and the stripes within this same structure can lead to a sample that looks more enlarged and somewhat less detailed. The only alteration with this piece is the number of rows knitted with each colour of yarn. Instead of knitting 2 rows before bringing needles out into the hold position and changing colour, 4 rows are knitted.

This means the last needle in hold position will need to be wrapped. See the box on page 34 for more information on wrapping needles. This builds up some bulk on the needle by the time it is reintroduced, but not enough to affect the working of the needle.

Altering the number of rows knitted with each colour and each needle placement will alter the size of the stripes. In this sample the stripes are larger, which alters the graphic effect of the knit. *Yarn A: Green 3-ply wool. Yarn B: Purple, three ends 2/48NM wool. Tension: 6.*

Partial Knit and Intarsia Effects

Finally, to conclude our explorations with colour and partial knit, we can experiment by using partial knit as a type of intarsia to create blocks of colour within the samples. These are not limited to geometric shapes; however, in these samples we will use geometric shapes to create colour blocks.

This first sample is essentially a repeat of a previous sample but including a third yarn colour in the piece. This allows us to begin to incorporate block colours and sections into the knit, which in turn can create an intarsia effect.

Cast on 40 needles with colour A: this will act as the striped yarn between the partial-knit sections.

Introducing more colour into the sample and also shaping in specific areas can build up an intarsia effect. *Yarn A: Blue 3-ply wool. Yarn B: Lilac, three ends 2/36NM cotton–wool blend. Yarn C: Light blue, three ends 2/36NM cotton–wool blend. Tension: 6.*

Similarly, by repeating sections of shaping and then alternating the side that they are made on, a shaped piece can be built up. This piece was striped every two rows with a repeat of seven sections before the direction of shaping was altered. *Yarn A: Cream 3-ply cotton. Yarn B: Green 4-ply mercerised cotton. Tension: 6.*

Once the weights are on and the knit is established with the carriage on the right-hand side, change to colour B.

Using colour B, bring 2 needles out into the hold position for every row knitted, starting from the left-hand side working across to the right-hand side of the working area. Continue until all needles are out into the hold position. Take colour B out of the carriage and set to rest. You do not need to cut the yarn. It may be necessary to work one row with no yarn to take the carriage across to the opposite side of the bed. This can be done by disengaging the carriage or placing all needles into the hold position to ensure no needles are worked, thus avoiding dropping any stitches.

Now working from the left-hand side of the working needles across to the right-hand side, insert colour C and reintroduce into work 2 needles (on the left-hand side) in every row across the working area until all needles are back in the working position. Finishing with the carriage on the left-hand side, take out yarn C and lay to rest. Disengage the carriage and take it across, working an empty row (a row in which no needles are knitted but the carriage is moved). With the carriage back on the right-hand side, change to colour A and knit 4 rows with all needles knitting. This creates the dividing area between the shaping. Take the carriage back over to the left-hand side and reinsert colour C. Next, working from the right-hand side across to the left-hand side of the working area, bring 2 needles into the hold position on the right-hand side of the working area for every row knitted.

Once all needles are out in the hold position and the carriage is on the left-hand side, colour C can be cut and taken out of the carriage. Work an empty row to get the carriage across to the right-hand side and change to colour B. Reintroduce 2 needles every row working from the right-hand side across to the left-hand side.

Once all needles are back in work, change to colour A and work 4 rows with all needles knitting. If the sample is to be repeated, this process can then be continued for the desired length.

Variations of this can be made by changing the rate of the partial-knit shaping and also the direction. Areas could be built up on one another yet altering the colour, or the shaping could alter in direction. Additional yarns could also be placed into the shaped areas through stripes, as in the previous samples we have seen.

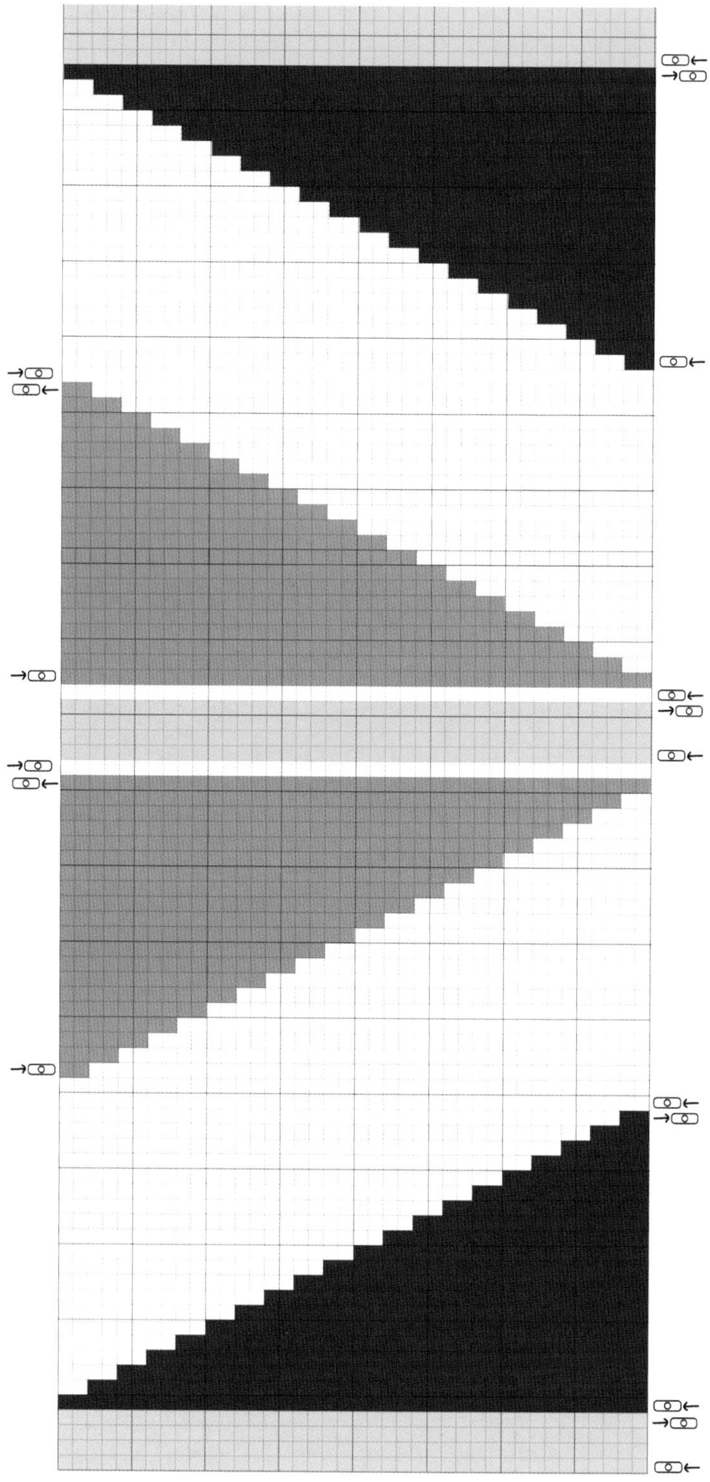

The changes of yarn are portrayed through the different shades within the graphic. This graphic shows the basic method of working partial knit as an intarsia-type technique but still using the basic methods we have previously covered.

Colour Blocks with Partial Knit

We can also create blocks of colour as a shape or pattern within a main piece of knit. The next method will create a diamond shape in the centre of a piece. This process is similar to working with the triangles whilst being more specific about which needles are worked.

The next two examples have been knitted identically: the only difference is yarn choice. The first sample has been knitted with each section in a separate colour. This helps to differentiate the sections and makes the structure much more visible. The second sample is knitted in the same manner but only two yarns have been used: one for the main background colour (sections A, B and C, and sections E, F and G) and one for the central diamond (D). Each individual section has been described. See the chart for instructions on each section.

This sample shows the structure of the partial knit with each section worked in a different yarn. This emphasises the structure that has been knitted rather than the intarsia effect. *Yarns: A variety of similar-weight yarns, approximately 3-ply. Wool and cotton blends. Tension: 6.*

Working with only two colours, an intarsia effect is given. *Yarn A: Light blue, three ends of 2/48NM wool and cotton blend. Yarn B: Dark blue 3-ply wool. Tension: 6.*

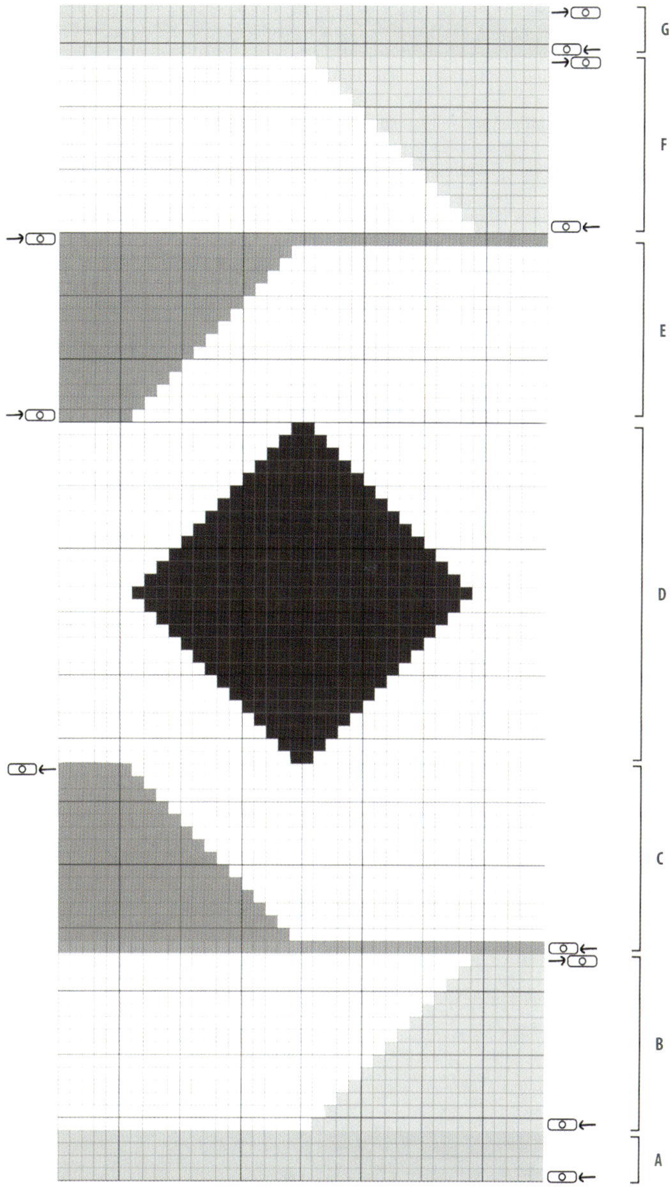

Initial carriage direction is shown for the main sections of the knit but not for the diamond shape in the centre. This is because the diamond can be knitted with the carriage starting on either side. The sections are lettered according to the instructions.

Section A: Cast on 40 needles with yarn A and establish the knit.

Section B: With the carriage on the right-hand side, change to yarn B. Bring into the hold position the left-hand side 21 needles (L20–R2). This will be just over half of the working needles on the left-hand side of the working area. Knit 1 row.

Now push 1 needle into the hold position on the left-hand side of the working needles for every row knitted, until 6 needles remain out in the working area on the right-hand side (R14–R20). This is the first section complete. Carriage finishes on the right-hand side.

Section C: With the carriage on the right-hand side, change to yarn C. Knit 1 row across all needles to get the carriage across to the left-hand side.

TIP

When inserting a new colour in the middle of some partial knit, place the yarn on the inside of the needles to be worked, and on top of the needles that are in the hold position on the side of the carriage. This will ensure the yarn is placed into the needle hooks when the carriage is passed. If the yarn is placed into the carriage but kept outside of the whole working area, the yarn might not be knitted into the needles, resulting in the stitches being dropped from the centre needles.

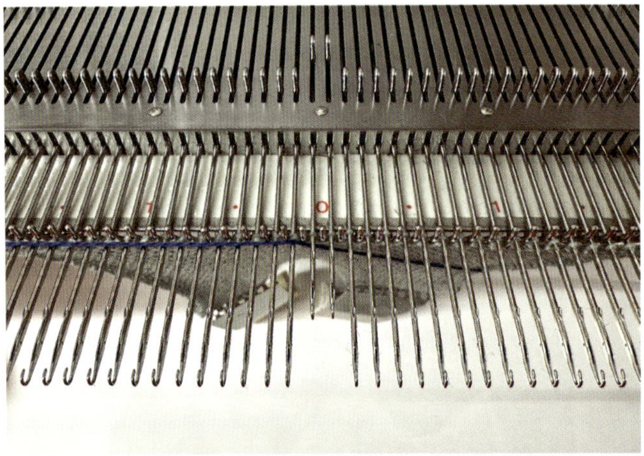

In this instance, the carriage is on the left-hand side of the working area. The yarn is brought to the inside of the needles that are to be worked and left to rest on top of the needles in the hold position. If the yarn is sitting under the needles in the hold position, there is a chance that the needle in work may not catch the yarn in the yarn feeder.

Bring the right-hand side 21 needles (L2–R29) into the hold position.

Knit 1 row, ending with the carriage on the right-hand side. For the next and following rows, bring 1 needle out on the right-hand side of the working needles until 6 needles remain on the left-hand side (L20–L14).

Section D: It does not matter which side the carriage has finished on. Change to yarn D.

Bring into action the centre 2 needles (L1–R1) and knit across.

For the next and following rows, introduce 1 needle for each row knitted on both sides of the knit area until there are 28 needles working in the centre of the knitted area (L14–R14).

Then, for the next and following rows, reduce the number of needles worked by bringing 1 needle on each side of the working needles into the hold position until there are only 2 working needles in the centre of the knit. Those two needles can then be brought out into the hold position. Remove yarn D.

Section E: The carriage is on the left-hand side. Change to yarn E. Bring back into the working position the left-hand side 6 needles (L20–L14) and knit across. For the next and following rows, bring 1 needle back into the working position until the left-hand side 19 needles are back in the working position. The carriage should finish on the left-hand side. Knit all needles using yarn E, to take the carriage across to the right-hand side.

Section F: Change to yarn F. Bring the right-hand side 6 needles back into the working position (R14–R20) and take the carriage across. For the next and following rows, bring 1 needle back into the working position until the right-hand side 19 needles are back in the working position. The carriage should finish on the right-hand side.

Section G: Change to yarn G and work all needles, knitting the final section of single jersey.

The whole sample should now be complete. Knitting the same piece but with all sections in the same yarn apart from the central diamond will give an intarsia effect.

Repeated Colour Blocks

To further this, we can repeat the diamond across the knitted material and also vertically. Follow the chart for each section knitted; note that they are knitted in the same method as the single diamond.

Working with a similar method of breaking up the material into sections, we can use partial knit to replicate intarsia, creating geometric shapes that are repeated on the vertical and horizontal dimensions of the material. *Yarn A: Green 3-ply wool. Yarn B: Bright green 4-ply mercerised cotton. Yarn C: Light pink, three ends 3/36NM cotton–wool blend. Tension: 6.*

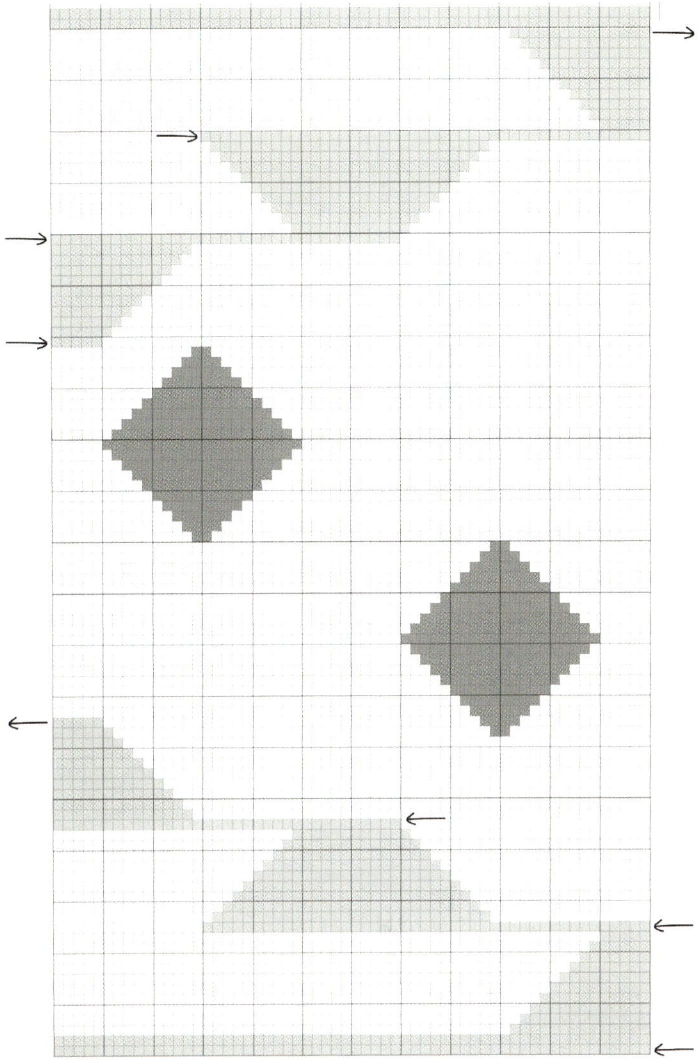

The needles used and carriage direction worked when repeating the diamond shaping across the horizontal. This graphic only shows two colours of yarn and the directions in which it has been knitted.

WRAPPING NEEDLES WITH PARTIAL KNIT

You may find that when you are working partial knit some lace holes might appear in areas next to the partial-knit areas. This is completely normal, and these lace holes will not ladder and unravel your knit. These holes are created because you have begun to add more rows into a specific area that is not connected to the adjacent needle. That initial row that you were working has now become unbalanced with more rows in one area rather than a straight and continuous row across. This disruption creates a little shaping hole.

If you find this unsightly, you can wrap the adjacent needle that is in the hold position on the same side as the carriage with the yarn from the carriage, before you take the carriage back across. This will close up the hole and make it unnoticeable. Generally, the yarn will sit on top of the needles in hold, so just moving the yarn underneath the last needle creates a wrap.

There is one exception to this rule which means we do not need to manually wrap the needle. This is when we bring out one needle into the hold position on the same side as the carriage. This will automatically wrap the needle as you take the carriage across. This works the same when reintroducing the needle back into the working position. You do not need to wrap when introducing a needle on the same side as the carriage.

To show the difference between the shaping details, for these samples 30 stitches were cast on and a few rows knitted to establish the material. Yarn for both samples is a 2/15NM wool at a stitch size 5.

Please note that for all samples I have not wrapped the needle unless this is directly stated within the method.

Automatic wrap. For the first sample, one needle has been brought into the hold position on the same side as the carriage, and two rows knitted. Once all needles across the working area were brought into hold, they were reintroduced into the working position again, one needle every two rows, the same side as the carriage.

No wrap. This second sample was worked in the same method as the previous sample, but the shaping was made on the opposite side of the carriage. An extra row has been knitted before the shaping began to get the carriage across to the correct side.

A GENERAL RULE FOR PARTIAL KNIT TO AVOID FLOATS

A rule that I teach students for partially knitted areas is to check that the last needle knitted (or a needle very close to it) should be the first needle to be knitted when removing or introducing needles from the working position. If this is off by a few needles because you have brought them into the hold position before taking the carriage across, this is okay; but there would be more of a problem when working in groups of needles (as we will do further on in this chapter) that contain larger numbers of needles.

By checking which needle was last to knit and which is the first to knit on the next row, the needles are worked in the correct order, ensuring the yarn will not skip or float over needles that are still in the hold position. For example, if I wanted to bring needles into the hold position on both edges of the working area to knit only in the centre, and my carriage is on the right, I would bring out the needles into hold on the left-hand edge of the knit. Then, knit one row so the carriage moves across the right-hand edge needles and middle needles but leave the left-hand edge needles in hold. Next, I would bring out the right-hand edge needles, meaning that I can now work in the middle needles. To simplify, use a group of needles on the opposite side of the carriage, whether moving them in or out of the hold position, to avoid floats.

If I had brought both sets of edge needles into the hold positions before the first pass of the carriage, the carriage would have finished knitting on the last needle on the right-hand side; but now, as that needle is in the hold position, it will begin to knit again on the first needle on the right in the central section of needles that are still in the working position. This will create a float from the last needle on the right-hand side to the first needle just knitted in the centre. Hence, the last needle to knit should (thereabouts) be the first needle to knit on the next row after bringing needles out into the hold position.

When moving from one section of working needles to another, if there are needles in the hold position in the middle that should not be worked, all needles (including the original section, the middle section that is in the hold position and the new section) must be worked.

Please note, this method will be used throughout this chapter to avoid floats, even if it is not stated explicitly.

This image shows the incorrect positioning of the carriage when introducing needles back into the working position from hold. The first needle to knit on this next row was not the last needle to knit, therefore a large float would be made over the needles as they are brought back into work.

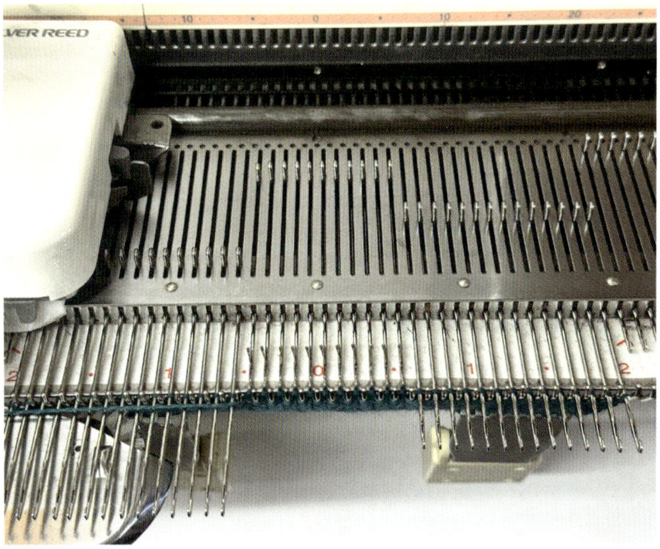

This image shows the correct positioning of the carriage when introducing needles back into the working position from hold. The last needle knitted whilst in hold will be the first needle to knit again, which results in no large float over the working area.

PARTIAL KNIT FOR THREE-DIMENSIONAL FORMS

Using partial knit to create three-dimensional effects is one of the easiest methods to create shape within your work. This is done using the same method as previously stated, by bringing one or more needles into the hold position with each pass of the carriage.

Choosing where we bring needles into the hold position will alter the final appearance of the fabric. If we hold needles in the middle of the sample, the sides of the material will build up, creating flare and dimension; in comparison, if we hold the side needles and work the central needles, a build-up of material in the centre will be created.

Creating flared sides to a piece can open out the form. This first sample was cast on over 40 needles. When the carriage was on the right-hand side, all needles apart from the right-hand 15 were brought into the hold position, and the carriage placed into hold. Then 1 row was knitted; then 3 needles for each row are brought out into the hold position from the centre of the working area outwards, until only 3 needles on the right-hand side edge were working. This will be a total of 4 shaping rows.

Still with the carriage in the hold position, we will next introduce 3 needles at a time from the right-hand edge, until we are back to the original position of working with the far-right-hand 15 needles. The carriage should end on the right.

Holding the needles on either side of the working area, material can be created in the centre, which will create a bulge. *Yarn: 4-ply mercerised cotton. Tension: 7.*

Holding the needles in the centre and working additional rows on the edges of the working area can create a flared effect. *Yarn: 4-ply mercerised cotton. Tension: 7.*

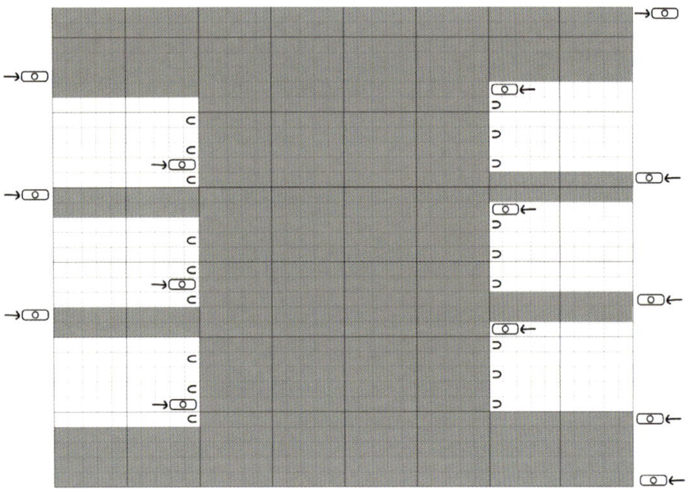

Working over the centre needles to build up material. This graphic shows the carriage direction and needles worked.

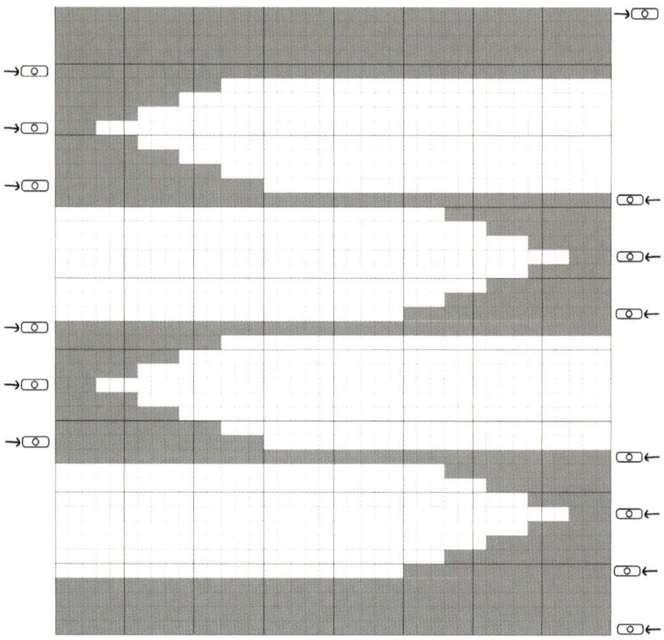

The course of the yarn over the shaping of both the right side and left side, in which fabric is built up on each side.

Take the carriage across, knitting all needles, so it ends on the left-hand side. Repeat the shaping on the left-hand side with the far-left-hand 15 needles. You will notice that the centre 10 needles do not have any shaping or extra rows added to them at any time. This section will be the base and will have the least amount of material built up on it.

Repeat the shaping on both sides for a total of 6 times to create a similar shape to the sample shown. To alter the sample, you could work more or less shaping sections.

To create the sample in which the material bulges out of the centre portion of the knit, we will work over the centre section, rather than working at the side as we did previously.

Cast on 40 needles and knit to hang the weight. With the carriage on the right-hand side, the left 10 edge needles are brought into hold. With the carriage in hold, pass the carriage across the selected working needles; the right 10 edge needles are then brought into hold, leaving the middle 20 needles in work. Wrap the end needle in hold with the yarn from the carriage.

Knit 6 rows just on these centre 20 needles, wrapping every row – this includes the first row in which the right-hand needles were brought into hold. This is the build-up of material in the centre.

Once the 6 rows are complete, the carriage will end on the right-hand side. We can reintroduce the left-hand side needles that are in the hold position before we take the carriage across. Knit carefully over this row, as the needle with all the wraps will be quite bulky.

Finally, knit all the way back over to the right-hand side to complete the first of the shaping sections. Repeat this shaping section in full 6 times to create the same build-up of material in the centre as shown in this sample.

Variations

Slight variations in both these first samples can be made through the amount of shaping. For the first sample, in which material was built up on the sides of the piece, a similar build-up of material to the second sample can be created but this time by keeping the same number of needles out in the hold position and wrapping the end needle for each row. This is potentially an easier method to try out for a first attempt, and the shaping of the material is more pronounced.

Similarly for the second sample, where the shape is built up in the middle, the number of needles worked can be slightly decreased so the working area decreases before being brought back into action.

To understand the shaping qualities, experiment with small samples to see what shaping variations you feel comfortable with.

In this variation, the sample has been shaped within the partial knit. Needles have been brought into the hold position throughout the process of shaping, and then reintroduced to build up the bulk in the centre of the piece rather than knitting straight over the centre needles. *Yarn: 4-ply mercerised cotton. Tension: 7.*

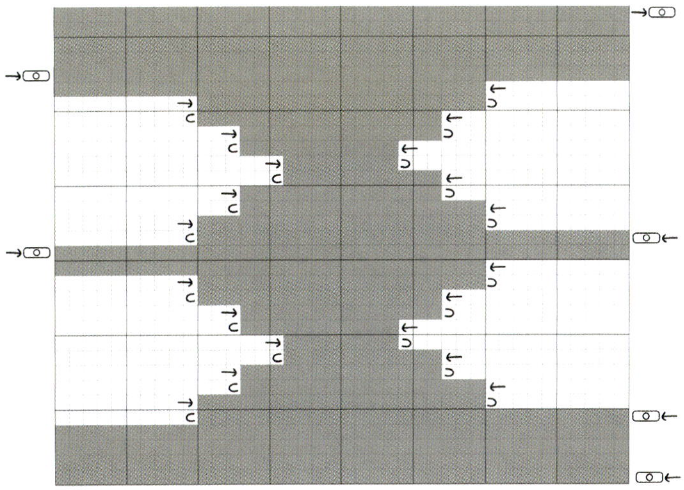

The build-up of material in the centre of the knit is clear. The carriage direction and wrapping of needles is shown.

Similarly, the variation in this sample shows no shaping within the outer flared sections, but the last central needle in the hold position has been wrapped to close up the material. *Yarn: 4-ply mercerised cotton. Tension: 7.*

Godets are triangles of knit which, in this case, are formed within the middle of the material, giving it dimension and form. *Yarn: One end Jamieson's Of Shetland, Spindrift. Tension: 7.*

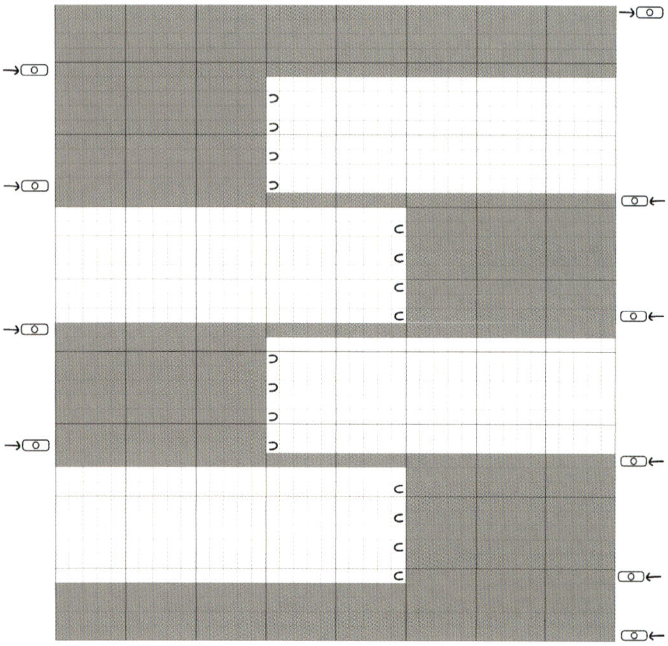

This graphic shows a variation of creating material on the edges of the knit. This sample has less shaping but the same amount of material builds up over the same number of needles.

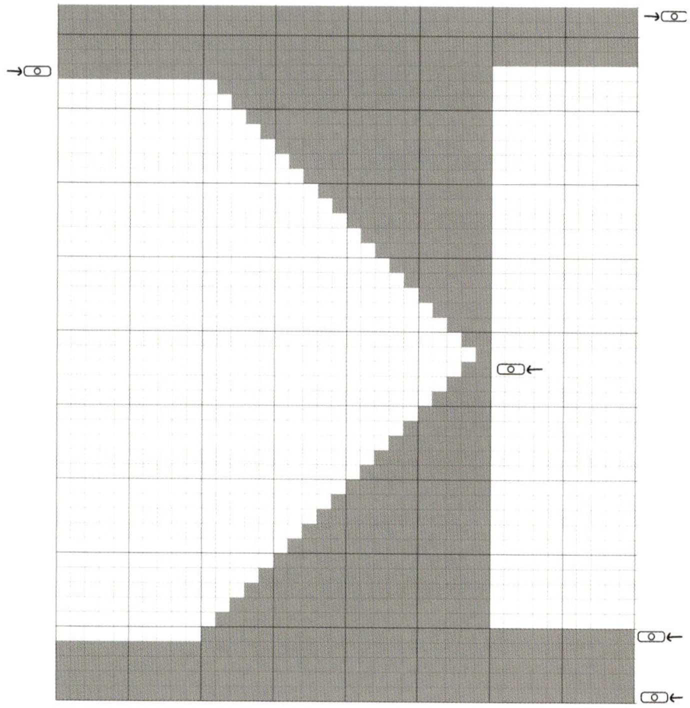

Building up knit on one side of the material to create a godet.

Godets

Continuing this exploration of building material in certain areas, we can use the knowledge developed in this early part of this chapter to turn the shaping into formed godets. These godets are shaped on one side and open on the other. As with all other shaping using partial knit, the positioning, size and rate of shaping can all be adjusted and altered for your design.

In this first sample to create godets, a total of 40 working needles were cast on, knitting a few rows to hang the weights before starting the shaping. The left-hand side 10 edge needles are brought into the hold position and the carriage placed into hold, then the carriage passed over to the left, knitting the needles except for the left-hand 10 needles. Before the shaping, the 10 right-hand side edge needles are then brought into the hold position, so we are only working on the centre 20 needles.

Next, 1 needle was brought into the hold position on one side of the centre working needles (it doesn't matter which side, as long as it is the same side for each godet) for each pass of the carriage until 1 needle remains. Then, 1 needle was reintroduced with each pass of the carriage, again on the same side. I finished with the carriage on the right, with the last needle being brought back into work on the next row. At the same time as bringing back this last needle, I reintroduced the left 10 edge needles to work. Taking the carriage across to the left, this knitted the last needle that was reintroduced on the godet, and the 10 edge stitches on the left. With the carriage on the left, it was placed back into normal knitting and a full row of all needles was worked. Now that all needles were back working, 4 full rows were knitted before beginning the next shaping in exactly the same way, but alternating the side of the shaping relative to the middle needles.

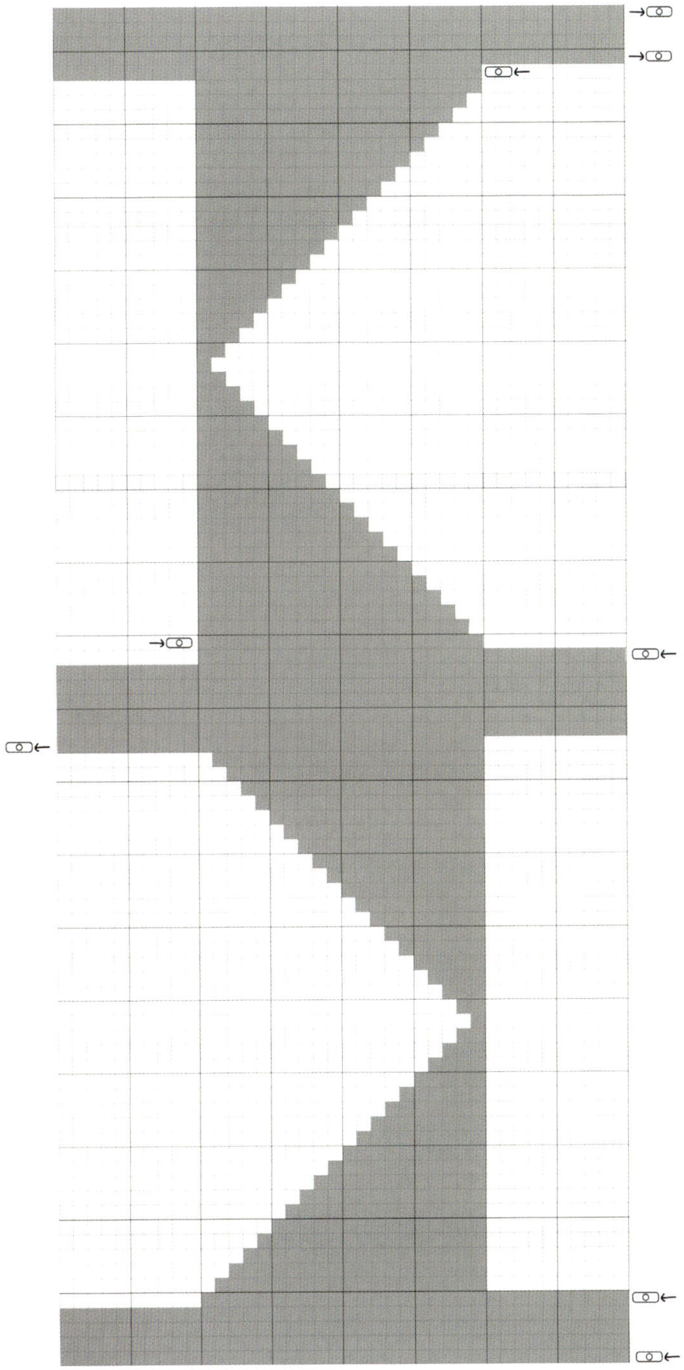

This shaping is working on opposite sides to make godets with alternating open sides.

This shaping creates an open area on one side of the godet, and a triangular shape if it is pressed flat. You can see the shaping marks of the partial knit along the ridge of the godet when you look at the sample face-on. By altering which side the shaping of the godet is worked, the side that is open can be controlled. Variations of this technique could develop to include different colours, different size godets, and even different placements.

Building on the basic version, only the colour of the godet has been changed. There is a horizontal repetition of the godet, however, alternating colours to add more detail. A secondary yarn simply replaces the main yarn, and the knitting continues as previously instructed, exactly like striping. *Yarn: Jamieson's Of Shetland, Spindrift. Tension: 7.*

Peaks

Developing onwards from godets, we can begin to add even more shape into the material. Keeping to the same technique of working in a central part of the working needles and holding one needle in each row, we can build up a three-dimensional shape. The difference with this technique is that, instead of holding one needle on only one side with each pass of the carriage, we can bring out needles into hold on both sides, meaning that we are alternating the side where the needle is brought into hold. Alternating the needles in this way, we build up material in the centre of the knit which ultimately pushes out into a form similar to a three-dimensional triangle.

Peaks, in a similar way to godets, can be knitted into the textile at any point. It would be best to start by knitting one peak in the centre of your work before working several to get acquainted with the technique.

Start this first sample by casting on 40 needles, hanging weight and knitting some rows to form a bottom border. We are only going to work the centre 20 needles into a peak, so place the carriage into hold. On the first row, bring out the 10 needles on the far-left-hand side and take the carriage across with the carriage in hold. Once the carriage is on the left, we can bring into hold the furthest right 10 needles, but also the first needle on the left of the 20 needles of the peak. Then, with each pass of the carriage, bring a needle into hold, carriage side, until you have 2 needles remaining. The carriage should finish on the left.

A singular shaped peak is steamed flat against the main material. Shaped with one needle in hold in every row on the carriage side. *Yarn: One end 2-ply Shetland wool. Tension: 7.*

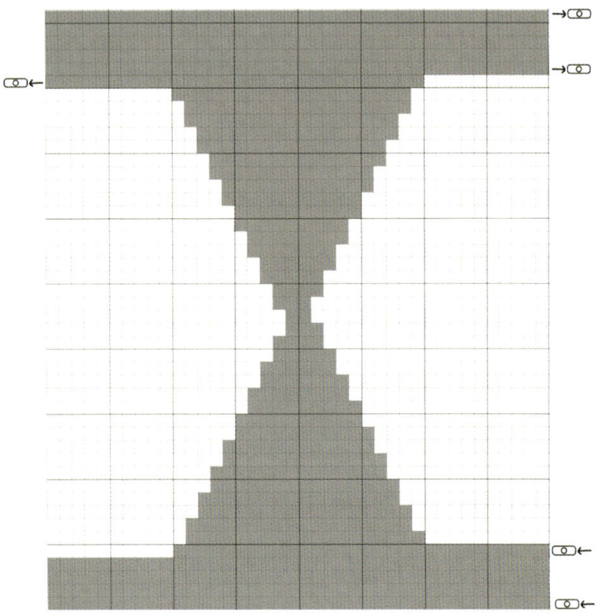

The shaping on both sides to reduce the knit area down to a couple of needles in the centre of the knit before the needles are then reintroduced.

Next, reintroduce the needles one by one on the same side of the carriage until you are back with 20 needles in the centre of the working position and 10 either side in hold.

When the carriage takes the last pass back across to the left, reintroduce all 10 needles on the left-hand side. Lastly, we can take the carriage out of the hold position and back to the right, reintroducing all remaining needles in hold ready to continue with the pattern.

Variations of this technique can include sizes of the peak, different colours, different placements. Here are some notes on those variations:

Peak size

The peak is not limited to bringing out 1 needle into the hold position on every row to make the shape. More rows that have been knitted before a needle is brought into hold will elongate the peak; similarly, bringing more needles into hold on every row would shorten the shape of the peak. It may be preferred to wrap the end needle with yarn before shaping or taking the carriage across to avoid lace holes in the peak, but this isn't a necessity. In the sample pictured, I have wrapped each edge needle to close up the hole.

Increasing the number of rows within the shaping and also wrapping the end needle increases the overall length of the peak. This elongated peak has been repeated and staggered in placement. *Yarn: One end 2-ply Shetland wool. Tension: 7.*

Alternatively, working fewer rows and less shaping in the peak, the size is decreased. These peaks have also been repeated and staggered in placement. *Yarn: One end 2-ply Shetland wool. Tension: 7.*

Knitting Multiple Peaks

We can repeat the peaks across the whole knitting area by repeating the process of making one peak. We are unable to make the peaks simultaneously as this would build up a series of floats across the held needles, therefore we start with a peak on the furthest edge of the knitting area on the carriage side and work across that row, one peak at a time.

For example, if we are starting with the carriage on the right-hand side, our first peak would be knitted on the right. Once finished, on the last pass of the carriage to the left for that peak, we would introduce the needles in between any peaks and also the needles for the next peak along. Then, on the first pass of the carriage back to the right, we would bring into the hold position the needles from the previous peak and any needles in between the peaks, to make sure they do not knit whilst we are shaping this next peak.

This process is continued across the entire working area from either right to left, or left to right depending on the starting direction.

Smaller peaks have been worked in place across the working area. One needle every row was brought out into the hold position compared to the original sample, and the graphic shows the difference in shaping rates. *Yarn: One end 2-ply Shetland wool. Tension: 7.*

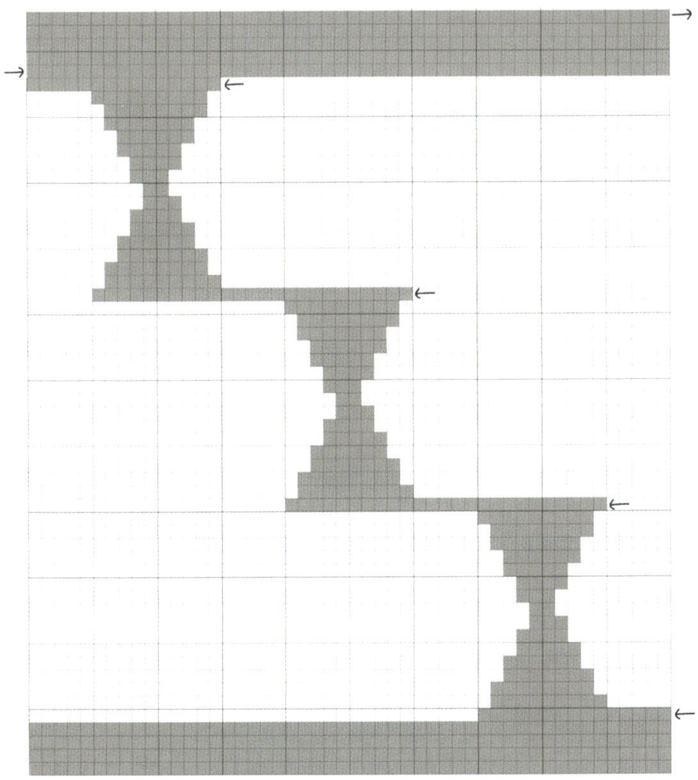

Showing the working needles with a carriage direction through arrows, to create multiple peaks across one row. This chart is for a sample with one colour rather than multiple colours, and is for a peak size of the original one peak with one needle in hold on every row.

Stripes, Pattern and Placement

Adding stripes to the shaping can add a colour element and contrast to the overall technique. In this sample, the peak has been made over fewer needles and with fewer rows. This gives a less dimensional effect with a subtle texture. The stripe can be used to highlight the peaks, either the shape or the position of them. Striping during the shaping will allow for the full peak to be a different colour simply by replacing the main yarn when the shaping of the peak begins.

Pattern can also be placed into either the peak or the background material with the use of a punch card or any other hand-manipulated technique. The working of the peak is isolated to those particular stitches at that particular time, therefore any other technique within the material is undisturbed.

Multiple peaks knitted into a sample with an incorporation of different colours along with a separate background colour. The peaks are staggered in placement. *Yarn A: Pink, one end 2-ply Shetland wool. Yarn B: Blue, one end 2-ply Shetland wool. Yarn C: Grey, one end 2-ply Shetland wool. Tension: 7.*

Working multiple smaller peaks with a simple stripe and a staggered placement, the stripe becomes a focal point in the knit, creating waves out of a plain knit. *Yarn A: Yellow, one end 4-ply merino wool. Yarn B: Pink, one end 4-ply mohair. Tension: 7.*

CHANGING COLOUR AND PARTIAL KNIT

It is easier to knit a peak in a different colour compared to the same colour as the main material as you no longer need to consider your needle placement and whether you will unintentionally create floats or not. When changing colour, the first needle knitting with yarn B will be a part of the peak, therefore we can bring all needles we will not be knitting out into the hold position and immediately start knitting in the centre of the peak.

This is different compared to knitting the peak in the same yarn as the main surrounding fabric. In this instance, we have to consider the last needle that was knitted and the first needle to be knitted, to avoid floats over needles that are in hold. This means potentially working needles on the same side as the carriage that are to be held before they are brought into hold. If needed, check the earlier box 'A General Rule for Partial Knit to Avoid Floats'.

The placement of the peaks worked alongside stripes can give a very subtle form to the material, but more a graphic effect. Here the peaks are relatively subtle in size. However, due to their structure they add shape to the textile, and by alternating the position of the peaks through the piece along with the inserted stripe, the overall texture becomes more decorative and wavy. Using colour combination, you can highlight either the stripe or the structure of the peak.

In this instance, a wool yarn was used for the main structure of the peak and then a mohair for the stripe. The mohair could be brushed out to bloom and add even more texture to the sample.

Throughout all the samples of peaks, the position of them has been staggered. This is purely to show the structure and positioning of each peak. They can, however, be built up in the same position on the needle bed. Again, this is a design detail which you should develop further to explore all the possibilities within peaks and partial knit.

PARTIALLY KNITTED SECTIONS

Through this part of the chapter we will explore working within sections across the knit to develop textures that replicate the look of braids, or vertically curved knitted columns. These are worked in sections over the machine, knitting in groups, in sequence across the machine bed, using the same method as knitting multiple peaks. As you can see in the selection of samples that are included here, there are many ways to work this method, which produce different results and effects. This technique can be either left to relax into its natural state or it can be stretched out to reveal the structure.

Colour can be incorporated into this technique in many different elements which both enhance the texture and can also include a pattern. Striping is the easiest way to include colourwork into these structures; however, you are encouraged to play with different methods including working with a punch card or changing colour at different points when knitting each group.

This first sample is the foundation upon which most of the samples in this section are based. See it as the master technique. These samples build up quickly despite working each section separately, meaning this is a great method to create an interesting structure in a short amount of time.

A basic sample of working in partial knit and in groups across the needle bed. The knit leans in the direction of the carriage. This sample has been stretched and pinned into position before steaming to set the structure. *Yarn: One end 4-ply mercerised cotton. Tension: 8.*

Each group will be numbered and worked accordingly. See the chart below for the alphabetically labelled groups. All of the following samples will be instructed in a similar method.

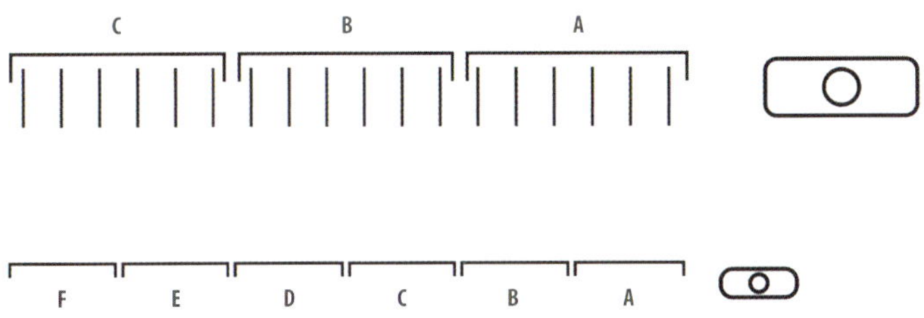

All of these next samples will be explained using alphabetically named groups of needles. Looking at this diagram, the groups begin on the right-hand side of the working area as this is the assumed position of the carriage when beginning.

Having cast on in multiples of 6 (in this instance 7 groups equalling 42 needles) and with the carriage on the right after hanging weights, work each group of 6 needles from the right to the left across all sections, and then back again over the working needles from left to right. The placement of the carriage after each section is stated as follows:

COR: Carriage on the right
COL: Carriage on the left

When a group is not being worked, it is placed into the hold position so the carriage will ignore it and only knit the stated groups.

Work the following:
1. Group A: Knit 6 rows COR.
2. Groups A and B: Knit 8 rows COR.
3. Groups A, B and C: Knit 1 row COL.
4. Groups B and C: Knit 7 rows COR.
5. Groups B, C and D: Knit 1 row COL.
6. Groups C and D: Knit 7 rows COR.

Continue this pattern across the working needles until all groups have been knitted, placing groups back into work and then out into the hold position. Once you have reached the left side and all groups have been knitted, the carriage should finish on the left-hand side of the working needles. If it is not, add in an extra row to take the carriage to the left. That one extra row will go unnoticed once the knit is off the machine.

Work backwards across the knitted sections in exactly the same pattern, introducing sections back into work and then bringing them into hold after being worked. This rhythmic process is then repeated to build up the length of the material. Once off the machine and relaxed, the direction of lean in the knit will relate to the carriage direction during construction.

The decorative holes in the knit are made from the number of rows knitted over each section. The more rows knitted, the larger the decorative holes will be. The number of needles used will determine the width of each section. All of these elements are variables within the construction process and, although they are explored in depth through this chapter, they are open to your own experimentation.

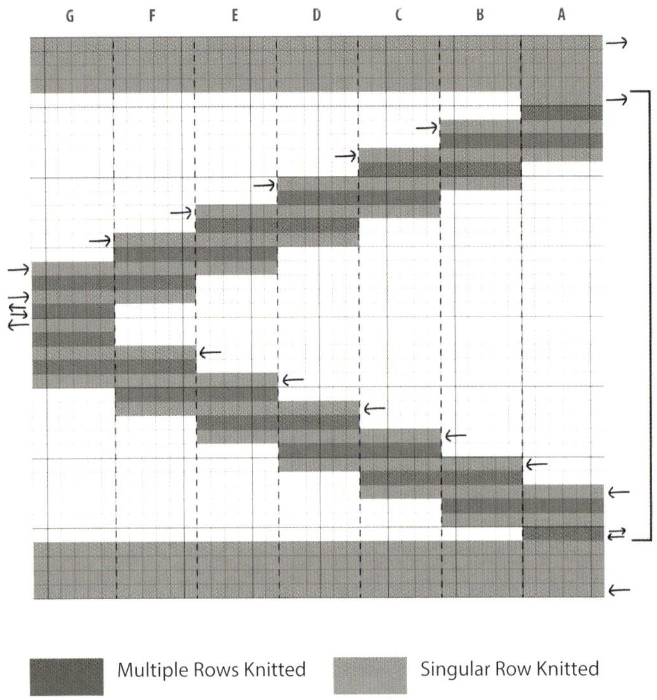

The chart shows the structure for the partially knitted sections. Note that the change in shade represents multiple or single rows over those groups. Carriage directions are included. Check the instructions for the number of rows.

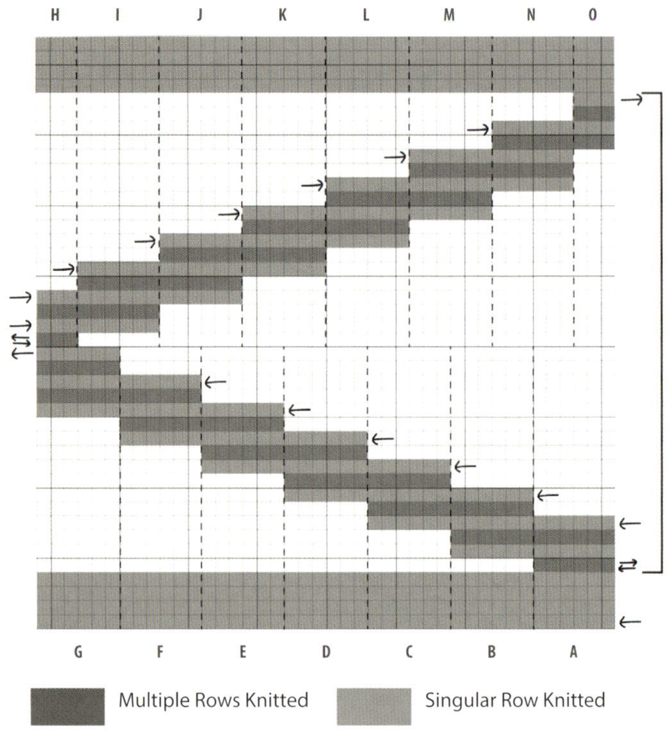

The chart to represent the slight alteration in structure. Note the positions of the groups and how the groups change in needle placement.

Creating Twisted Sections

Altering the groups slightly and staggering them every other full row creates a twisted effect with the sections. Note that the groups of needles are different when the carriage moves over to the left, compared to back over to the right. This also shows the difference in effect when the sample is encouraged to relax rather than being pinned and stretched.

A slight alteration in the workings of the groups can give a twisted effect to the sample. Allowing the sample to relax encourages each section to create the twist effect. *Yarn: One end 4-ply mercerised cotton. Tension: 7.*

This next sample showcases the difference when working over a different number of rows and also needles whilst still making the structure. Starting with groups of 8 needles, each group was reduced by 1 needle after every 2 full shaping rows (when the carriage is returned to the right-hand side after working all groups of needles to the right and then back to the left), and shortened by 2 rows:

- Group of 8 needles = 12 rows knitted
- Group of 7 needles = 10 rows knitted
- Group of 6 needles = 8 rows knitted
- Group of 5 needles = 6 rows knitted
- Group of 4 needles = 4 rows knitted

The variation of size of the knit can be experimented with to explore needle number and row count and the shape in relation to the needles and rows knitted. It is not necessary to decrease the number of stitches simultaneously as decreasing the number of rows; however, it proves to be a fun experiment with pattern and form.

In terms of the decrease over the groups, I decreased equally rather than favouring one side. For example, transferring to decrease the left stitch of each group and then on the next decrease transferring the right stitch to decrease. Decreasing always on the same side can add an alternative detail.

Now we have reminded ourselves of the basics, we can begin to alter needle placements, yarn combinations and the number of rows or working needles to alter the basic shape.

Needle Placement

In the next sample, needles have been placed out of action from the cast-on across the working area to create a needle placement. The vertical sections of knit become more defined as floats are introduced into the structure over the out-of-action needles. These floats become visible as 'bridges' between the sections. The more rows knitted over 2 sections, the more floats there will be, and vice versa with fewer rows knitted.

In the next samples, 42 needles were cast on in groups of 5 working needles with 3 needles out of action in between each working group. The same process as the last sample has been worked to knit each of the groups.

With the carriage starting on the right-hand side, knit the following:

1. Groups A and B: Knit 8 rows COR.
2. Groups A, B and C: Knit 1 row COL.
3. Groups B and C: Knit 7 rows COR.
4. Groups B, C and D: Knit 1 row COL.
5. Groups C and D: Knit 7 rows COR.
6. Repeat through all groups of needles.

Work your way across all the groups until the carriage finishes on the left-hand side, and then work your way back again, working the groups in reverse. Again, if needed knit an extra row on the last group to finish with the carriage on the left.

It should be noted that for this sample, each end group of needles are not knitted on their own, but always with the adjacent group. This is to help keep a flat and neat border to the piece. If each end group has 8 rows knitted into it, the side edges will become loose due to the additional rows in those groups. It is not detrimental to the sample structure if you knit each end group, purely a method to clean up the sample edges, so test this to see if it is the effect you want.

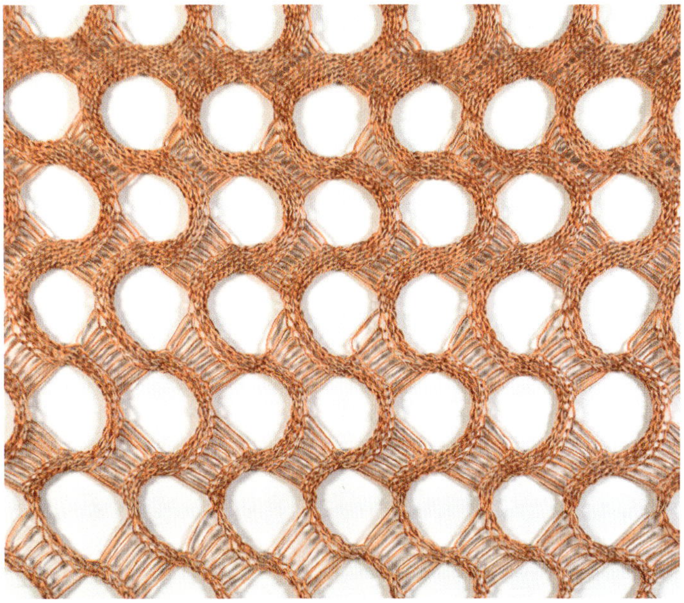

In this sample the number of needles that each group is worked over decreases, as does the number of rows. This creates a lacy effect with a striking structure dominated by the shaping holes *Yarn: Three ends (different colours) 2/16NE mercerised cotton. Tension: 6.*

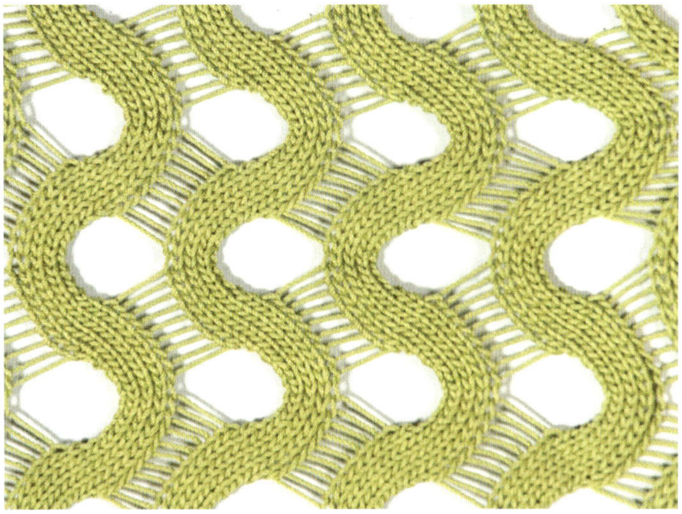

Incorporating a needle placement into the structure gives an openness to it and also emphasises the direction of the knitting. *Yarn: One end 4-ply mercerised cotton. Tension: 8.*

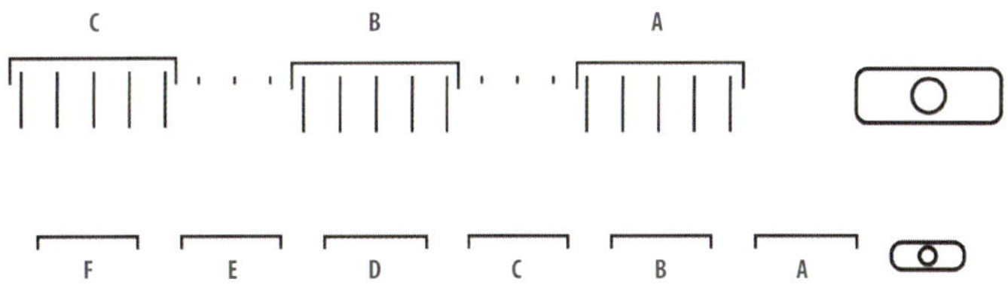

The needle placement for the sample. Refer to the original chart at the beginning of this section to see the carriage direction and groups worked.

The size of the floating areas can change depending on the number of rows knitted when bridging, or knitting two groups. The more rows knitted, the larger the bridge sections will be, and likewise the fewer rows knitted, the smaller the bridge sections will be.

We do not always have to follow the knitting pattern shown previously, of working with multiple groups at one time. Instead we can knit over a single group after working a bridge between two groups. This will alter the overall look and texture slightly by making it yet more open, even when working with all needles.

Working individual groups will open up the material more and define each group. This piece did not have a needle placement, yet is just as open as a piece with a needle placement. *Yarn: One end 4-ply mercerised cotton. Tension: 8.*

Cast on in multiples of 6 needles: in this sample there are 36 needles. Work in groups from the right to the left; the bridges will be worked over 2 groups of working needles.

1. Group A: Knit 8 rows COR.
2. Groups A and B: Knit 5 rows COL.
3. Group B: Knit 7 rows COR.
4. Groups B and C: Knit 5 rows COL.
5. Group C: Knit 7 rows COR.

Continue across the groups of working needles in this sequence to bridge 2 groups before knitting 1 on its own, again working back in reverse after the carriage has worked all the way to the left, to bring the carriage back to the right-hand side, completing 2 full rows of the sequence.

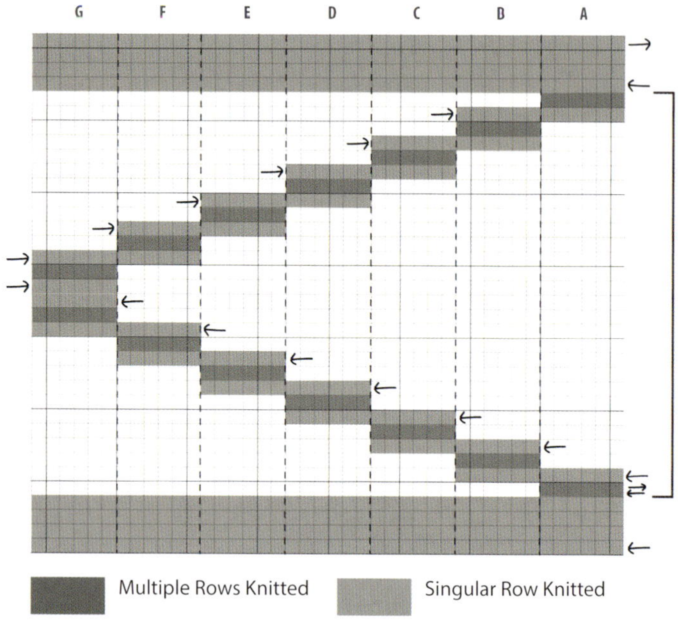

Again, the different shades represent multiple rows or singular rows knitted for the chart in which each group of needles is knitted separately.

Incorporating Colour

Colourwork, in the form of stripes, can be included to help define the structure even more; for example, working two full rows of the partial-knit shaping before changing colour. Two full rows would mean working the carriage all the way over to the left-hand side working all groups (first full row) and then knitting all the groups again taking the carriage back to the right-hand side (second full row). It does not mean two passes of the carriage within the partial-knit shaping over one group. Groups of six needles were worked with twelve rows over each group to build up a substantial amount of material. When the colour change is implemented, the structure is emphasised further. This can be done either when knitting one group at a time, or two (refer back to the original sample).

The change in yarn does not have to be for an alteration in colour, but could be for an emphasis in form. The next sample has been knitted using the same technique as a previous sample but includes some single-jersey rows in between each of the partial-knit shaping rows. In this instance, the full rows of a single jersey were knitted using an elastic with a smaller tension.

Colour changes, such as stripes, help to define the structure. This sample is knitted with each group individually rather than combined groups. The yarn colour was changed after every two full rows and the carriage ended all the way back over on the right-hand side. *Yarn: One end 4-ply mercerised cotton in each colour. Stitch size: 7.*

Knitted using exactly the same method as the very first sample in this section with combined groups. The colour was also changed every two full rows when the carriage ended on the right-hand side of the working needles. *Yarn A: Gold 3-ply mercerised cotton. Yarn B: Green 4-ply mercerised cotton. Tension: 6.*

Similarly, changing colour after every full row and working with the twisted technique creates an undulating effect. The yarn is cut and reinserted after each full row as the yarn finishes at the opposite side that it started. *Yarn A: Purple, one end 4-ply mercerised cotton. Yarn B: Gold, one end 3-ply mercerised cotton. Tension: 6.*

Another piece in which the sections were altered slightly to encourage the knit to twist; however, the colour changed after each full row, directly alternating the colours. Therefore each time the carriage was travelling across the needle bed through the groups to the left, yellow was being worked; and each time the carriage worked back to the right through all the groups, purple was used. The yarn was cut and reinserted after each full row. *Yarn A: Yellow 4-ply organic cotton. Yarn B: Purple 4-ply mercerised cotton. Tension: 7.*

Stripes using a yarn with different properties can emphasise the structure of the piece. A shrinking yarn over the single-jersey rows can shrink the areas, condensing the general structure. *Yarn A: Three ends 2/48NM wool. Yarn B: Shirring elastic. Tension over the partial knit areas: 6. Tension over the shirring elastic: 5.*

The back of the sample shows the stripes with the shirring elastic which help to constrict the knit into form.

Mirroring Sections

Mirroring each sample will enable you to create the wavy pattern of the structures we have just been focusing on, but in a symmetrical structure rather than with each of the sections moving in the same direction. It is another detail to the pattern and an element that can be translated across all elements of working with partial knit in sections. This is often best presented when the piece is stretched after its completion to emphasise the structure, rather than allowing it to relax. The additional process involved to mirror the structure can make the basic samples more complicated to knit, therefore planning their structure is a necessity. Once you are in the rhythm of the knit, you will begin to see where you are, but start with mapping out the piece.

To create a mirrored piece we will need to split the knit up even more than just into groups of needles. As the direction of the knit is determined by carriage direction, we will divide the knit up to work one set of needle groups in one carriage direction and the other set of needle groups in the opposite carriage direction. This cannot be achieved with only one length of yarn, therefore we will need to work intarsia into the sample. We do not need an intarsia carriage.

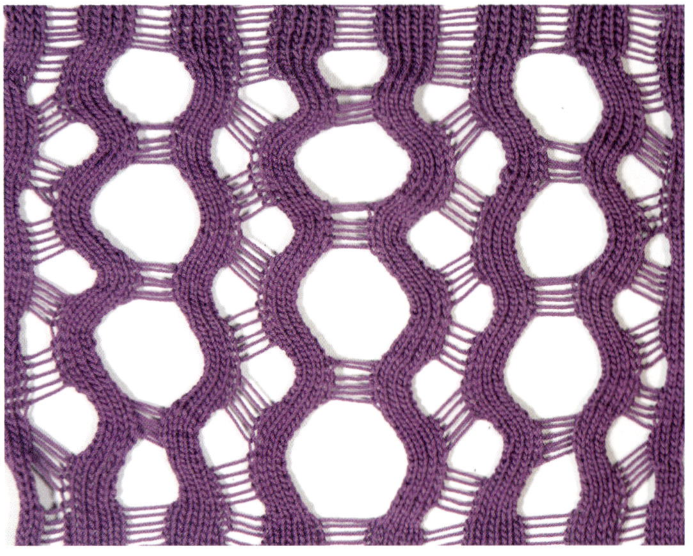

Mirroring the direction of the section is not as easy as simply altering the carriage direction mid-knit. Although this sample seems as if it has been knitted with one yarn, two cones of the same yarn were used in the same colour. *Yarn: One end 4-ply mercerised cotton. Tension: 7.*

Working a type of intarsia and splitting the pattern in half, we can mirror the sample and the direction of the vertical waves. This can be seen in the image as either side is worked in a different colour. *Yarn: Both colours, one end 4-ply mercerised cotton. Tension: 7.*

We will keep it simple to begin with the basics before yet again advancing the sample. For this example, cast on multiples of 5 working needles and 3 out-of-action needles. We will use an even number of groups, in this instance 6 groups. Groups A, B and C on the right will be worked using one cone of yarn, and groups D, E and F worked in a second cone. To make it easier to see, in this sample the two cones are different colours of the same yarn.

We start with the carriage on the right-hand side and working with yarn A. Work the right-hand 3 groups towards the centre in the following pattern.

1. Group A: Knit 8 rows COR.
2. Groups A and B: Knit 8 rows COR.
3. Groups A, B and C: Knit 1 row COL.
4. Groups B and C: Knit 7 rows COR.

Take out the yarn and disconnect the carriage so no needles will knit. Take the carriage across to the left side of the machine. The best way to achieve this without dropping stitches or disturbing live stitches is to place all needles into hold and move the carriage. Remember to place the next group of working needles into the upper working position before knitting the next group.

1. Group F: Knit 8 rows COL.
2. Groups F and E: Knit 8 rows. COL.
3. Groups F, E and D: Knit 1 row. COR.
4. Groups E and D: Knit 7 rows. COL.

Now we need to join the two sections together by working the two groups in the centre of the sample.

Take out the yarn and take the carriage over to the right. Insert the yarn from the right-hand side. Knit groups B and C, 1 row. Before taking the carriage back to the right, wrap the first needle on the right of group D, and also bring group B into the hold position so we are now only working group C. Knit back across group C; the carriage ends on the right.

Take the yarn out and take the carriage across to the left. Insert the yarn from the left-hand side. Knit groups E and D for 1 row. Bring group E into the hold position so we are only working group D. Wrap the centre needle and knit back across group D to the left.

Take out the yarn and take the carriage across to the right so we are working group C again. Repeat working each section individually whilst wrapping the end needle of group D, until 8 rows have been knitted in total over the middle 2 sections.

After this central section has been knitted to join the two separate cones of yarn, we will work each side separately and in reverse order, similarly to the previous steps.

1. Groups C and B: Knit 7 rows COL.
2. Groups C, B and A: Knit 1 row COR.
3. Groups B and A: Knit 8 rows COR.
4. Group A: Knit 8 rows COR.

Continue through each group in reverse with the yarn on the right-hand side until the carriage has knitted the last group. Work an extra row to finish with the carriage on the right.

Next, place all the needles into the hold position to take the carriage to the left-hand side and work a section picking up the left-hand yarn in the centre of the working area.

1. Groups D and E: Knit 7 rows COR.
2. Groups D, E and F: Knit 1 row COL.
3. Groups E and F: Knit 8 rows COL.
4. Group F: Knit 8 rows COL.

Once that is complete, you will be back at the starting position with a yarn on the far-right-hand side and a yarn on the far-left-hand side, and an even amount of material that has been built up over the cast-on needles.

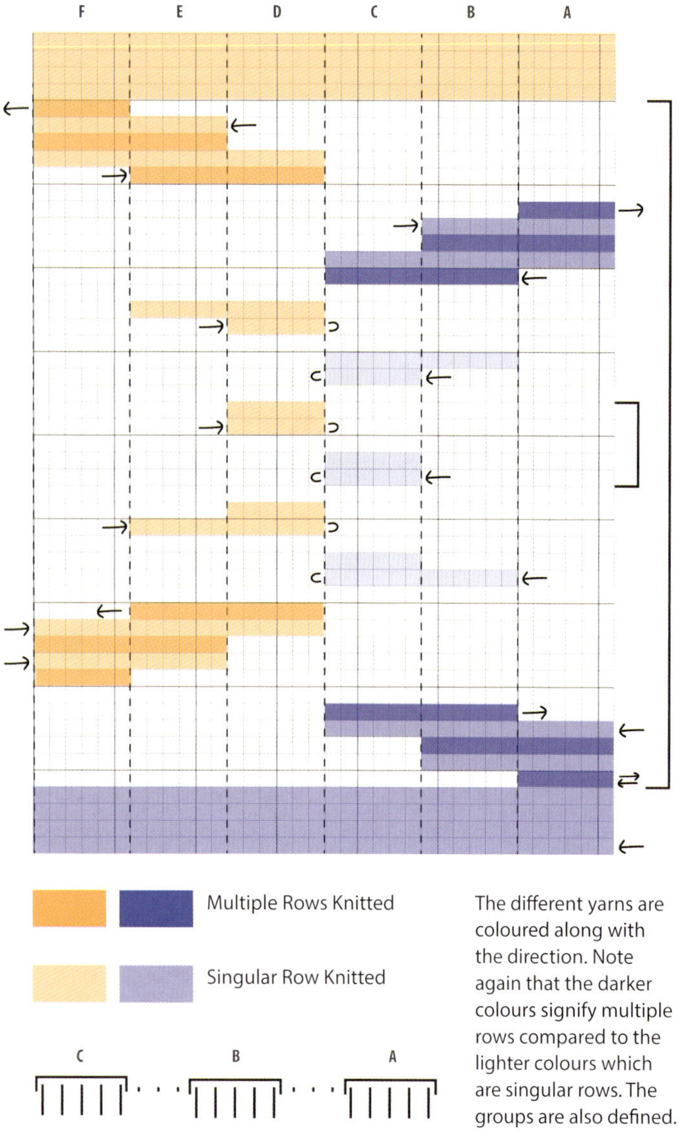

The different yarns are coloured along with the direction. Note again that the darker colours signify multiple rows compared to the lighter colours which are singular rows. The groups are also defined.

This whole process is repeated to build up the main material. See the chart for one repeat of the process.

Note: When using only one colour of yarn (but two bobbins) you only need to wrap the end needle once when joining the two central sections. Wrapping with each colour as previously mentioned is to ensure the sample is fully symmetrical with no colour dominating the structure and no extra central floats.

You can mirror with as many bobbins as you like and also with whichever structure you choose from the Partially Knitted Sections part of this book. It would, however, be advisable to plan the structure prior to casting on so you know how many bobbins of yarn you will need and the general layout of the structure you are mirroring.

This sample has been worked in an identical method to the previous sample, but a different needle layout was used and the number of rows knitted over each group varied. It was still only split into two groups with a central mirror point. *Yarn: One end 4-ply mercerised cotton. Tension: 7.*

The number of bobbins used to create more mirrored sections is up to you. Personally, I wouldn't use too many because the time it takes to knit up a sample can become quite lengthy. This last image was worked using four bobbins of yarn with each bobbin worked over two groups. It took about four hours to complete and I had to keep a very close eye on my position in the pattern and which sections I had already knitted.

This larger piece was worked with 4 groups of 6 needles and 3 needles out of action in between. Each group and bridge were knitted over 8 rows. Keeping the number of rows the same became one element less to think about.

After the first couple of repeats, it became easier to see which section was to be knitted next, and thus which sections were to be wrapped together to bridge them. Counting up the shaping holes from the cast-on row also helped me to make sure I was working at an even rate across the whole piece.

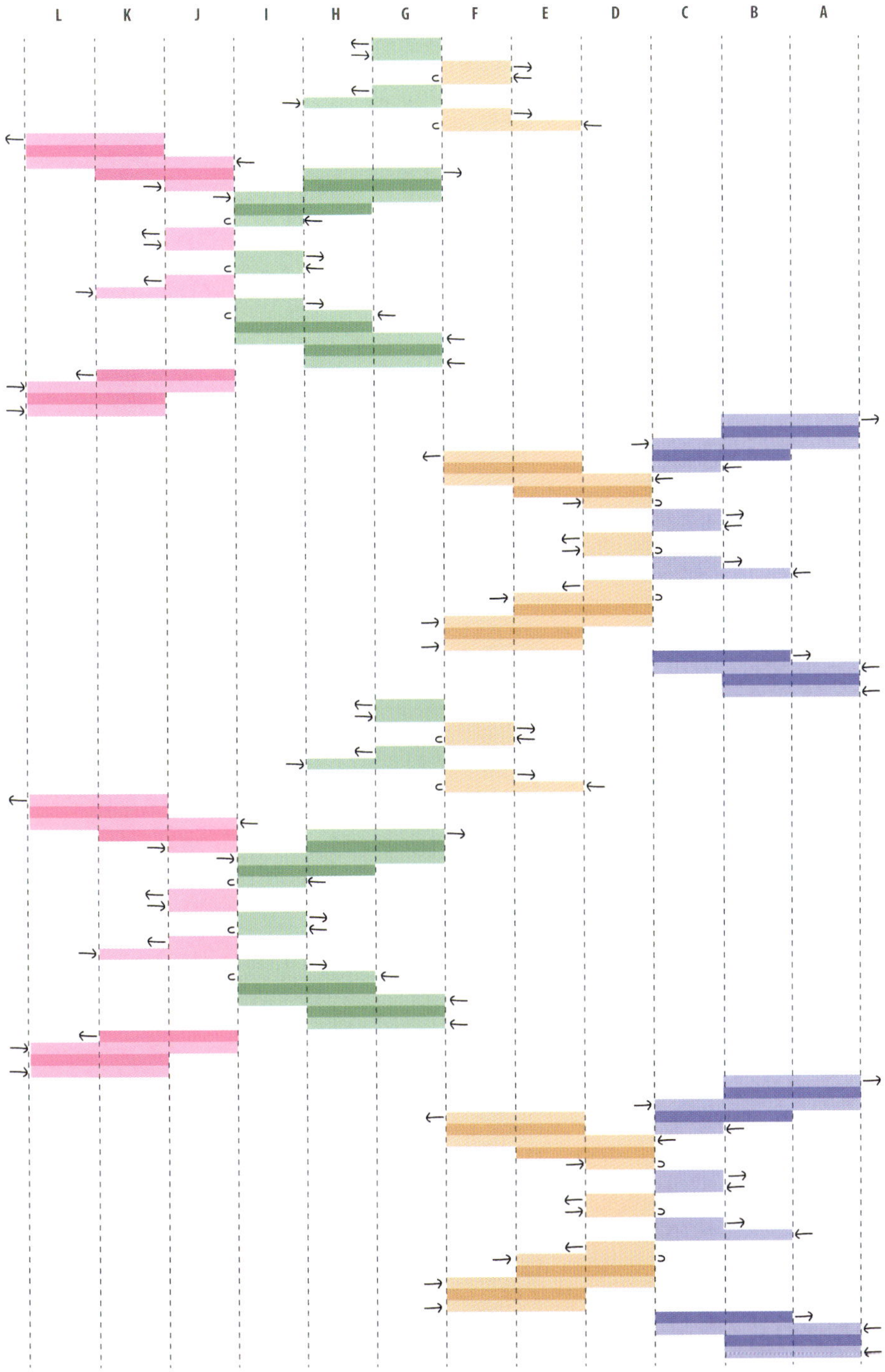

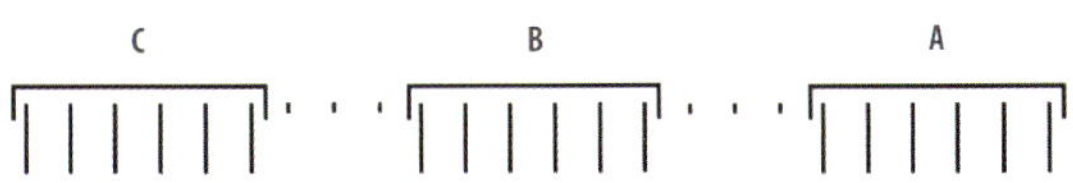

A much more complicated chart for the mirrored section with four bobbins. This has been simplified slightly compared to the first chart for the mirrored sections with fewer empty carriage rows. Colour-coded for the bobbins and also for the single or multiple rows. In the sample image, eight rows are knitted.

Technically, the number of mirrored sections within the structure is not limited, therefore some intricate structures can be built up. *Yarn: Three ends 2/16NE mercerised cotton. Tension: 6.*

BRAIDS

By working in sections of the needles, we can create loops within the knit that can then be interlocked together, either joining sections of knit together or creating a texture within the textile sample. This is a very similar technique to one that will be covered in the next chapter; each of the techniques is versatile in many ways and can be adapted with the simplest adjustment.

These loops that form the braids can be made over any number of needles, with any number of rows, and at any point within the main structure of the material. It should be noted that each of these samples that use braids has different-sized loops. This is not only to show the difference between the size of the loops, but also to test various structures and sizes to find the size that best suits your design. The main element to consider is whether the loop is large enough to stretch to the next loop and interlock, or whether there are enough rows knitted in between each loop. There is no rule for this apart from trial and error, and testing the tightness of the braids after they have been looped together.

Working with loops of knit, they can be interlocked and joined either as a fastening of the material or as a surface pattern and texture. These loops were linked in a criss-cross pattern over the surface rather than following the columns or rows that they were created in. *Yarn: 2/16NE cotton. Tension: 5.*

This first sample is a basic series of loops that can be interlocked in several different directions. Each loop is made over 5 needles with 4 needles in between each loop. Each loop is knitted for 30 rows.

Cast on in multiples of 9 plus 4 edge needles and knit some rows to establish the knit.

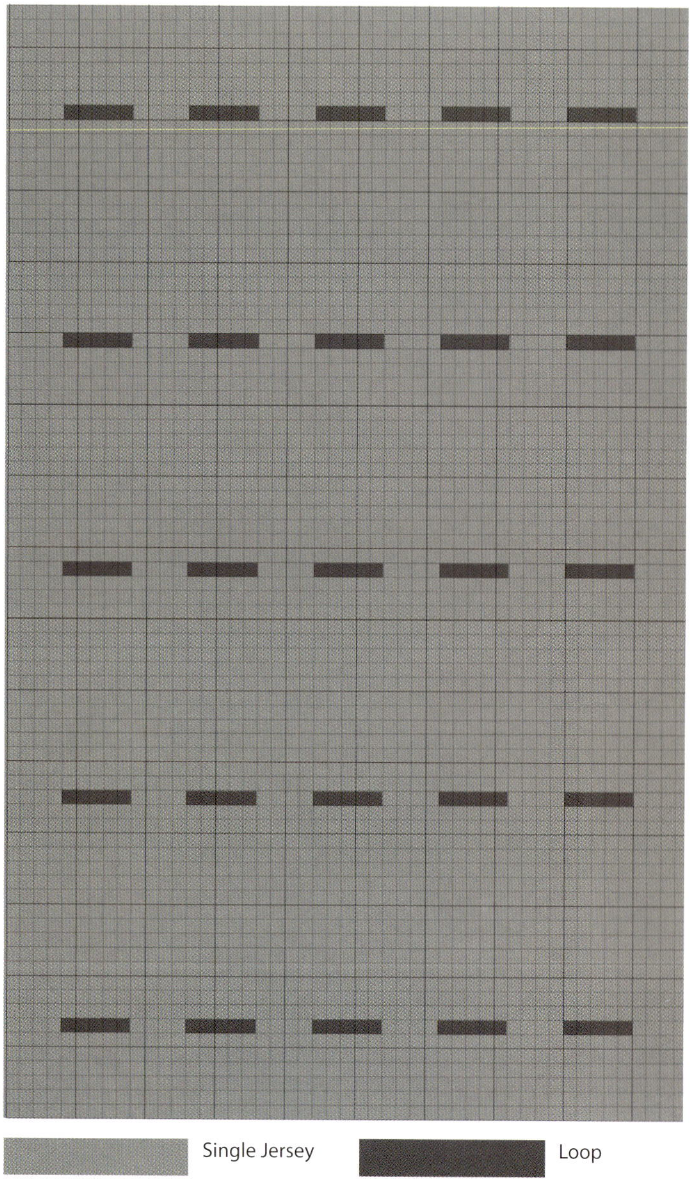

The chart shows the placement of the loops across the surface of this sample. Each darker area represents a loop placement and not the loop structure.

Working with partial knit, with the carriage on the right, place the carriage into hold and bring into the hold position all needles apart from 9 needles on the right-hand side.

Take the carriage across to the left, over the 9 needles, and then bring out the furthest right-hand side 4 needles. We are now only knitting over 5 needles.

Knit 29 rows over these 5 needles. It will be imperative to keep a check on the weight over this section of knit. I use my hand to manually hold the knit down, acting like a weight; however, you can use a claw weight as long as it is moved up regularly, and placed only on the section of 5 needles.

Once 29 rows are knitted, the carriage will end on the right-hand side. We can now introduce the next 9 needles (the next loop of 5 needles and the 4 needles in between each loop). Take the carriage across what are now 14 needles in the working position on the left-hand side.

Bring out the right-hand side 9 needles so we are now only working on the 5 needles for the loop, and knit the loop in the same way as previously.

Repeat this across the working needles until all loops have been formed across the cast-on needles, ending by knitting the last 4 needles as you take the carriage across to the left. Take the carriage back to the right-hand side, knitting all needles.

Next, knit 14 rows of all-needles knitting to create vertical space between the loops. Repeat the row of loops in the same placement as the previous row.

For this sample, the loops were repeated 5 times on the horizontal and 5 times on the vertical before being cast off.

Once cast off, the loops can be interlocked across the sample to join them together, creating a braid within the material. This is done by taking the second loop in line through the first loop; then continue the process by bringing each loop through the previous loop and making a chain.

The last loop that is passed through will need to be secured to the main knit to make certain that the braid does not undo over time or through handling of the material. This can be done by working a few hand stitches at the top on the underside of the loop so it is not seen from the front side of the braid.

We can alter the initial sample by changing the colour of the loops, working with different sizes of loops (both the length and the width), and also the placement to interlock. *Yarn A: Pink 2/16NE cotton. Yarn B: Green, one end 2/15NM wool.*

To work the loops as a series of fastenings, in order to join two pieces together, the loops should be worked on the edge of the material. The technique is exactly the same as working the loops in the centre of the material, just using the edge needles.

Cast on the width of the material needed plus 6 needles for the loops on the right-hand side, and knit to establish the stitches on the needles. At the point for the first loop, bring into the hold position all needles apart from the 6 right-hand edge needles.

Bring the carriage into the hold position and knit 20 rows only on the 6 right-hand side needles, to create the loop. Ensure the weight over the loop is monitored and either moved when needed, or work the weight of the loop manually to ensure the loops are held away from the needles.

With the carriage finishing on the right-hand side, bring the carriage back to knit all needles and pass it across all working needles and knit 6 rows of single jersey. This is the part separating the loops.

By only working the loops on the edge stitches, we can create loops that can be used to join two pieces of material together. *Yarn A: Pink, one end 4-ply cotton. Yarn B: Green, one end 3-ply worsted wool. Tension: 6.*

Having loops on both sides of the working material allows us to create a material that can be fastened together with a second, third, fourth etc. piece of material that also has loops, by braiding them together. The loops are made longer here to give a looser connection. Depending on the tightness of interlock you want, the loops can be knitted to length. *Yarns vary from 3-ply wool to 2/16NE cotton.*

After this first loop is formed, we repeat the same process of creating the loop on the same right-hand side, building up a series of loops on the same side.

Once the length of material required has been made, the second side of the material needs to be knitted. In this instance, it has been knitted in a different colour which allows you to see the braiding more clearly.

Another difference is that the loops will be knitted on the opposite side to the previous sample. This might mean that an extra row needs to be worked to take the carriage across to the opposite side, then you bring all needles apart from the far-right-hand 6 needles out into the hold position in preparation for the first loop on the left-hand side.

With the carriage in the hold position, knit a loop of 20 rows on the working 6 needles.

Once the 20 rows have been knitted, work 6 rows of knitting with all needles to create space in between the loops. Work the same number of loops that were knitted on the first section so there are an equal number of loops to link together along the edge section.

Once both pieces are off the machine, starting from one edge, the first loop on one piece can be brought through the first loop on the second piece, then continue interlocking each loop by passing it through a loop on the opposite side.

To further this idea of connecting pieces of material together, loops can be worked on both sides of the material, allowing us to create a material that can be braided on either side. This allows us to create an unlimited width of material as we are joining multiple lengths together.

Creating braids around the outline of each sample means they can all be joined together to create a larger piece that is similar to patchwork. Each piece within this sample has a loop made over six needles with four needles in between each loop on the horizontal, with eight rows in between each vertical loop. *Yarns vary. Tension: around 6 but slightly adjusted for each yarn.*

Connecting on the Horizontal

Not only can pieces be joined together through the vertical edges of each material by connecting them through loops made on each side, they can also be connected on the horizontal using the cast-on and cast-off edges, also through loops made just after the cast-on and just before the cast-off. This allows a much larger piece of material to be created, similar to a patchwork blanket, with a variety of yarns, textures, colours and also patterns.

Each piece should be made with a similar yarn weight in a similar tension to ensure that the loops will join up and link together. If two very different yarns are used with different stitch sizes, this could alter the positioning of the loops on both the vertical and the horizontal. Having said this, explore the differences in yarn and contrasts to observe the different textures.

If the material tensions are very different and this is intentional, it would be advisable to do a couple of tests, or to make some tension samples and calculate the number of rows and stitches needed in between each loop to ensure they will loop at the correct position. It may also be necessary to calculate the number of rows in each loop to make them long enough.

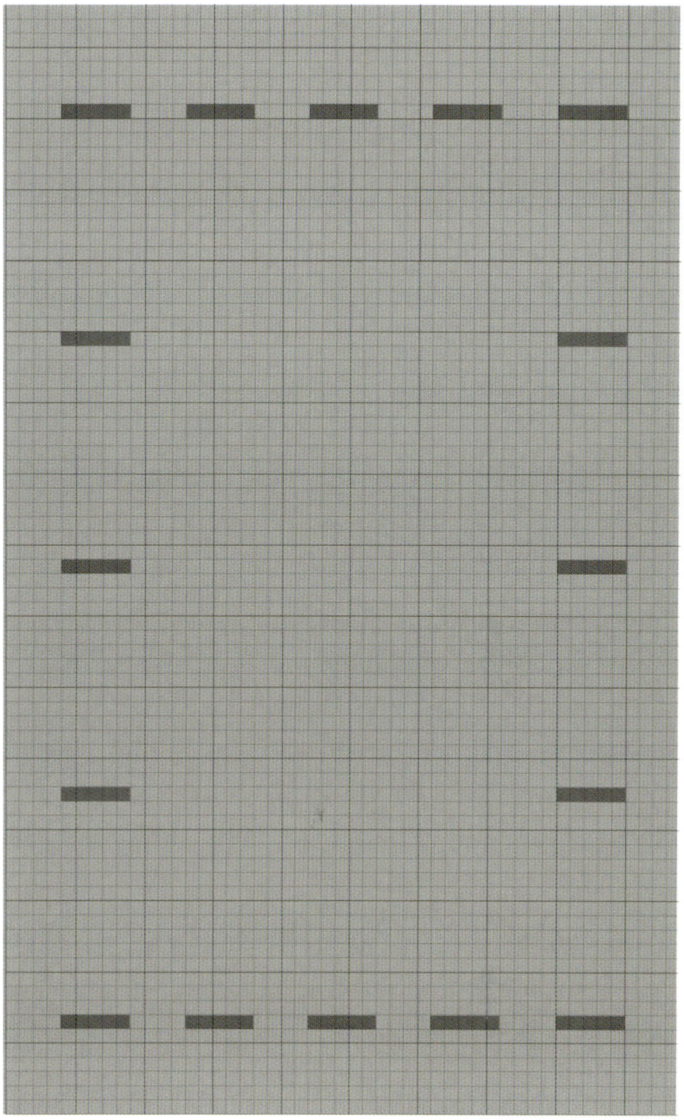

Single Jersey — Loop

The placement of the loops to create a patchwork-type sample where individual pieces can be connected together to create a much larger piece. The darker areas signify a loop, but not the rows within the loop.

The process to knit a border with loops is to combine both the first sample within this section, and the sample working the loops of both edges. Once the length of the piece has been knitted, repeat the horizontal row of loops a couple of rows prior to casting off.

POCKETS

Pockets have been included within this chapter because, whilst not directly using partial knit to be constructed, we are selecting needles to be either worked or left out of action, therefore using an element of partial knit.

Pockets within knit can be created for many reasons, from creating a quilted effect for garments or blankets, through to sensory products within textiles. This technique is one that cannot be created on an industrial machine as there is no opportunity to stuff the pocket unless it is fully off the machine. This technique is possible on a V-bed machine using high- and low-butt needles for the needle selection; however, only two colours can be used and worked as stripes rather than a pattern placement. This method will not be covered in this chapter as we are working more with hand-manipulated techniques. These pocket techniques have been constructed on the domestic Silver Reed machine with a ribber attachment. You would only be able to recreate the colour placement with a domestic machine and not a V-bed machine due to needing the ability to select particular needles, which is not possible on a V-bed machine.

Methods to create pockets with a punch card or using electronic software and slip stitch are also possible, and may cut down the time it takes to knit, but all the samples in this section have been manipulated by hand.

One-Colour Pockets

We can start with a basic one-colour pocket method. The pockets in this sample have been positioned in a repetitive placement to allow you to trial the method first and become accustomed to it.

We will start by casting on multiples of 11 plus 3 needles on the double bed. Out of these working needles, 3 needles on either side will act as closing stitches to ensure the material becomes whole rather than a piece of tubular material. There will be pockets of 8 needles with 3 needles dividing each pocket.

After the basic double bed is cast on, place the carriage straight into circular (or tubular) as this will be the main carriage position for the one-colour pockets. Working in circular after a double-bed cast-on will effectively create one large pocket across the whole working area. To split it up and create smaller pockets, when the carriage only knits on the front bed, we will bring the 3 dividing needles on the main bed (or back bed) into the forward working position.

As these needles are in the forward working position, the needles will be forced to knit when the carriage is taken across. This in turn creates the smaller individual pockets that can then be stuffed. Once the pocket is made to the desired length (in this sample 12 full rows, or 24 passes of the carriage), the ribber bed can be dropped, opening up the pocket so that it can be stuffed. Raising the ribber attachment and knitting a full row of all-needle knit closes the pocket.

Pockets can be any number of rows in length and any width or shape as the control is down to the knitter. We can begin to play with this and incorporate more colours into the pockets, although the method alters slightly.

Using only one colour to create a structured pocket fabric that can be filled with anything from scrap yarns to stuffing or more sensory fillers such as rice or beads. *Yarn: One end 2-ply Jamieson's Of Shetland Spindrift wool. Tension: 7.*

Basic circular knitting creates one large pocket over the cast-on needles.

Bringing the needles into the forward working position will create closed knitted sections which give the pockets structure.

The row being knitted in the front bed only will also use the needles that are brought into the FWP on the main bed.

Dropping the ribber bed allows you to access the pockets to stuff them.

Knitting a full row of double jersey closes the pockets.

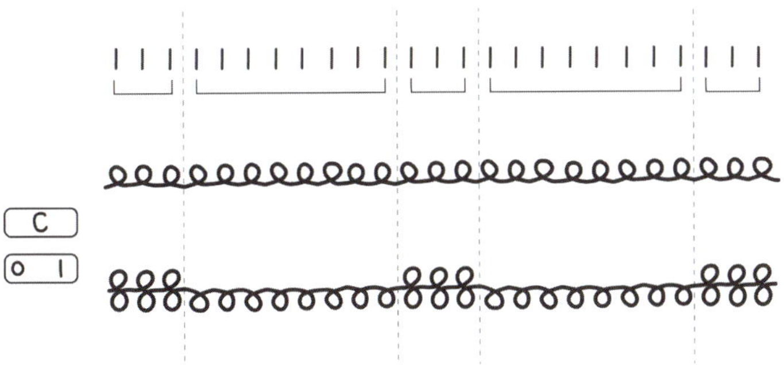

C Carriage
O I in circular

The working of the yarn over the needles when the pocket is in construction. This makes obvious the circular structure along with the pocket dividers made using the back bed.

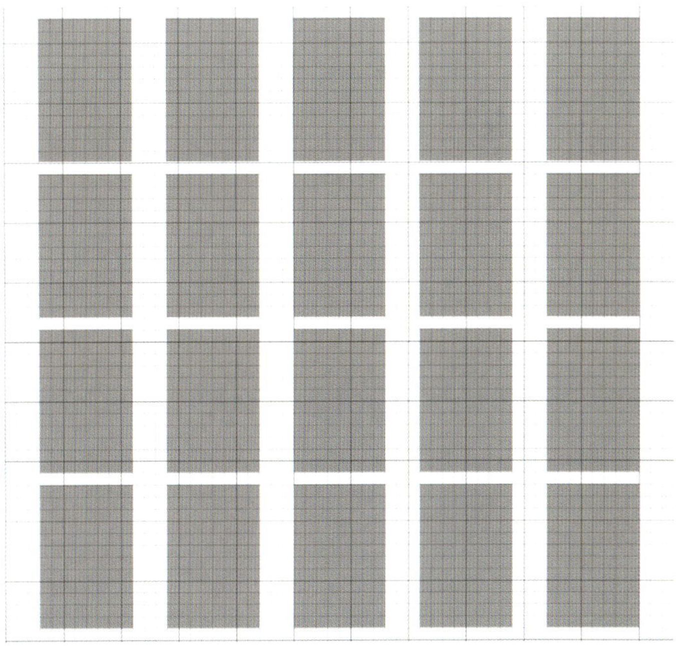

Pocket
Pocket Dividers

The placement of the pockets. In this instance the pockets are evenly spaced apart and the same height in rows.

Two-Colour Pockets

Now would be the opportunity to set up the colour changer with the double bed if you have one, as we will introduce two-and three-colour pockets. Although you can change colour without a colour changer on the double bed, it becomes a little more complicated as you will need to take the yarn out of the carriage manually and feed in the next colour.

For this sample we will keep the same set-up as the previous sample (multiples of 11 needles plus 3 edge needles). Cast on and hang the weights on the double bed.

Starting with the carriage on the left (to enable the use of the colour changer) and using colour A, disengage the back bed and knit 2 rows on the front bed only. Return the carriage to the colour changer to change to colour B.

Re-engage the back bed and disengage the front bed to only knit on the back bed. Bring up into the forward working position on the front bed 3 needles on each edge of the knit and 3 needles after 8-needle intervals throughout the working area, to join the front and back bed together. These needles that are manually brought up create the divides in the pockets. Alternating between knitting on the front and back bed creates the pocket structure instead of circular working where the front bed is knitted and the back bed on the second pass of the carriage. For pockets with 2 or more colours, 2 rows of one bed are knitted before you change to the opposite bed. This builds up the structure.

Follow the chart for the needle placement.

After a few rows, drop down the main bed to check that you are creating both open areas to be stuffed and the joining sections where there is the vertical pocket divide.

Working with selected needles, two colours can be incorporated into the pocket structure. The spacing between the pockets will be striped and the main pocket colour solid. The pockets can all be the same colour (as pictured) or each pocket alternating in colour. *Yarn: One end 2-ply Jamieson's Of Shetland Spindrift wool in each colour. Tension: 7.*

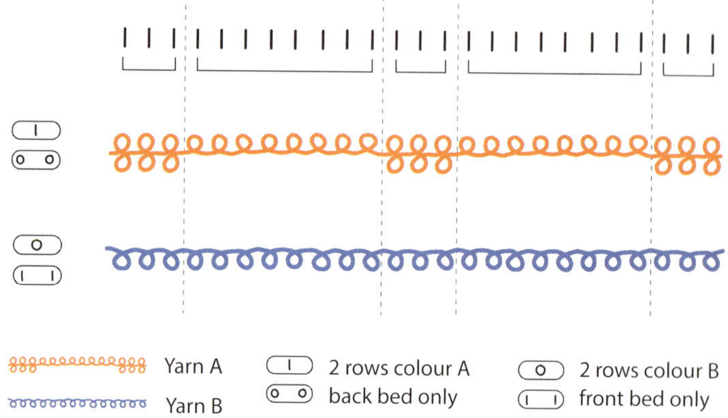

The placement of the yarn over the needles and the carriage positions for the two-colour pockets.

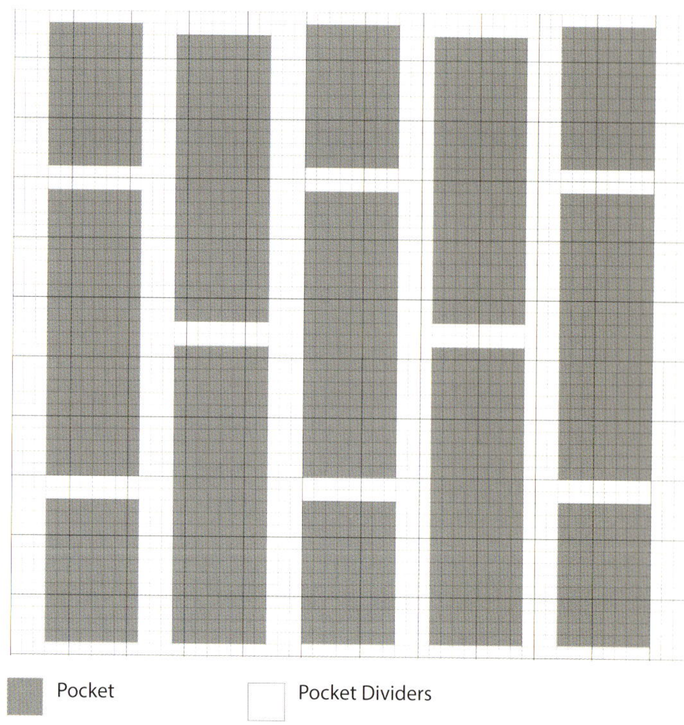

The pocket placement on the knit sample. All the pockets are the same colour and the background a second colour.

As you change colour every 2 rows, technically you will also be knitting the front bed with yarn A and the back bed with yarn B. This is a useful reminder of which bed you are knitting next and with which colour. Where the needles are brought into work on the front bed when knitting with yarn B, this will not only create the structure of the pockets, but also a colour detail. The pockets are predominantly in yarn A, and the joining structures in striped A and B.

For this sample, each pocket was closed at different times to create a stacked effect. Counting the rows, the first, third and fifth pocket were closed after 12 circular rows, continuing on with the second and fourth pocket for another 12 circular rows. Because closing pockets is done by bringing all the needles across that pocket into the forward working position, this can be done at any point in the knit, and can be done quite randomly to create a more organic shape to the pockets if desired.

Pocket Placement

Now we have explored the basics of handmade pockets, we can experiment with placement and shaping the pockets. The pocket shape does not have to stay rectangular and can change with your design.

One element to note which may need to be taken into consideration is that we are technically knitting the needles that combine the front and the back twice, and those that make the pocket once. Therefore, if you are trying to make a pocket in the centre of a piece with flat surroundings, the surrounding area will be twice as large as the pocket area.

You can see this quite clearly with the colouring that has been used in the next sample. The pocket area is purple and the surrounding area striped white and purple.

To reiterate about the structure of the pocket, the separations and closings of the pockets are due to us forcing selected front-bed needles to work when working a back-bed-only row. Bringing the needles into the forward working position whilst the front bed is deselected will force the needles to work and create stitches. These needles are then reintroduced into the working position when the carriage is passed, bringing them back into the non-selected state as that side of the carriage is turned off. This means that we can change the needles selected at any point whilst the fabric is in construction.

If knitting a single pocket area, the surrounding knits may be twice as large as the pocket area. This is because the front and back of the pocket are knitted in circular over two passes of the carriage (the front for one pass and the back for the second) yet the sides are knitted in double jersey therefore a row with each pass.
Yarn A: Cream, one end 2-ply Shetland wool.
Yarn B: Purple, one end 2-ply Shetland wool.
Tension: 7.

A chart has been drawn up that replicates this sample in which the shape of the pocket alters from a basic rectangle. Following it, the needles that are brought into the forward working position to close the sides of the pockets alter every few rows.

Altering the main needle placement by increasing and decreasing will alter the main pocket shape. This allows for placement of both colour and texture within the main material and the pockets. *Yarn: One end Jamieson's Of Shetland Spindrift in each colour. Tension: 7.*

Shaped Pocket   Pocket Dividers

The pattern of the pocket placement with the moved stitches. Four stitches are used in between each pocket.

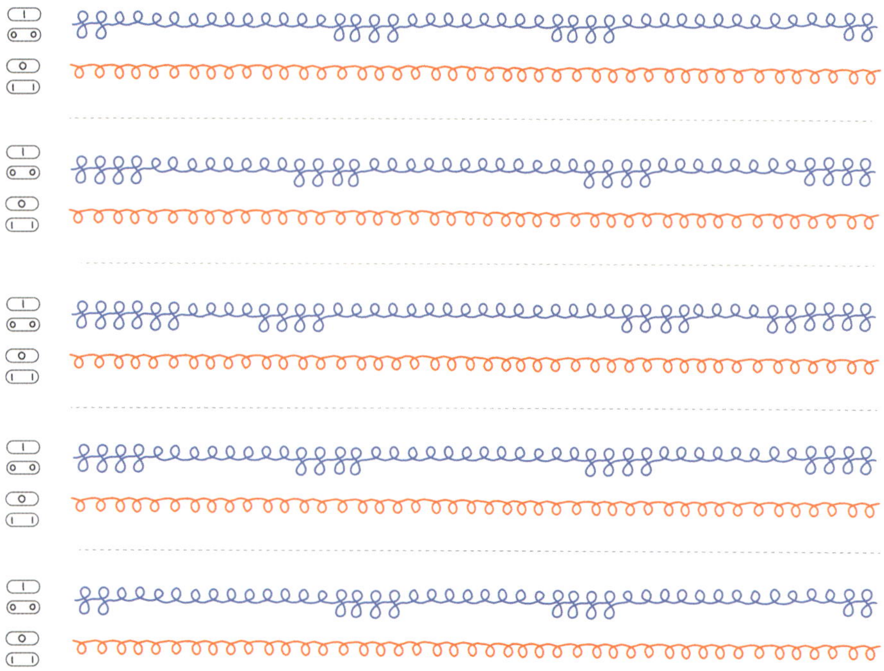

The stitches that would be built up when creating a shaped two-colour pocket. Notice how the stitches move when they are forced to knit on the front bed. This is due to manually choosing which needles will be worked on the front bed to make the pocket shape.

Yarn A

Yarn B

2 rows colour A

back bed only

2 rows colour B

front bed only

Shaping the Main Material

Now that we are happy shaping the pocket section, we can develop the idea further by increasing and decreasing the working needles to create a shaped piece. This next sample shows one large pocket that has been shaped. The transfers to increase and decrease happen on both beds after the front-bed-only row, and before the main-bed-only row that incorporates the front-bed needles in the forward working position. Increase and decrease as you usually would: either by bringing up an empty needle and knitting over the empty needle to create a stitch, or transferring a stitch over. As you are effectively working with the single bed, multiple increases or decreases should be cast on and cast off rather than worked as the double bed with a double jersey.

Shaping pockets can be achieved similarly to shaping for a garment, by increasing and decreasing the number of needles that are worked. The process is the same as changing the needle placement for the pocket shape, however, it is worked on the outer stitches. *Yarn: One end 2-ply Jamieson's Of Shetland Spindrift wool yarn in each colour. Tension: 7.*

Three-Colour Pockets

To increase the complexity a little further, we can add a third (or fourth or fifth if desired) colour into the design. This, along with shape alterations, can open up many possibilities for the pockets. In this example I have shown a variation on the first sample – to walk before we run!

The main difference with this alteration is that partial knit needs to be looked at in a different way. Partial knit will be used to work a sort of intarsia to create the different colours of the pockets, but as a type of reverse partial knit. Instead of using the forward working position to hold the needles and not knit, we will be using the forward working position to force the needles to knit whilst the needles in the working position will rest. This is very similar to working the pocket divides in the previous samples, but here for the main body of the material as well as the pocket details.

For this method, the carriage will be set to slip on both beds which means we must always bring the needles into the forward working position to knit. If we take the carriage across without selecting the working needles, the carriage will simply not knit.

Needles in the FWP will be forced to knit on the front bed even when the front bed is disengaged.

After the carriage passes, the needles in the FWP are brought back into work.

As the colour placement will be worked on the front bed, we will disengage the front-bed carriage and have it turned off for the full duration of the sample. The back bed will continue to alternate between engaged and not engaged to make the back side of the pocket material. This also means the back of the sample will be one colour whilst the front will be the colour detail over the pockets.

Follow the chart for the placement of the colour and the sequence of yarn usage.

More than two colours can be included with the pocket technique when the function of the needles and carriage are used in this slightly different method. Pattern or block colour is possible as you are controlling which needles are knitting, therefore controlling the pattern build-up. *Yarn: One end 2-ply Shetland wool in each colour. Tension: Front and back bed 6.*

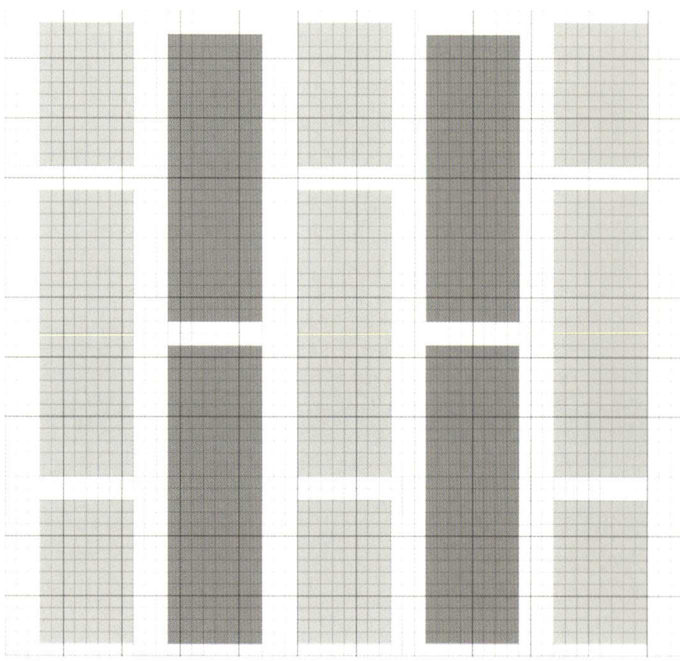

The pocket placement and the colours used for the three-coloured pocket. Working with this chart, make your own and create a design for a three-coloured pocket.

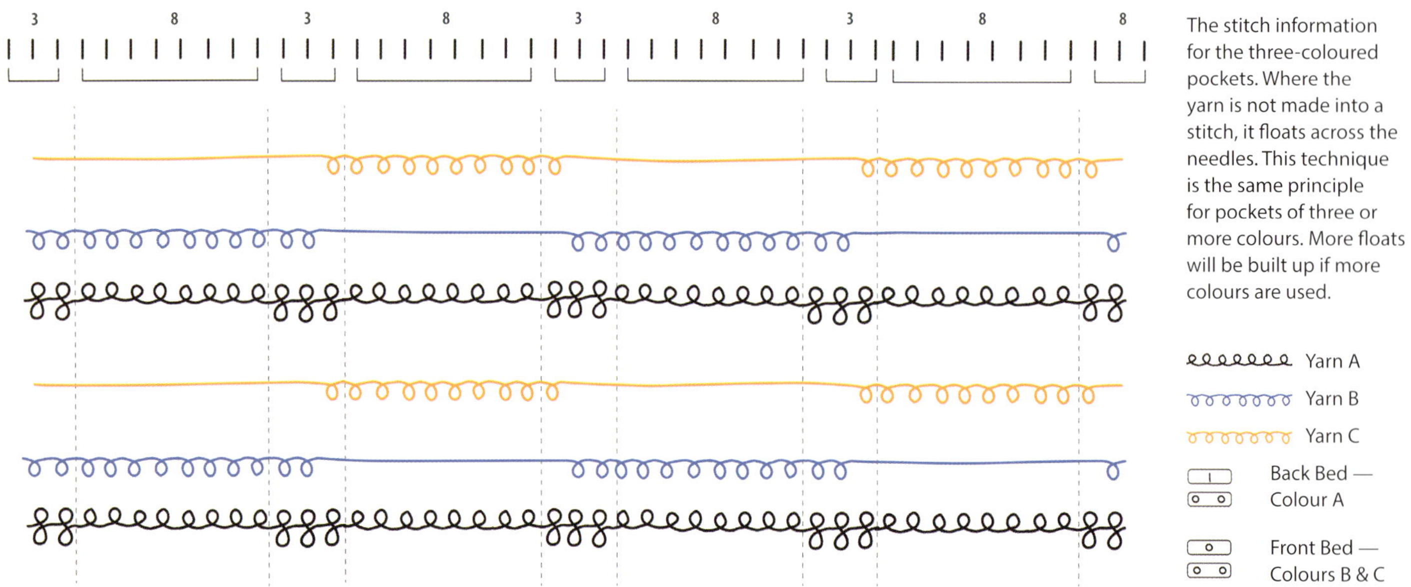

The stitch information for the three-coloured pockets. Where the yarn is not made into a stitch, it floats across the needles. This technique is the same principle for pockets of three or more colours. More floats will be built up if more colours are used.

B

Cast on the same needle placement for the two-colour pockets (multiples of 11 needles plus 3 end needles).

1. Rows 1 and 2: Front bed only – bring into FWP on the front bed colour blocks A, C and E, knit across.
2. Rows 3 and 4: Front bed only – bring into FWP on the front bed colour blocks B and D, knit across.
3. Rows 5 and 6: Back bed only – bring into FWP on the front bed the pocket edge needles, knit across.

The needles for yarn A are brought into the FWP to be knitted on the front bed. Knit two rows with this needle selection.

The needles for yarn B are brought into the FWP to be knitted on the front bed. Knit two rows with this needle selection.

The build-up of the structure is more obvious when the front bed is dropped down, revealing the pockets.

Once they are ready to be stuffed, the pockets can be filled with any material. Here, old toy stuffing is being used and compacted with the transfer tool.

Two rows of double jersey are worked to close all the pockets when needed.

Repeat these 6 rows for the duration of the sample.

To close the pockets, again bring the front-bed needles over the pockets to be closed into the forward working position when you are working a back-bed-only row. Where a colour is not knitted, it will float over the resting needles. This float will then be tucked into the pocket along with the stuffing, so will not be visible.

You would follow the same process if you were to add a fourth or fifth colour into the sample. This could also lead to working with a pattern in the pockets rather than leaving them plain.

Using the same process as the three-colour pocket, we can create a four-colour pocket with a pattern detail – in this instance, a stripe. This pocket has also been shaped rather than left as a rectangle. You can plan the pocket details using squared paper. *Yarn: A mix of Spindrift and a 3-ply wool. Tension: Both front and back beds 6.*

Finally, there is a general rule within machine knitting that may need to be considered when working with multiple colours and groups of needles out of action. Floating over more than an inch (roughly 2.5cm), or the same number of needles as the gauge of the machine, can become problematic as the yarn in the feeder can rise slightly. This increases the risk of the yarn not being placed into the needle hook correctly, which can potentially lead to dropped stitches. To avoid this, try not to float over too many needles, especially when you are forcing needles to work and leaving groups of needles out of work. The methods for pockets with three or more colours will naturally begin to float over a larger area of needles so work slowly. You can also help the yarn by holding it gently down against the needle bed as the carriage comes from left to right until it has worked the first stitch.

CHAPTER 2

LIFTED STITCHES AND OTTOMAN

The content in this chapter works well in conjunction with other techniques. It will be broken up into two sections: lifted stitches and rolls. These are two different techniques but they give very similar results, which is why they have been grouped together.

Ottoman, also known as rolls or ripples, is seen as a double-bed technique as we use one bed to create the material of the main fabric, and the second bed to create the roll and texture.

Lifted stitches, on the other hand, are seen as a single-bed technique as we will be rehanging knitted stitches back up onto the machine to create the form. Therefore we need access to both the material that is in construction on the machine, and also to the needle bed. It would be harder to reach the fabric if the second bed is in action due to the material being constructed in between both beds. If you do not have a ribber attachment for your domestic machine, lifted stitches give the same results as Ottoman.

MACHINE TYPE

It should be mentioned that the V-bed machines (such as Dubied, Universal, Stoll) can be a little limited with these techniques. Ottoman that is created on a V-bed machine is structured and clean but can be limited to around four to six rows in depth. This, of course, is not a rule, and there are methods in which the depth knitted can be much bigger, but in this chapter we have used lifted stitches on the single bed for those techniques.

The difficulties come from weight on the knit and the structure. When working on one needle bed to build up material we lose the weight, meaning the stitches are not held down when the needles rise as the carriage is taken across. This can result in yarn being placed into the needles when the original stitches have not passed the latch of the needle, resulting in no new stitch being made, but excess yarn in the needle. In this chapter, both machines are used to create the samples; however, you will notice the V-bed machines have been used more than the domestic machines for the Ottoman samples, whereas the domestic machines have been used only for the lifted stitches.

SUGGESTED YARNS

Yarn choice becomes quite an important decision when working with rolls and lifted stitches. For Ottoman we are generally looking to create a relatively dense material, therefore a yarn that would have allowance for some shrinkage, or a strong yarn where we can create quite tight stitches would be ideal to use for the main material. This is not a rule, but a factor that could enhance the structure and surface texture. We will explore many different yarn types through some of the Ottoman samples to see what happens when we change one of the yarns for a different type.

For lifted stitches, yarn choice is not such an important factor considering that we are hand manipulating the material as we knit it. Therefore, even with the tightest of stitches we would be able to manipulate the textile. Yarn choice would be more of a texture play or preference when knitting. Again, we will look into different options for yarn as we experiment with the technique.

OPPOSITE: Dense ripples worked with an elastic yarn create a structured and three-dimensional material.

LIFTED STITCHES

We will start with lifted stitches on the single bed. Lifted stitches, being a hand-manipulated technique, can be applied at any time in the knit structure and at any point of the sample. It is one of the only techniques that cannot be directly replicated on an industrial machine due to the fact the knitter has to have access to both the knitted material and the needles. It works best on a single bed as the knitter manually picks up stitches from the knitted material on the machine and rehangs the stitches onto the needles in work. Depending on the placement of the rehung stitches, the material can twist, bulge and gather, transitioning the knit material into three-dimensional form quickly and easily.

Lifted stitches occur on the back side of the material as this is the side that the knitter can access when knitting. The knitter can lift all the stitches across one row, or a select few, depending on the desired outcome. The material on the front side of the fabric then becomes a roll or bulge within the textile. There are no rules to lifting stitches. You could lift and rehang the corner of the knit, the cast-on edge, or even live stitches from another piece to join two pieces of knitted material together.

A main difference between Ottoman and lifted stitches is the number of rows that can be inserted into the roll. We are limited to approximately six rows (depending on the yarn) on a V-bed machine when working Ottoman technique, compared to no limitation on the single bed with lifted stitches. This is due to the take-down of the knit on the machine and the complications that can arise when one side of the material is held as the other is worked over, compared to knitting as usual and then rehanging the made material back up onto the needles. There is more coverage of this in the Ottoman section further on in this chapter.

An example of a lifted-stitch piece where the number of rows is not limited to six. In this instance, up to 150 rows have been knitted into the piece before the stitches were lifted and rehung. Partial knit was also used simultaneously to create additional form, but the large rolls came from the excessive number of rows knitted into each section. This piece took around 34 hours to knit.

LIFTING THE STITCHES

Step 1: Finding the heel of the stitch on the row you would like to rehang (in most of the samples it will be on the change of colour): using the transfer tool, insert the points of the tool into the stitch.

Step 2: Place the transfer tool on the needles onto which you are rehanging the stitches.

Step 3: Pull out the needles and lift the stitches onto the needles. There will now be two stitches on the needles: the existing stitches from the last row knitted, and now the stitches from the needles that were rehung.

Step 4: The needles can either be brought into the forward working position and forced to knit with the next pass of the carriage, or moved back into the normal working position and knitted as normal.

The main constraint would be the stretch of the knit on the needles. For instance, you would not be able to lift adjacent stitches in opposite directions as the stretch would not allow it. You are, however, able to lift and gather in material from points towards each other.

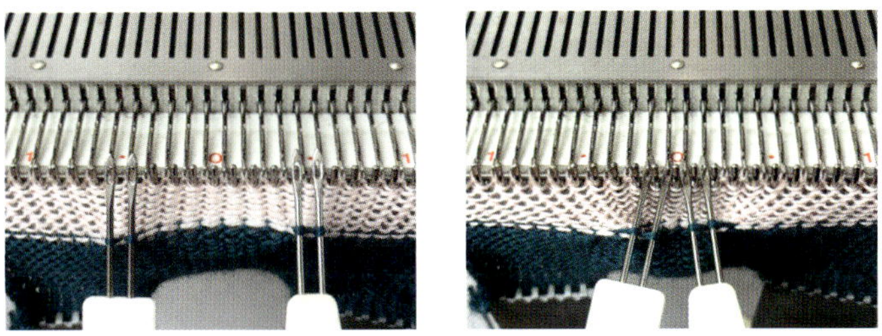

You can pick up the heels of stitches and move them both in towards each other and rehang in a different position.

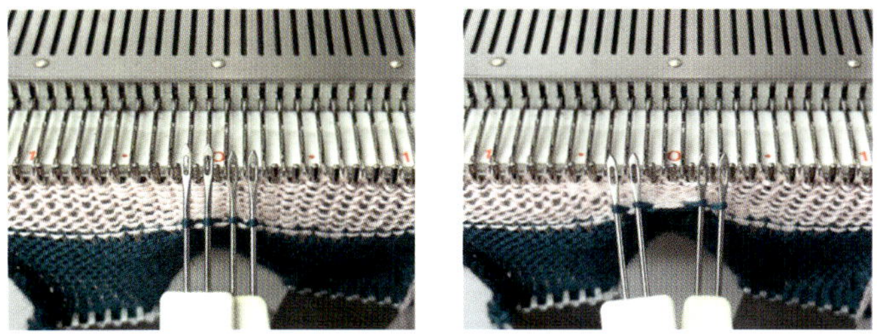

However, you cannot pick up the heels of stitches and rehang them in opposite directions to each other, due to the stretch of the yarn and the yarn needed to space them out away from each other.

Lifting Selected Needles

This section will focus on choosing specific stitches and bringing them back up onto the needles across the whole working area, rather than lifting stitches to create rolls. This will create both patterned effects and also very similar structures to Ottoman. If there is a structure that you like that is created through Ottoman, but you do not have a double-bed machine, this option would be perfect for you.

Creating patterns within lifted stitches is all about pre-planning where you will lift your stitches. We can work with squared paper to plan the pattern, but you can also decide as you work on the machine, creating an organic and spontaneous pattern in the piece.

Working over 50 stitches, changing colour every six rows and rehanging onto the needles two stitches with a gap of eight stitches. This basic lifted-stitch sample is the first to explore. *Yarn A: Yellow, one end 4-ply organic cotton. Yarn B: Light blue, one end 4-ply organic cotton. Tension: 7.*

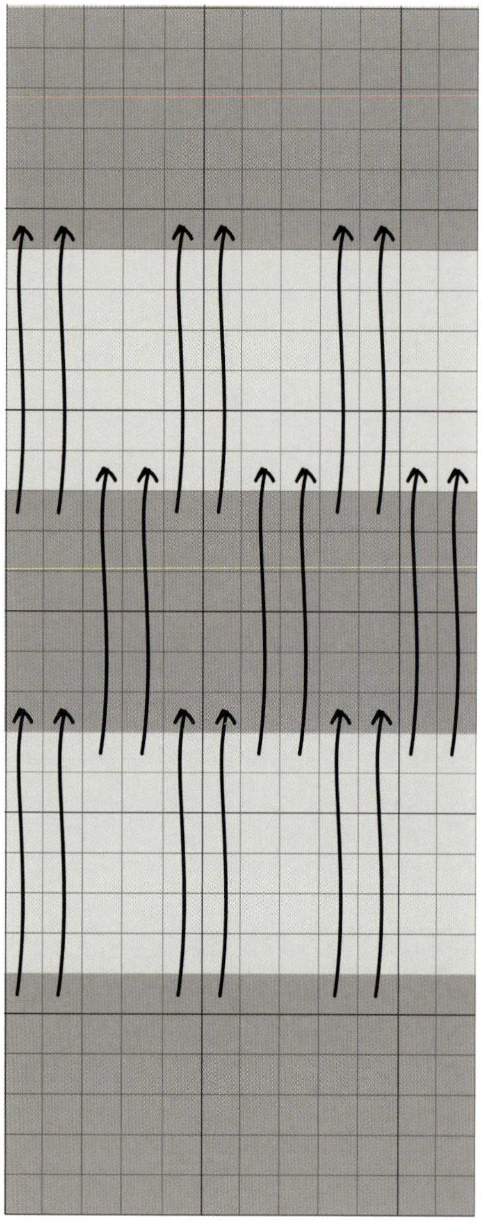

This chart shows the change of colour of yarn through the different shades, and the positions where the stitches are lifted through the arrows.

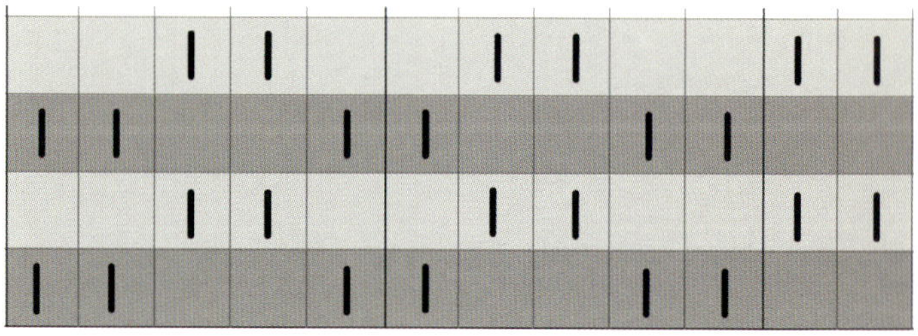

A simplified version of the chart above. Here, the chart shows the same needles that will be lifted but does not show each individual row. Most of the charts for the lifted-stitches section will be like this.

To begin with a simple piece, cast on over 50 stitches and work with a repeating pattern throughout the lifted stitches. Stripes of 2 colours make the stitches easier to see when picking them up, and will also increase the colour element within the pattern.

Once there is enough fabric knitted to hang the weights, change to yarn B and knit 6 rows.

Using the transfer tool, return to the last row of yarn A, pick up and rehang onto the needles 4 stitches with intervals of 10 needles. Usually, we pick up the heel of the stitch, or the 'bump', but as this is a technique where the structure is not dependent on the part of the stitch that we rehang, we can technically pick up any part of the knit to place back onto the needles. Rehanging the heel of the stitch creates the most even and high-quality structure. In the box 'Lifting the Stitches', you can see which part I rehang.

Change back to yarn A, proceed to again knit 6 rows. Again, find the last row of yarn B and rehang onto the working needles 4 stitches with intervals of 10 needles, but in the alternating position relative to the previously hung stitches.

Repeat this process of knitting, changing colour and rehanging the stitches to build up the main material.

This alternating pattern of rehung stitches creates areas within the knit of closeness and openness and incorporates a pattern on both the front and rear sides of the sample.

If we are to work on a smaller scale, a smaller honeycomb pattern would be created. In this instance, 40 stitches were cast on, then every 4 rows the colour was changed; 2 stitches were hooked back up onto the needles with an interval of 2 stitches across the whole working area and repeated throughout the knit.

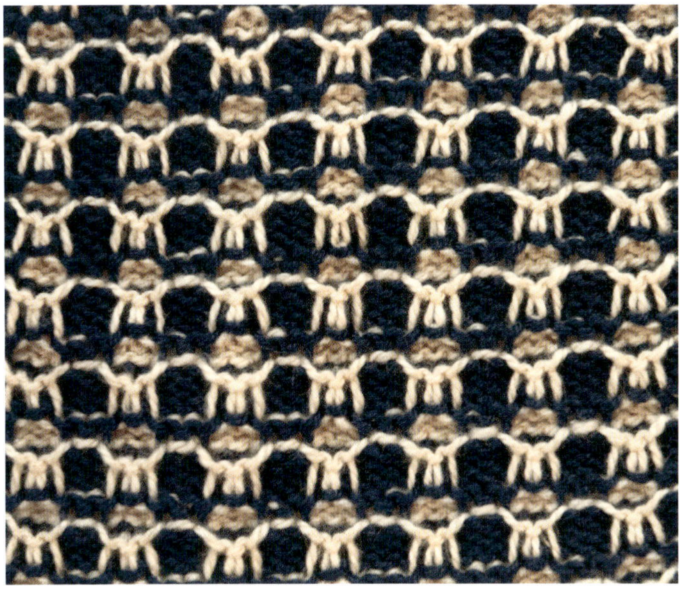

Hooking up every other two stitches across the working area and then knitting four rows in between. A change of colour every four rows adds to the honeycomb effect. *Yarn A: Dark blue, one end 4-ply merino wool. Yarn B: Pink, one end 4-ply cotton. Tension: 7.*

Working with larger areas of lifted stitches and more rows knitted, larger structures within the knit are created. This is the front side. *Yarn A: Purple, three ends 2/48NM wool. Yarn B: Green, one end 2/16NM wool.*

The back side shows the placement of the lifted stitches.

Alternatively, we can hook up larger areas that have more rows knitted within them, or only hook up a few stitches knitted over fewer rows for a more detailed look.

This larger shape is probably the simplest and quickest of the hook-up samples, due to the amount of knit created in between each section lifted – useful if you want to make a larger surface area.

Working with multiples of 6, 66 needles are cast on in yarn A on the single bed with weights hung.

Change to yarn B, and knit 20 rows.

Return to yarn A. Working in multiples of 6 from the left-hand edge, lift the stitches from the last row knitted in yarn A; 18 stitches are left before the next group of 6 stitches are lifted.

Work 20 rows with yarn A and then change to yarn B.

The next row of lifted stitches will start 12 stitches in. The next 6 stitches are lifted with the next 18 left resting. This pattern creates a staggered effect, always with 6 stitches not lifted in between the lifted areas.

The effect viewed from the front of the material is almost a three-dimensional smocked effect. Playing with the placement of lifted stitches and rows knitted between each lifted area can create further interesting effects. In contrast, lifting fewer stitches and knitting fewer rows creates more detail in the rear side of the knit, but less form overall.

With these samples, the colour of the stitches that are to be hooked up is also the colour of the next stripe. This means that it becomes easier to know where you are in a pattern and which colour you should be knitting with, or which colour of stitches you need to hook up next.

TIP

To ensure these needles will knit with the additional lifted stitches, it is advisable to bring the needles that have rehung stitches on them out into the forward working position to force them to knit.

If you are working alongside partial knit and combining the two techniques, the needles in the forward working position will not knit, therefore bring the needles with rehung stitches into the upper working position in which the stitches just pass the latch. This ensures that the forward working position needles will not knit when the partial knit is engaged on the carriage, yet will force the needles in the upper working position that have the extra bulk on them to knit.

Pattern Placement

Outside of the typical honeycomb patterns that have been sampled, placement of the lifted stitches can be worked and experimented with to create more interest. We alternated the hook-up stitch positions in the last couple of samples, so now we can begin to look into creating patterns and placement with the hook-ups.

Like all patterns, these can be charted. You can begin to draw out your own charts for specific pattern placements; otherwise, there are several included throughout this chapter that you can use to directly copy the samples shown.

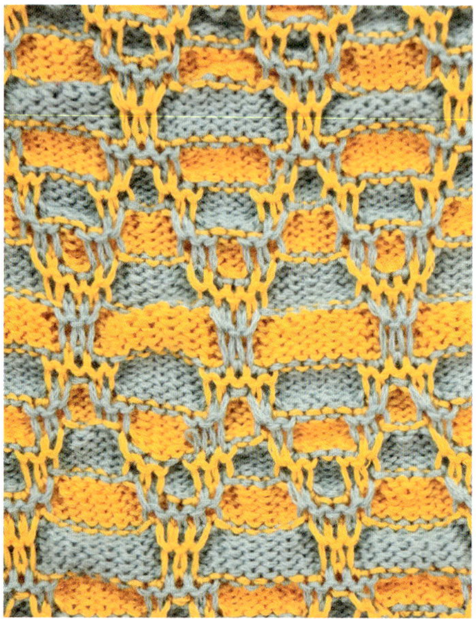

Introducing a pattern with the lifted stitches can increase the visual and tactile effects of the sample. Six rows were knitted in each colour before the stitches were lifted. *Yarn A: Yellow, one end 4-ply organic cotton. Yarn B: Light blue, one end 4-ply organic cotton. Tension: 7.*

The front-facing stitches and the slight gather that is created from the pattern on the reverse side.

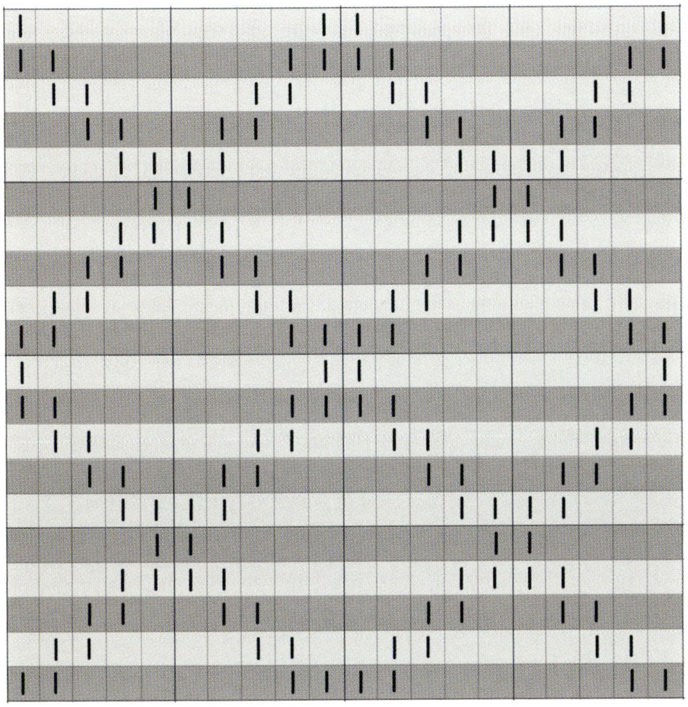

The chart for the pattern of lifted stitches. Again, this chart shows the colour change and the lift placement, but not each individual row. This allows you to alter the number of rows knitted for each colour before the lift.

This form is mostly visible on the back side of the knit structure where the lifted stitches are visible and become a little stretched. On the front side, the material becomes gathered in the areas of the lifted stitches. Depending on the number of rows knitted before lifting the stitches, the gathers are either subtle or can become large rolls.

1. Cast on 50 stitches in yarn A and hang weights.
2. * Change to yarn B and knit 6 rows.
3. Following the pattern in the chart, hook up the heel of the stitches of the last row in yarn A.
4. Change to yarn A and knit 6 rows.
5. Following the pattern in the chart, hook up the heel of the stitches in the last row of yarn B.
6. Repeat this process from * to make the length you would like the knit to be, or until the pattern is complete for one repeat.

If this pattern is to be cast on over a much larger scale, repeat the pattern across the working area of the knit, centring it with needles L1–R1.

Contrasting Yarn Qualities

In order to increase the texture element, we can experiment with yarns that have opposing qualities. Alternating between a heavier-weight yarn and a finer-weight yarn will automatically give a texture similar to a horizontal rib, in that the heavier-weight yarn will push out towards the purl side of the knit, compared to the finer-weight yarn that will collapse more into the purl side. By simply striping with these two different weights of yarn, we can already gain texture in the fabric. There is more information on this in Chapter 4: Pleats and Folds.

To alter a basic sample using this technique, we can use a similar pattern to the previous sample shown: one with a diamond effect. However, instead of knitting an equal number of rows between the change of colour, fewer rows can be knitted with the heavier-weight yarn and more rows can be knitted with the lighter-weight yarn. This will equal out the potential differences from the two different weights of the yarn. An additional quality of this technique is that the fabric has an appearance similar to garter stitch. Not only were the contrasting yarns of different weights, but also different fibres: one was a wool mix and the other a polyamide that contains a slight stretch and shrinks slightly once off the machine. This means that the elasticity from the yarn helps to draw the stitches together, with the result that the 6 polyamide rows are the same size as the 2 rows knitted in the wool mix.

A difference in weight of yarn can add to the structure. This is better viewed on the back side in which a garter-stitch effect is given. *Yarn A: Dark blue, one end polyamide. Tension: 4. Yarn B: Gold, one end 4-ply alpaca and wool mix. Tension: 7.*

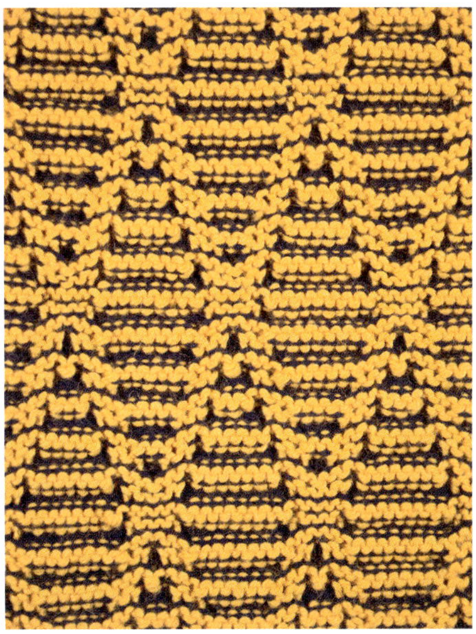

Further to this initial exploration of using different yarn qualities, we can incorporate a third yarn, but simplify the lifted stitch pattern. This sample has been knitted with very slight differences in the yarn; however, the overall effect is still very much visible.

Three separate yarns and colours have been used, yarn A being a light 4-ply pink cotton, yarn B also a 4-ply cotton in a light blue, and yarn C is a 4-ply merino wool. Despite all three being 4-ply yarns, the merino wool is actually a little heavier than both the cottons, which means this will act as the yarn that will push towards the purl side once knitted. All three of these yarns have been knitted using the same tension, T6. A slightly smaller tension would not be noticeable; however, it will activate the heavier-weight yarn a little more as the stitches become denser and have less space to bloom.

1. Cast on 40 stitches in yarn A and knit to attach the weights (at least 6 rows).
2. Change to yarn B: Knit 6 rows.
3. Change to yarn C: Knit 6 rows.
4. *Hook up the heel of the stitches in the last row of yarn A in groups of 3 across the working area, leaving 10 needles in between.
5. Change to yarn A: Knit 6 rows.
6. Hook up the heel of the stitches in the last row of yarn B in groups of 3 across the working area, leaving 10 needles in between.
7. Change to yarn B: Knit 6 rows.
8. Hook up the heel of the stitches in the last row of yarn C in groups of 3 across the working area, leaving 10 needles in between.
9. Change to yarn C: Knit 6 rows.
10. Repeat this sequence from *.

Differently weighted yarns begin to increase the tactility of the sample by 'pushing' out the denser knitted areas. *Yarn A: Pink, one end 4-ply cotton. Yarn B: Light blue, one end 4-ply organic cotton. Yarn C: Dark blue, one end 4-ply merino wool. Tension: 6.*

The placement of the lifted stitches on the rear side is regular and even.

Within this knit, the placement of the lifted stitches will always be the same. This creates a continuous area of lifted stitches and an even pattern on both the front and back side of the knit. The added texture has come from the differently weighted yarns. Whilst still visually subtle, it becomes more pronounced when you explore the piece physically by touch.

Developing on from this, more colour can be integrated and the positions of the hook-up stitches altered. Using 4 colours instead of the 3, and hooking up in adjacent positions, the effect on the front of the knit incorporates more areas revealing the colours used. The patterning on the back side has a stepped diagonal striping effect in which the lifted stitches join each striped section.

This sample has been worked over 50 needles. To begin, cast on in yarn A and work 4 rows with each yarn to create a striped material. Once back to yarn A, hook up 2 stitches of the last row knitted in yarn A (which will now be 12 rows below our current row of stitches) across the needle bed with 8 needles in between each hook-up.

Knit 4 rows in yarn A. Change to yarn B, and similarly hook up 2 stitches of the last row that was knitted in yarn B across the needle bed, but this time picking up the adjacent stitches to the stitches hooked up previously.

Knit 4 rows in yarn B. Continue this same process with yarns C and D by hooking up 2 stitches on the last row knitted in each yarn.

Once one repeat through all 4 colours or yarn variations has been knitted, repeat the steps as described above, always picking up the adjacent stitches to the previous picked-up stitches. This will create a diagonal patterned effect on the back side with all the hooked-up stitches, but also a diagonal waved effect on the front side.

Giving a more undulating and 'conceal and reveal' effect by using four colours and hooking up in different places. *Yarn A: Yellow 4-ply organic cotton. Yarn B: Dark blue 4-ply merino wool. Yarn C: Light blue 4-ply organic cotton. Yarn D: Pink 4-ply cotton. Tension: 7.*

The reverse side shows the placement of the lifted stitches.

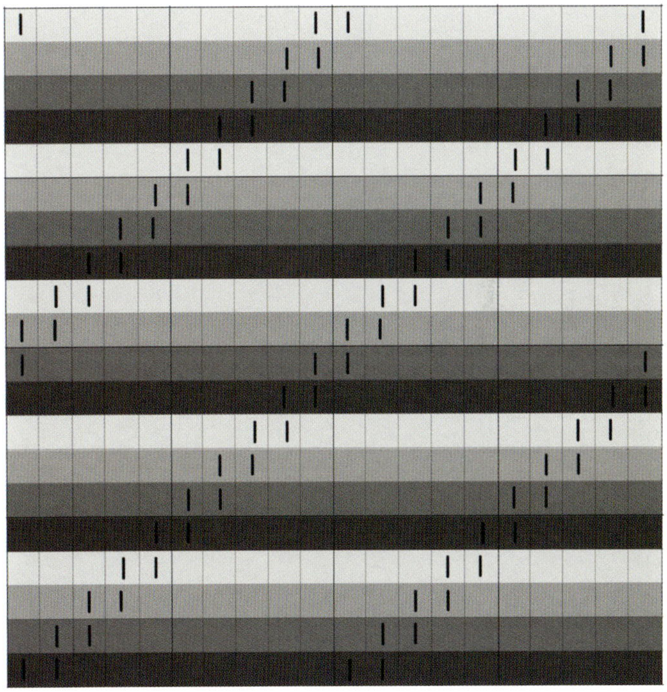

Chart to show the lifted-stitch placement but also the change of colour. This is represented by the greyscale.

Block Patterns

To further this structure, altering the number of rows knitted with each colour and combining it with a pattern spread over a larger area, the lifted-stitches pattern can become more interesting still. These next variations are the single-bed versions of some techniques covered in the Ottoman section of the book. Despite needing more time to hand manipulate, and considering we are only working with one bed rather than two, the overall effect of the two techniques is strikingly similar.

This sample was knitted over 50 stitches. Yarn A was used as a main yarn that was hooked back up onto the needles, whereas yarn B was striped and used as the yarn to create the textural ripple. Depending on the type of pattern, a yarn with some elasticity or shrinkage will help to emphasise the pattern and the rolls as it will shrink the side of the fabric with the lifted stitches.

Introducing a block pattern for the lifted stitches along with a change in the number of rows being knitted alters the surface texture and structure to create an undulating 'conceal and reveal' type of effect. *Yarn A: Dark blue, one end 4-ply merino wool. Yarn B: Pink, one end 4-ply cotton. Tension: 7.*

The back side shows the placement of the lifted stitches.

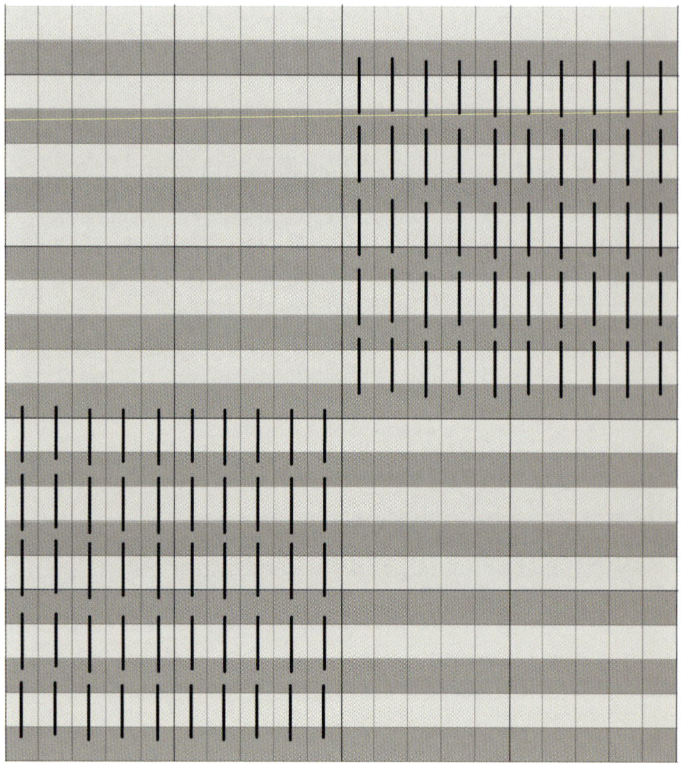

Using this chart, hook up in block sections over the working area to create a more graphic pattern. The pattern is clear on the back side with the lifted stitches; however, on the front side an undulating effect with the ripples appears. It brings a softness to the sample despite the geometric pattern on the rear side.

Using the graph, the indicated squares are hooked back up onto the machine after every ripple and after changing back to yarn A. The size of the ripple in yarn B can be as large as you like; in this sample, 12 rows have been worked.

This pattern of lifted stitches on the back side can also be altered for your own design. Lifting stitches in a more organic pattern on the back side will produce a softer effect with less organised texture compared to a pre-planned geometric pattern. It is recommended to lift stitches in blocks to create more dynamic patterns within the sample. Lifting a small number of stitches over larger areas can diffuse the overall effect.

Another option to try out is shown in the following chart. This has been knitted in an identical method to the previous sample but using different hook-up positions.

Another example of blocked areas to lift stitches over the back side of the sample, but worked as a pattern. *Yarn A: Dark blue, one end 4-ply merino wool. Yarn B: Light blue, one end 4-ply organic cotton. Tension: 7.*

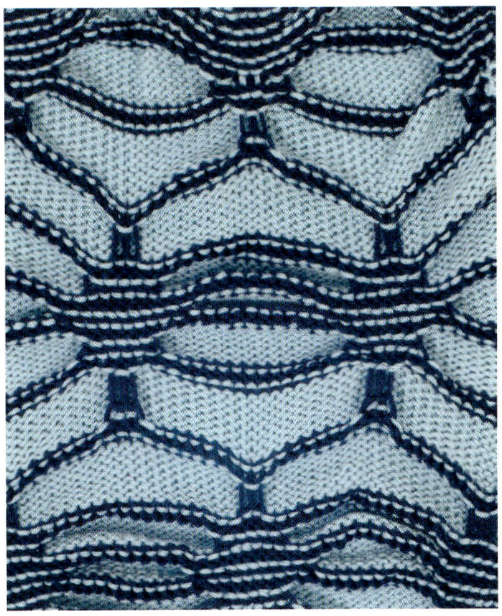

The placement of the lifted stitches on the reverse side.

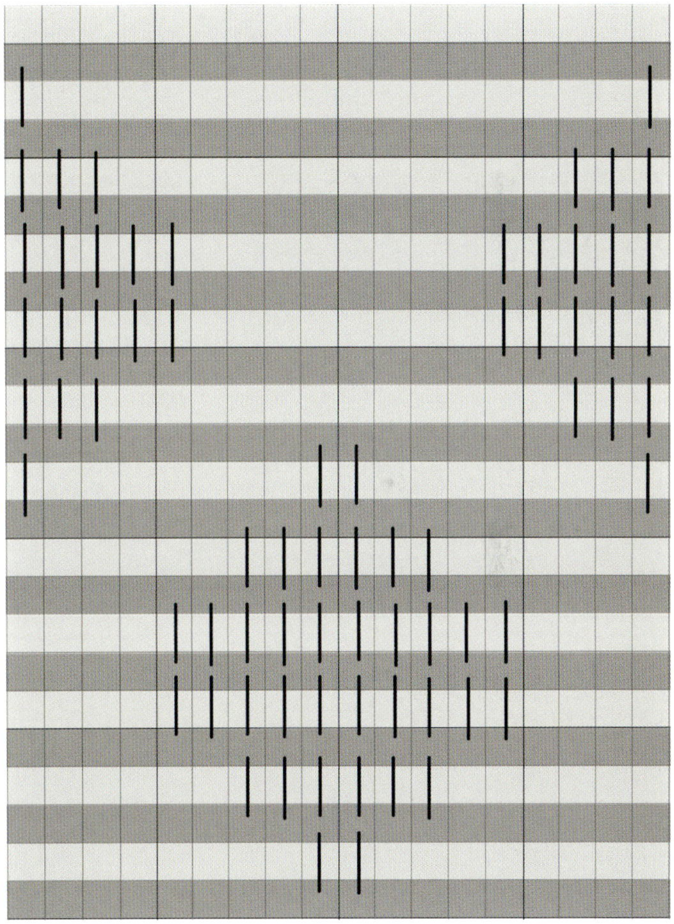

Working a pattern into the lifted stitches can create more interest on the lifted side of the material and, depending on the pattern, additional texture on the front side.

Lifting in Directions

Lastly, before we move on to lifting full rows and also Ottoman, we will briefly explore lifting stitches and moving needles. In these instances we will not only lift stitches as previously explored, but move the stitches to neighbouring needles to create a natural twist within the knitted sample.

Here, after every 6 rows, the last row of the previous colour is lifted back up onto the needles whilst also moving them across 3 needles either to the left or the right. The direction alternates between the left and the right with each row lifted, which results in a wavy pattern on the front. If all stitches are lifted in the same direction, a definite single direction will be visible on both the front and the back of the sample.

It is important to note that, generally, you can only lift stitches in one direction across the lifted row. It is possible to lift in multiple directions, but only if the lifted stitches are being moved towards each other rather than away from each other. This is due to the limited stretch within the structure of the stitch being insufficient to pull them apart and lift away from each other. Explore this in multiple directions to understand further how the direction makes a difference with lifted stitches.

Moving the lifted stitches across to other positions can incorporate an added undulating and twisting effect. *Yarn A: Dark blue, one end 4-ply merino wool. Yarn B: Light blue, one end organic cotton. Tension: 7.*

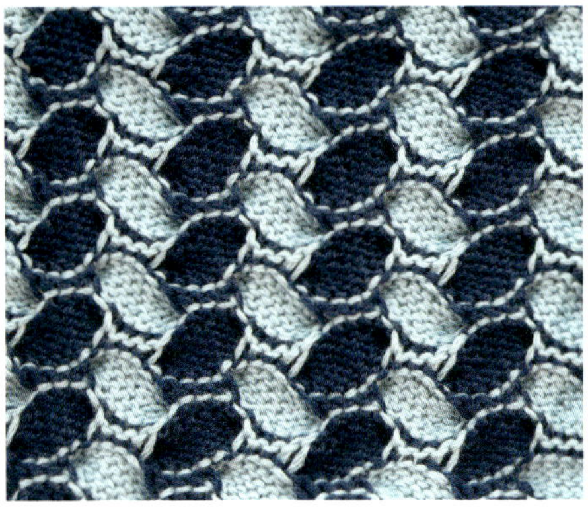

The lifted stitches on the rear side of the sample.

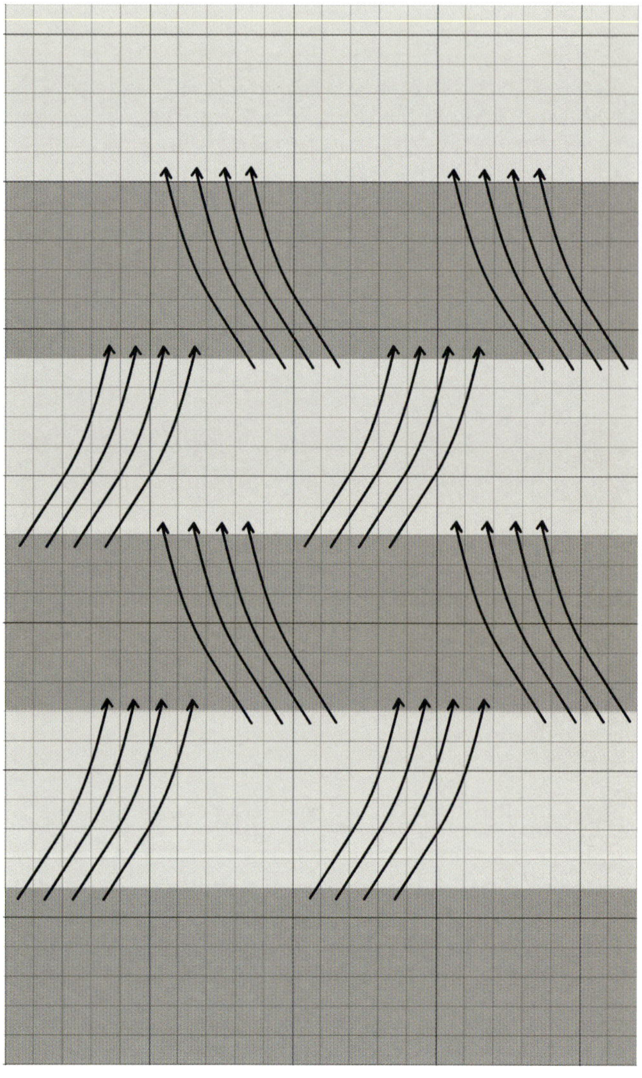

The chart to represent the direction of the lifted stitches.

REHANGING LOOPS

Having explored lifting individual stitches, the process of combining techniques to create dimensional loops can be explored. This combination is one of the first dimensional techniques I learnt that combines the two techniques to create form and thick texture, and I still use it in many of my pieces today. Its simplicity means it is very easy to experiment with – including variations in colour, texture and pattern – whilst you become more comfortable with the stitch.

The process of creating loops is exactly the same as the method covered in Chapter 1: Partial Knit. Loops can be made over any number of needles and for any number of rows. The number of rows knitted determines the length of the loop, and the number of needles that a piece is knitted over determines the width. Loops can be made across the whole working area or only in one section. As you have complete control over the placement of the loop, the area of loops can be anything from one loop in the centre to loops covering the entire piece. They can also be in completely different colours, sizes and patterns.

The process of lifting the stitches back up onto the machine after the loop has been made closes the fabric rather than leaving gaps from the process of the partial knit, which we were working with in the previous chapter.

For this first sample, cast on 40 stitches and knit 18 rows as a bottom border. Working in groups of 4 needles using partial knit, knit 30 rows over the 4 working needles before proceeding along to the next group of needles to be worked as a loop. Here, 2 needles were left unworked in between the groups of 4 needles to space the loops out. Once each group across the working area has been knitted with the 30 rows, the heel of the stitch from the last row before the loop was rehung back up onto the needle.

The carriage is to finish on the left-hand side after knitting all loops before the stitches of the last row are rehung. Then knit across all needles for 5 full rows to get the carriage to finish back on the right-hand side. This allows for the stitches with extra bulk to be knitted away from the needles and space created in between the loops.

Due to working a large number of rows over the partial-knitted areas, I would suggest pulling the loop you are knitting through to the back of the material (which is the side closest to you) to allow you either to manually hold the knit down away from the carriage, or to place a claw weight on that particular part of the knit. Without adding extra weight to those 4 working needles, the stitches have the potential to rise up and pop off the needles, dropping the stitches.

Using one yarn, a series of loops has been knitted over the working area, creating texture and form. The last stitch before the loops were made was then lifted to close the loop. *Yarn: One end 3-ply mixed wool.*

Using elastane as the main yarn creates a dense main material that in turn shrinks the backing area, creating a dense surface texture with the loops. *Yarn A: Pink shirring elastic. Yarn B and C: Blue and beige 3-ply wool. Tension: 6.*

The placement of the rolls created by lifted stitches can be played with and explored. It does not have to be in a static position. As you can see in the previous samples, the loops have been staggered through the rows rather than being vertically aligned. This can aid density, if that is an element you wish to develop, or pattern, but also can help with making the loops appear to be placed randomly rather than in a linear position.

Altering the main yarn for the sample can also create a much denser material. In the last sample, elastane, or shirring elastic, has been used on its own whilst the second and third yarns used within the piece for the loops have been made from wool. The elasticity of the main yarn has then greatly constricted the knit sample, condensing the loops. If a dense area of loops is positioned within the knit, this would give a very intricate area of texture.

Alternatively, if a natural fibre were preferred, one could knit this sample with 100 per cent wool and felt the piece as a post-knit process. This will not only shrink the material to create a generally dense fabric, but will shrink the areas in between each of the loops, which therefore increases the density of the loops. You can see this in the images to the right.

To play with this felting process and explore further options, a difference in yarn between the backing material and the loop could be used. For example, if a wool was used for the backing area and a cotton for the loops, the backing would felt, increasing the density of the material yet allowing the loops to keep their structure. Differences in size of the loops could also be achieved. Increasing and decreasing the number of rows knitted over the loops can alter the visual and textural pattern of the piece.

These two samples show the differences of a felted structure of loops and an unfelted structure of loops. The density is increased through the felting of the wool. This is the felted version.

Despite being knitted on a 12gg Shima Seiki machine, the overall effect is identical to that produced on a domestic knitting machine. This is the unfelted version. *Yarn: One end 2/28NM Zegna Baruffa Cashwool. Loop length: 80 rows.*

Lifting full rows: A practice piece enables us to gauge the height of the rolls we will create and the juxtaposition with the spacing in between each roll (instructions overleaf). *Yarn A: Orange, one end 2/17NM lambswool. Yarn B: Purple, three ends of 2/25NM cashmere–cotton blend. Tension: 3.*

LIFTING FULL ROWS

To become a little more accustomed to creating rolls before we move on to the use of colour and placement, we can work another simpler sample that explores the size of the rolls and spacing between them. After this we can then begin to see the effect of working larger or smaller rolls in the same piece and how they reveal the backing material.

For example, this sample plays with the size of the ripple. A little further on in this chapter we will introduce working with partial knit where the direction of the ripple along with the shape is explored.

1. Cast on 30 needles using yarn A. As whole rows of stitches will be lifted, the number cast on can be limited as this is a practice piece.
2. Knit to hang the weights. Change to yarn B and knit 10 rows.
3. Hook up the last row of yarn A back onto the needles. Knit 6 rows.
4. Change to yarn B and knit 14 rows.
5. Hook up the last row of yarn A back onto the needles. Knit 6 rows.
6. Repeat the stripes and hook-ups by increasing each roll by 4 rows until 22 rows are knitted within one roll. Then, decrease the amount within the rolls by 4 rows each time until you are back to the original 10 rows within a roll.

This sample is shown on the previous page. Variations of this sample could include larger differences of rows with each roll; altering the number of rows knitted in yarn A in between each roll; or adding decoration in either the roll or the section in between with lace holes, stripes or punch-card techniques.

LIFTING STITCHES AND PARTIAL KNIT

Incorporating multiple techniques within one sample often gives the most interesting forms and textures. Now that we have explored hooking up full rows of stitches, we can, again, refer back to Chapter 1: Partial Knit and further incorporate the two techniques.

As touched upon within Chapter 1: Partial Knit, the technique is generally only suited to a single bed on the domestic machine and is very limited on the double bed due to limitations with the take-down. As it also cannot be worked with the V-bed machine due to the carriage restrictions, the combination of the lifting of rows and partial knit will only be worked on the single-bed domestic machine. Despite the following techniques resembling Ottoman quite closely, you might be tempted to try them with the double bed with partial knit. Whilst I encourage all explorations and experiments using all these techniques in the book, the process with partial knit cannot be replicated so well due to the take-down problems. This is the reason why lifting full rows is the preferred method to work with partial knit rather than Ottoman.

With regard to the take-down of a knit when working with lifted stitches on the single bed, it can be easier overall to remove the weights completely from the knit. Certainly, removing the weights whilst rehanging the stitches will help to locate the stitches that need to be rehung and to insert the transfer tool. To then replace the weights once the chosen stitches are rehung could be seen as unnecessary when you can manually hold the knit down and away from the needles by hand. If you are using a weight bar, to rehang this evenly could be more problematic than it would be to use individual claw weights.

Working with lifted stitches and partial knit combined, we can shape the knit much more than just working on the flat without the partial knit. The direction of the ripples can be altered, we can stack the ripples in a pattern, or we can even create a form including a colour pattern within the piece. Again, this section starts with a simpler sample, then the samples increase in difficulty through the section.

Working with ripples and partial knit can alter the positioning of the ripples so they are no longer horizontal, but at an angle. *Yarn A: Orange, one end 2/17NM lambswool. Yarn B: Purple, three ends 2/36NM cashmere–cotton blend. Tension: 3.*

1. Cast on 40 needles with yarn A. Knit a border of approximately 16 rows. This will just serve as a border to the knit and is not functional.
2. With the carriage on the right-hand side (COR), place it into the hold position and bring out all needles except for 4 needles on the far-right-hand side of the working area. These end 4 needles will be worked over to create the first ripple.
3. Change to yarn B and knit 10 rows on the right-hand end 4 needles only. Finding the last row of yarn A, hook up the heels of the 4 stitches directly back onto the needles.
4. Change to yarn A and knit 4 rows, still only on the right-hand end 4 needles.
5. COR. Introduce 2 needles into the upper working position (UWP) so you now have 6 working needles on the right-hand side.
6. Change to yarn B and knit 10 rows on the right-hand edge 6 needles. Finding the last row of yarn A, hook up the heels of the 6 stitches just worked to create the second ripple.
7. COR, change to yarn A and knit the dividing 4 rows between each ripple.
8. Repeat this process by reintroducing 2 needles into the working position for every ripple until all needles are knitting across the full working area.

Now half of the shaping has been worked. Next, the working needles to create the ripples are decreased by 2 stitches for each ripple starting from the right-hand side. This means the working area is decreased over towards the left-hand side.

1. With the carriage starting and finishing on the right with each ripple, bring out 2 needles on the far-right-hand side of the needle bed into the hold position.
2. With yarn B, work a ripple of 10 rows. (In this sample, this would be knitted over 38 needles on the left-hand side). Finding the last row of yarn A, hook up the heels of the 38 stitches directly back onto the original needles.
3. Knit the dividing 4 rows with yarn A.
4. Introduce 2 needles into the hold position on the far-right-hand side and repeat the ripple and lifted stitches.

Repeat the process of introducing 2 needles into the hold position with each ripple until you have decreased the number of working needles down to 4 needles on the far-left-hand side of the working area. Once the lifted stitches have been rehung, the top border can be knitted and the piece cast off.

This slanting ripple is quite effective if one wants to create a fully rippled material working with a ripple that is not horizontal. To increase the length, continue to create ripples over the full working area with no partial knit. The partial knit created before and after the full knitted rows will give the ripples direction.

Variations on this technique can consist of repeated partial knit sections in the opposite direction, increasing and decreasing the number of rows knitted for each ripple or each dividing section. Changes of colour within the ripples or also in the dividing section between the ripples could also be incorporated to give a colour element, similar to the sample shown.

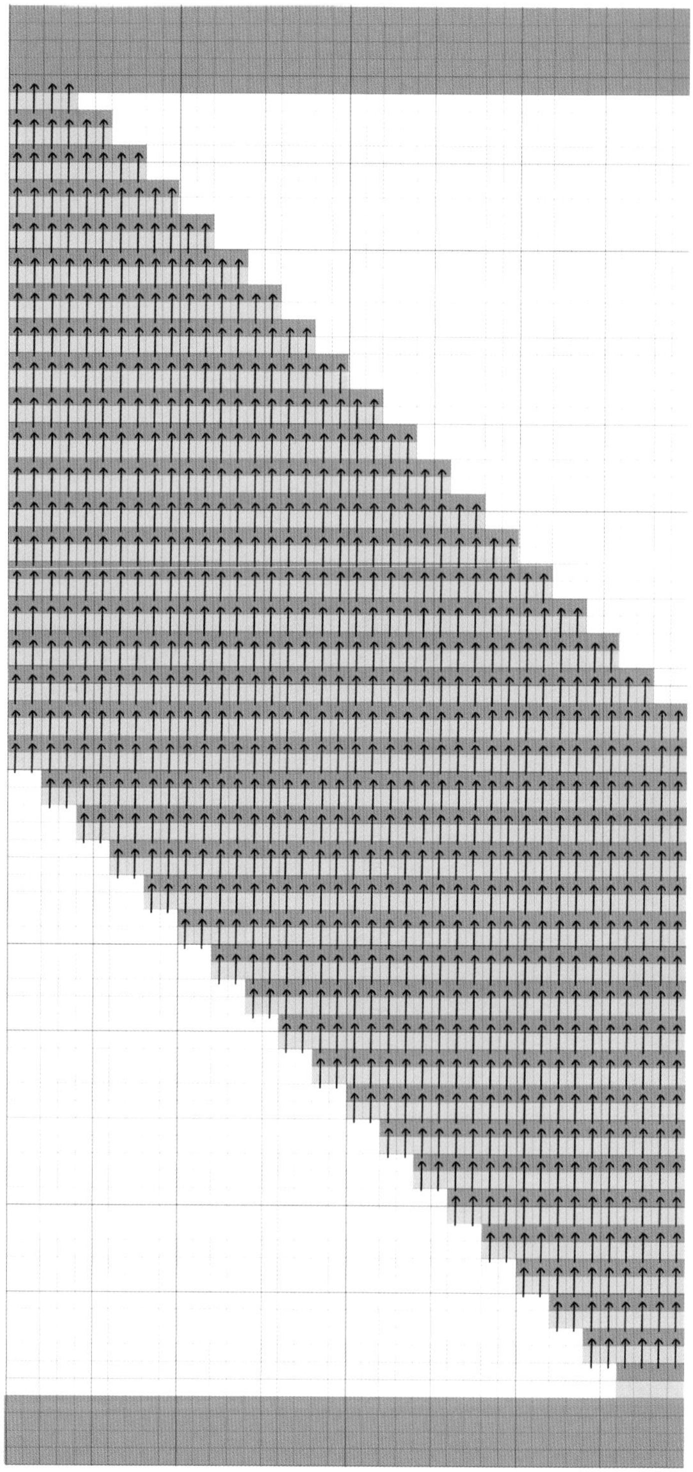

This diagram shows both the striping of the yarns through the different shades, the partial knit and working needles, and the lifting of the stitches. The lighter grey is the colour that the ripple is made with.

TIP

It should be noted that when you are placing the needles into the hold position for the second part of the shaping, it is advisable to ensure the yarn in the carriage sits on top of all needles in the hold position. By introducing two needles, the yarn from the yarn feeder in the carriage would naturally sit underneath the two needles just brought out into hold, and then on top of all other needles in hold. Rearrange the position of the yarn to ensure a smoother knit on the back side.

Whilst this is not absolutely necessary for this knit, it will help to diminish the floats that are naturally made when working partial knit over two needles.

Ensure the yarn sits on top of the needles when they are brought into hold.

To further this, we can work with ripples creating multiple directions within one piece. It does begin to get complicated planning-wise if one wants to achieve a flat sample; however, if it is not essential that the sample lies flat, you can experiment with creating hooked-up areas and partial knit.

The first instance of this approach will be a development from the previous sample. This is written in six parts as there are six shaped parts to this sample and each section will be explained individually. In your own exploration, there can be as many shaped areas as you would like within your piece. Ensure that you write down the shaping process in case you wish to replicate the sample later.

In this sample, partial knit has been used to create multiple blocks of leaning ripples. Partial knit can be used from either side to direct the knitting. *Yarn A: Green, one end 2/16NM worsted wool. Yarn B: Light green, three ends 2/36NM cotton–wool blend. Tension: 6.*

All ripples within this piece have been made with 12 rows knitted in yarn B before hooking back up the last row before the ripple in yarn A; and 4 rows have been knitted in yarn A in between each hooked-up ripple. Cast-on and cast-off have been worked in yarn A; 50 stitches were cast on to start with.

Section 1: Start from the right-hand side with the carriage on the right (COR). Bring all needles into the hold position except the right-hand 4 needles. Create a ripple over these 4 needles.

For the next and following ripples, increase the working area by 2 needles (by bringing them into work). Repeat this to create a total of 8 ripples.

Section 2: Start from the left-hand side with the carriage on the left (COL). Move the carriage across to the opposite side of the working area before beginning knitting. It may be necessary to break the yarn and reintroduce it on the opposite side.

Begin with all needles in the hold position except the left-hand 4 needles. Create a ripple over these 4 needles and then increase the next and following ripples by 4 needles (by bringing them back into work). Repeat this to create a total of 7 ripples.

Section 3: Starting on needles L2–R2, work a ripple. All other needles that are not knitted should be in the hold position. It doesn't matter which side the carriage starts from as this section is in the centre of the working area. You will need to break the yarn and reintroduce the yarn again in the centre.

For the next and following ripples, increase the working area by 4 needles on the right-hand side of the working area and 2 needles on the left-hand side of the working area (as above) (a total increase of 6 needles for each ripple). Repeat until a total of 6 ripples have been made.

Now we have completed 3 sections, we will begin again working from one side, then the other side and finally working in the centre.

Section 4: Start on the right-hand side with the COR. Begin with all needles in the hold position except the far-right-hand 4 needles (the same as Section 1). Make a ripple over those 4 needles.

For the next and following ripples, increase the working area by 6 needles for each ripple. Repeat this to make a total of 6 ripples.

Section 5: Start from the left-hand side with the COL. Move the carriage across to the opposite side of the working area before beginning knitting. It may be necessary to break the yarn and reinsert it into the carriage on the opposite side. Begin with all needles in the hold position except the left-hand 4 needles. Start by making a ripple over these 4 needles.

For the next and following ripples, increase the working area by 1 needle for each ripple. Repeat to create a total of 11 ripples.

Section 6: Start on needles R5–R10 (6 needles). All other needles that are not knitted should be in the hold position. It doesn't matter which side the carriage starts from as this section is in the centre of the working area. You will need to break the yarn and reintroduce the yarn again in the centre. Make a ripple over these 6 needles.

For the next and following ripples, increase the working area by 1 needle on the left-hand side of the working area and 2 needles on the right-hand side of the working area. Repeat to create a total of 11 ripples.

Once you have completed these six sections, you can continue in your own way now that the process should be more familiar, or you can cast off and plan your own pattern and sections.

It should be noted that the position of the ripples in the diagram is mirrored to the actual sample. When knitting, the back side of the knit is facing us rather than the front side. To help minimise confusion when working with diagrams, these are also drawn up as if we are looking at the back side of the knit, therefore mirrored to the image of the knitted sample.

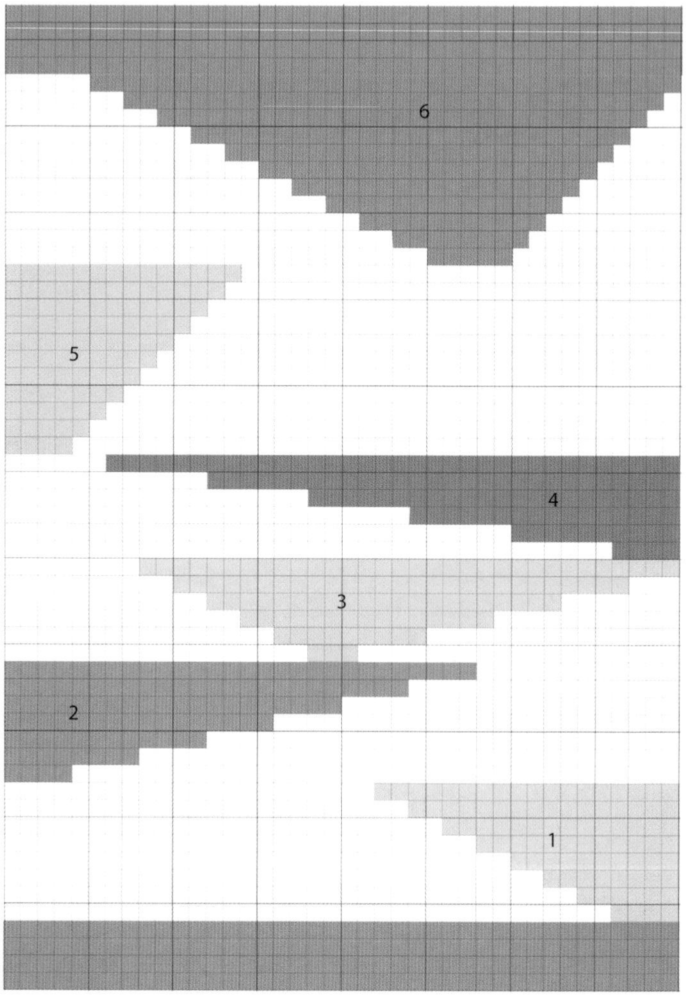

This chart only shows the placement of the working needles for the partial knit. The stripes and the lifted stitches are to still be included. Follow previous charts for this information if you are unsure.

Ripples created in different directions through partial knit, and then felted as a post-knit process.

The author's seat cover in use in her studio.

You can also felt a piece with partial knit and ripples. This sample has been knitted in the same method as the last one, working in sections across the knit, making ripples and then lifting them back up onto the needles. It was then felted as a post-knit process. This gives a softness to the material.

Peaks and Ripples

Adding more structure by integrating both partial knit and lifted stitches, the overall form can become a detailed and structural combination. It could act as a detail on a garment to draw attention to a particular area, to add structure into a piece without including an external form or additional skeleton. For uses beyond apparel, the tactility of the formed rolls and ripples can create volumed textures and weighted materials that are perfect for furnishings or interior pieces. I currently use a piece knitted many years ago as a seat cover.

Now that the combination of partial knit and ripples has been explored as the base of a material, developing a combination of them to highlight particular areas, or create a dimensional structure, is a natural progression for this technique. This first sample uses a basic partially knitted peak that was explored in Chapter 1: Partial Knit, elevating it by creating rolls over the peak area. The effect that it gives not only creates form and structure within the roll area, but a colour pattern also.

Cast on 30 needles in yarn A. This sample is to make one repeat on the horizontal. The shaping can be repeated across the horizontal multiple times by following the same principle that was covered in Chapter 1: Partial Knit, to knit multiple peaks. A small border was knitted at the base of the sample to help the take-down when knitting with partial knit; however, if you prefer to start the partially knitted roll immediately after casting on, this is also an option.

With yarn B, knit a ripple of 12 rows across all working needles (30 stitches). Lift the last row of yarn A, change to yarn A and knit 2 rows.

Change back to yarn B and place the carriage into the hold position. Bringing out into the hold position 2 needles on either side of the working area, work the 26 needles in the centre of the knit into the second ripple of 12 rows.

Again, lift the last row of the yarn A stitches back up onto the needles and knit 2 rows with yarn A.

This sample has been knitted in two contrasting colours to help decipher the hook-up structure, but also with some added partial-knit shaping in the main colour to help the sample lie flat. *Yarn A: Dark blue, one end 4-ply merino wool. Yarn B: Pink, one end 4-ply cotton. Tension: 6.*

This sample has an almost identical ripple and partial-knit combination. However, it is knitted in 100 per cent wool and then felted as a post-knit process. This in itself creates further structure and form within the sample. *Four ends 2/30NM wool. Tension: 5.*

Repeat the process of bringing out 2 needles at either end of the working area into the hold position for each ripple made. You will work ripples over fewer and fewer needles until you are using 6 needles in the centre. Take care to adjust your weight as you go. It may be necessary to work the take-down by hand over the smaller ripples, as the bulk of the material will be resting on the needles in hold.

Once a ripple of 6 needles has been made, begin to reintroduce the needles back into work: 2 needles per ripple. You can either rehang the stitches on the needles and place the needles into the WP, or return the needles into the UWP where they will be automatically knitted when the carriage is taken across. Continue until all 30 needles have been reintroduced and a ripple made across all 30 needles.

It is not fundamental to the sample to knit the following partial-knit section, but I did find it helped the sample to lie flatter once off the machine. The tension created due to the partial knit and ripples meant an excess of material in areas outside the ripples. In this sample, partial-knit shaping in between the ripples has been inserted with the intention of counterbalancing the tension from the shaping which has created additional form.

Knit 4 rows in yarn A over all the needles. Place the carriage into hold and needles L15–R1 into hold. With each pass of the carriage, bring 1 needle from the middle into the hold position until 4 needles remain working on the right-hand side. Take the carriage to the left, reintroducing and knitting over all needles. With COL, repeat the shaping, working

This combination of structure and partial knit to create the pattern makes a simple yet very effective knit. This was knitted all in wool.

needles L15–L1, and with needles R1–R15 in the hold position. Once shaped and COR, knit 4 rows with all needles.

If you feel this shaping described above is not necessary for you, knit a section of single jersey to separate the shaped ripples.

Repeat the shaped ripple and the section in between each ripple to knit the desired length – in this sample, it was repeated twice more before the sample was cast off.

Many elements in this sample can be experimented with, such as the size and length of the ripple and the exact positioning. Further colour development can be included to work with more than two colours, but also as an experiment with different yarn qualities to see how they could affect the results.

Another example with partial knit and lifted stitches is shown above, incorporating a different placement and size of ripple. Working in a systematic method across the working areas, a dense three-dimensional form is created along with a surface pattern. The undulation of the ripples made with the geometric pattern is what makes this piece interesting to look at and explore by touch. This was an initial idea that was developed within my master's research and where the technique first caught my eye.

Peaks and Lifted Stitches

Not only can partial knit be worked into the ripples for placement or size, but also for shape. Peaks have been worked into the structure of the material and then lifted to create a shaped ripple rather than a straight ripple similar to the previous samples. This sample is very similar to the original peak sample, but the back has been closed by lifting the stitches, which in turn creates a more stable structure with the peaks included.

This has been worked over 50 needles and splitting the working needle bed into three groups. Two groups will be worked in partial knit to create a peak on either side, and the third group of needles is worked in the centre of the working area.

Yarn A is used as the main yarn, and yarns B and C are used for the peak areas. After casting on with yarn A, yarn B is used to create a peak on the right-hand 15 edge needles. All other working needles need to be placed into the hold position to ensure they are not worked at this time.

This is only half a peak as one needle will be brought into hold on the left side of the working area every row rather than on both sides. Work 10 rows of shaping, and then return 1 needle back into the working position every row for 10 rows.

Once the right-hand side has been worked, take the carriage over to the left, working all needles. This is purely to get the carriage to the opposite side. Now work the same shaping on the left-hand 15 edge needles, bringing 1 needle into the hold position on the right-hand side of the 15 working needles with every pass of the carriage, and then similarly reintroduce them into work.

Partial knit has been used to create the three-dimensional form of the material, which has then been lifted back onto the needles. Another method that can be used with lifted stitches and partial knit. *Yarn A: Dark blue, one end 4-ply merino wool. Yarn B: Light blue, one end 4-ply cotton. Yarn C: Pink, one end 4-ply cotton. Tension: 7.*

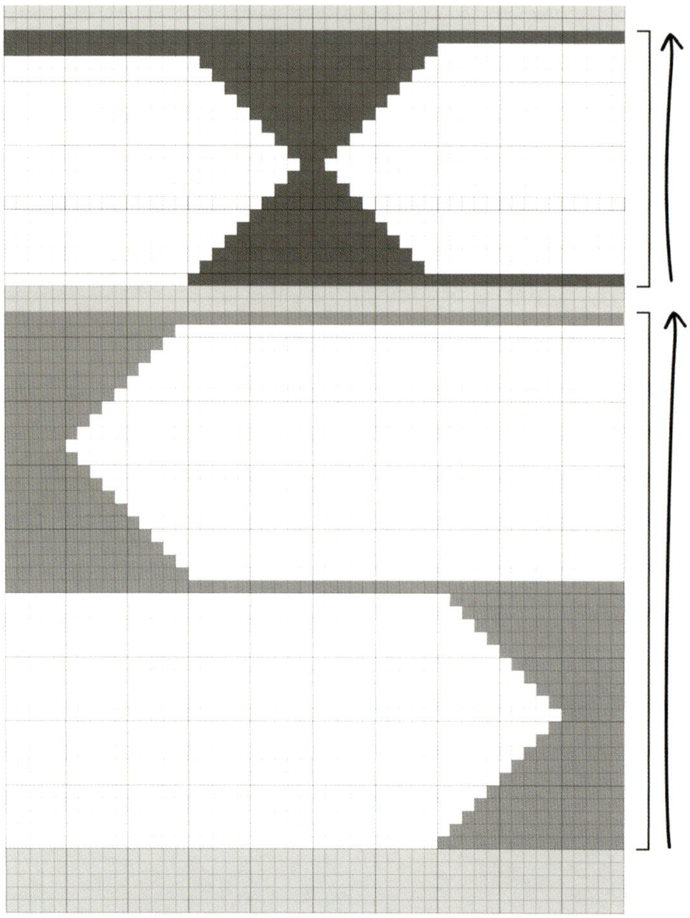

The graphic shows one repeat of the peak and the change of the yarn. The arrows on the right-hand side indicate that the whole section should be lifted once complete. For a more detailed chart, please refer back to Chapter 1: Partial Knit where these shapes are covered in detail.

Once the two edge shapes have been completed, the carriage should end on the left-hand side with only 15 needles on the left in work. Take the carriage across to the right, working all needles in yarn B.

Change to yarn A and lift the last row of yarn. You can choose whether to only lift the stitches over the peak areas to close that section of knit, or you can lift the full row. In the sample provided, only the stitches over the peak area have been lifted.

Change to yarn C and now work the centre shaping. Bring into hold position all needles on the left-hand side up to L10. With the carriage in the hold position, take the carriage to the left, knitting L10–R25. Next, introduce all needles up until R10 into hold. The shaping can begin by bringing 1 needle into hold on both sides of the working area for each pass of the carriage until we are left with 2 remaining needles. Now reintroduce the needles into work, 1 needle each side with each pass of the carriage until L10–R10 are to be worked. Once complete, the carriage should be on the right-hand side about to move to the left-hand side. At the same time as introducing L10 and R10 into work, bring all needles on the left-hand side of the shaped area into work and take the carriage across to the left-hand side, working R10–L25.

Return the carriage to all-needles knitting and knit across to the right-hand side.

Change to yarn A, lift the last row of yarn A, again only over the partial-knit area, and knit 2 rows.

Repeat these full instructions to create as much length in the material as you would like.

Possibilities for developing this texture are through yarn choice, the needles that are used for the partial knit, the number of rows knitted to shape the partial knit, the number of rows knitted with yarn A as a divider colour, and also yarn-colour options. This is the basis of a dimensional technique which can be developed in unlimited ways to create your own take on the technique.

Partial Knit as Background for Ripples

Considering partial knit had been included over the areas to create the ripples, partial knit can also be included to create the background material on which the ripples 'sit'. In this next example, the ripples have been made to partition the partial knit.

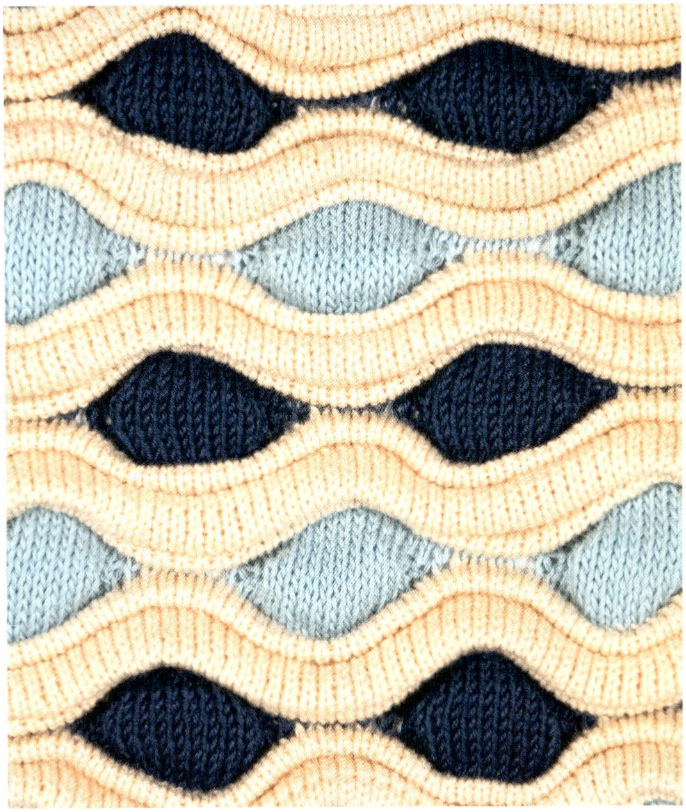

Partial knit has been worked to create the main backing areas of the material, whilst lifted rolls add a texture detail. *Yarn A: Light blue, one end 4-ply soft cotton. Yarn B: Pink, one end 4-ply soft cotton. Yarn C: Dark blue, one end 4-ply merino. Tension: 7.*

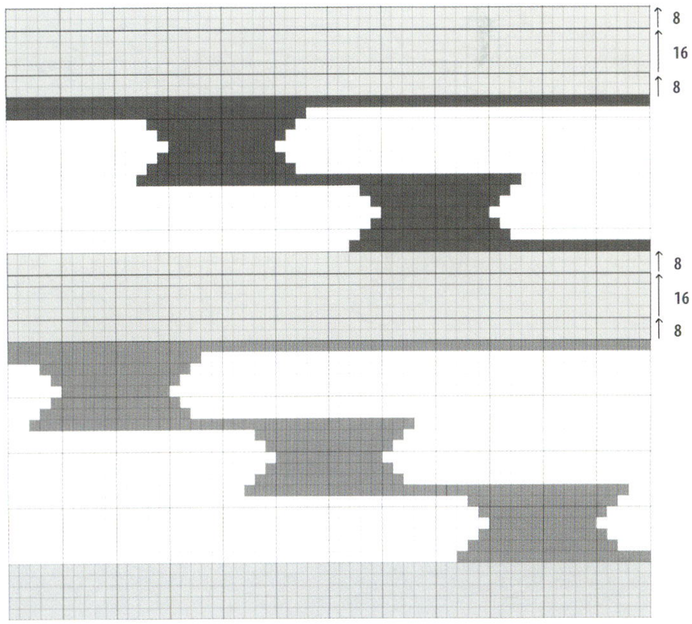

The process to create the partially knitted sample with lifted stitches for dividers between the partial knit. Again, the actual lifted stitches are not indicated but the partial knit is shown along with the ripple rows.

Partial knit can also be used to create both the lifted stitch area and the ground material. In this sample, partial knit godets were made and lifted back onto a triangle of material in a contrasting yarn.

Creating godet sections in the backing material and then full rolls across the working area to add colour or texture elements to the backing. This will alter the direction that the ripples lie in.

Each size of the flattened peak used for the sample on the previous page is 16 stitches wide with 4 needles as a spacer between the shaping, therefore multiples of 20 have been cast on. This sample has used 60 needles.

Using colour A, establish the knit and hang the weights, COR.

Working in partial-knit sections over 16 needles and using yarn B, bring all needles into the hold position apart from the right-hand edge 18 needles. Knit across to the left with the carriage in hold. Bring the end 2 needles on the right-hand side into hold, now working over 16 needles.

Bring 1 needle into the hold position for each row knitted on the same side as the carriage until 3 needles are in hold each side: a total of 6 passes of the carriage. We will not be creating such a dramatic shape as the previous sample and peaks.

Return the needles into work in the same sequence as they were brought out into hold. When the last needle is being brought back into work with the carriage on the right, introduce the next section of needles. There are 4 needles in between each of the 16 needles over the partial-knit shaping, therefore place into the working position the next 20 needles. Once the carriage is on the left, push into hold the first set we worked over plus the 4 separating needles.

Repeat this shaping across the whole working area. When the carriage has finished all of the partial-knit sections and has ended on the left-hand side, place it back into work and knit a full row across to the right, introducing all needles.

Change to yarn B. This is the yarn to create the ripple and the shape. There will be 3 ripples knitted and lifted. The first is knitted with 8 rows, the second with 16 rows and finally the third with 8 rows.

Once complete, change to yarn C as the partial-knit shaping will be repeated, this time in a staggered placement. The end needles will start with half the shaping, therefore 2 full shapings across that row will be complete and 1 half-shaping on either side. Follow the chart for clarification.

Working staggered areas of shaping will also create an extra shaped element within the lifted rolls. These will become wavy in effect, adding to the visual aesthetics. On a larger scale this could be repeated with differently sized ripples, differently sized partial-knit areas, and even more colours than in the sample.

OTTOMAN

Ottoman, also known as rolls, is the process of knitting on a double bed and then only using one needle bed to build up material in the horizontal direction whilst the other bed holds. It can be made on any knitting machine as long as it is a V-bed machine (or a domestic machine with a ribber attachment) as we work each bed separately to build up material on one side. Despite the fact that it is a technique that can be knitted on industrial machines, such as Shima Seiki or Stoll, there are still some limitations with the technique that need to be borne in mind. As I briefly mentioned previously when discussing lifted stitches, complications can happen due to the take-down of the material when working Ottoman technique.

The take-down (the force holding the knit away from the needles, whether these are weights on a Dubied or domestic machine, or rollers on an industrial machine) must be balanced well to hold the stitches down and out of the way of the moving needles. As the build-up of material occurs on one needle bed, more bulk of material is made there. As the side opposite the working needle bed is resting, the stitches will hold the material up near the needles rather than allowing the material to drop down away from the needles. This means that, if care is not taken, the material can rise up with the movement of the needle when the carriage is passed, eventually preventing the needle from creating a new full stitch. To avoid this, restrict the number of rows knitted on one bed, or manually push the stitches down the needle stem before they are knitted, to ensure the yarn is placed into the needle hook and the stitches are formed correctly.

Too much take-down applied, however, can mean the resting stitches can break as too much force has been placed onto them by the take-down. It is a delicate balance that needs to be watched and adjusted. This means that I often work the take-down manually by holding the knit down by hand on both the V-bed machines and the domestic machines to ensure that just the right amount of force is applied.

Needle selection (from a punch card, through DesignaKnit or from partial knit) is not possible on the V-bed machines. This means Ottoman rolls have to be worked across the entire working area. A needle selection is the only way to create structure with Ottoman rolls on the V-bed machines. Creating a shape or texture with Ottoman on the V-bed through a pattern placement will be achieved with manual needle selection by transferring stitches.

Whereas we have mainly explored samples made using domestic machines, the majority of the next samples will be knitted on a fine-gauge V-bed machine. This is purely to show the difference of gauge and how that can affect the knit both in detail and texture.

It is a personal preference to knit the majority of the double-bed techniques on the V-bed machines and single-bed techniques on domestic machines, rather than both on a domestic machine with a ribber attachment. This is due to the positioning of the needle beds, with those on the V-beds being closer together, therefore resulting in a finer and tighter double jersey compared to fabric made using the domestic machine and the ribber attachment. When working single-bed techniques on the domestic machines, the material is much more accessible as the front bed (whether a ribber attachment or the front bed of a V-bed machine) is not in the way.

It should be stressed that regardless of whether you are knitting on a V-bed machine or domestic machine, the process for knitting these samples does not change. The methods are the same and will be explained in a way that can be translated between machines without favouring one type. Please look to your machine instruction book for the basic positions for turning each bed off and back on again to produce a single jersey on only one bed.

Starting with a basic piece, within this we can get to grips with the carriage functions and working a basic Ottoman structure. These samples have been knitted with two or more colours to show the ripples more clearly, but the basic sample can be knitted with one colour.

Cast on 50 stitches on the double bed with yarn A; hang the comb and the weights.

Change to yarn B and deselect the front bed (turning the cams off so the carriage will not knit on the front bed) and knit 4 rows.

Change to yarn A and return the carriage to knit both beds, knitting 2 rows with all needles knitting.

Repeat the two steps stated above for as long as you would like your sample to be.

If the take-down is not sufficient when working Ottoman, the knitted material builds up and is not knitted properly. This results in unknitted stitches and potentially stitches coming off the needles.

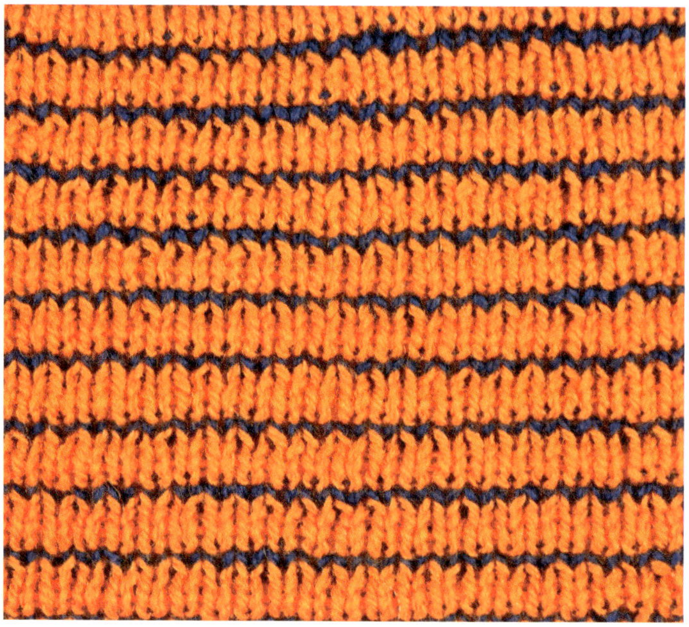

The first sample of Ottoman rolls, knitted on the Silver Reed domestic machine to get comfortable working with the process. *Yarn A: Dark blue, one end 2-ply worsted wool. Yarn B: Orange, one end 2/15NM lambswool. Tension: Plain 5, rib 4.*

Note that the stitch size on the domestic machine is adjusted slightly between the single jersey and the double jersey, partly because it is slightly easier to alter the stitch size between rows, but also due to the difference in space between the beds. As the domestic machine has a slightly larger gap between the main bed and ribber bed, it helps to produce a slightly better knit if the full rib is knitted slightly tighter than the single jersey. This step is not fundamental to the technique, only for a tighter knit overall.

Adjustments to this technique can include increasing and decreasing the number of rows knitted within the ripple or in between each ripple. This could also include changes of colour and yarns to alter the visual and tactile qualities of the sample.

To start, 50 stitches are cast on using the double bed with yarn A. Change to yarn B and knit 2 rows on the back bed only to create a ripple. Changing back to yarn A, knit 2 rows in double jersey – all needles knitting. Change to yarn C, knit 2 rows on the back bed only. Change to yarn A, knit 2 rows working double jersey. With the next set of ripples (a ripple with each colour) increase the ripple size by 2 rows, meaning each ripple in yarns B and C will be knitted with 4 rows, with 2 rows of yarn A in between.

The next set of ripples will then be with 6 rows, before returning to 4 rows and then 2 rows within each ripple.

Repeat the whole sequence of increasing the number of rows within one ripple and then decreasing them again twice, for the desired length of the sample.

A change of colour within the ripples can build up interesting colour elements. This sample changed colours within the Ottoman rolls but has a single base colour. The number of colours used throughout the rolls is not limited and can be as many or as few as desired. If you are not using a colour changer, tie on the new colour and pull through. *Yarn A: Dark blue, one end 2-ply wool. Yarn B: Orange, one end 2/15NM lambswool. Yarn C: Lilac, three ends 2/36 cashmere–cotton blend. Tension: Plain 5, rib 4.*

Double-sided Ottoman can be achieved on both the domestic and the V-bed machines when working with all needles on both beds rather than a needle placement. *Yarn A: Dark blue, one end nylon (count unknown). Yarn B: Orange, one end 2/15NM lambswool. Yarn C: Lilac, three ends 2/36NM cashmere–cotton blend. Tension: Rib 4, plain 5.*

The reverse side of the double-sided Ottoman sample, showing the secondary colour for the rolls.

The beauty with Ottoman and working with the double bed is that we are not limited to working on one bed of the machine, but can create material on both sides.

Perfect for lengths of material that may act as a room divider, blanket or any other piece of textile where it would be useful to have it double-sided, we can create Ottoman rolls on both sides of the material using both beds in turn. This works best when the ripple is made across all needles rather than if we were to have a needle placement, similar to some samples further on in this part of the chapter.

Using yarn A, cast on again 50 needles, or the width of the sample size you wish to make. With yarn B, knit 4 rows on the front bed only. Change back to yarn A and knit 2 rows of all-needles knit on both beds. With yarn C, knit 4 rows back-bed only. Change back to yarn A and knit 2 rows with all needles knitting on both beds.

Swapping between beds to create the Ottoman rolls, (working two rows with double jersey between each roll) will evenly distribute the ripples on both sides of the material. To create more of a pattern, you could repeat the rolls on each side any number of times before switching to the opposite bed to create a build-up of texture on one side of the bed. At least one row of working all needles on both beds needs to be knitted to close the rolls before working the next one.

Increasing or decreasing the number of rows within each roll or using colour can help to create an additional pattern or texture within the length.

Having knitted these last few samples on the domestic machine, I will now switch to working on the V-bed machine to create the following samples. This will give a contrast of gauge of knit but potentially also some constraints to the techniques with regard to pattern placement or size, considering that we have the ability to use partial knit on the domestic machines and to work with particular needles. Any of these techniques can be knitted on the domestic machines using the same methods. You can, however, incorporate additional techniques into the samples such as partial knit and lifted stitches if you are working on a domestic machine.

Creating more of a pattern with the ripples on each bed by altering the placement of the ripples, or the colour or size of the ripples, can enhance the length of the sample. *Yarn A: One end polyamide. Yarn B: One end 2/15NM lambswool. Yarn C: Three ends 2/48NM wool. Tension: single jersey 5, double jersey 4.*

The reverse side of the sample shows the secondary colour, but also the slightly elongated stitches where the ripples are made on the opposite side.

STITCH SIZE AND V-BED MACHINES

Samples knitted on the V-bed machine will not state a tension value due to the differences between using machine gauges and yarn types. Typically, I use around tension 12 for double jersey and 14 for single jersey on most machines, but in some instances have used tension as low as 10 and up to 18. The differences are completely due to the yarn and the gauge of the machine that was used. Tensions on the domestic machines are generally very similar between machine brands, and are more accommodating with the yarn choice.

I will also not state a number of needles to cast on as the samples made here are relatively large, therefore if you would like to knit a basic sample purely to get used to the technique, it is suggested that you work a smaller piece.

DECIDING ON WHICH BED TO WORK ON

Regardless of whether I am using a V-bed machine or a domestic machine, personally I prefer to work with the main body of the fabric on the back bed and the needle placement on the front bed. This helps when following a pattern as you do not have to mirror the pattern, and also helps with the ability to see the material better as it comes off the machine. This is also my preference when working with industrial machines such as Stoll or Shima.

If you are working on a domestic machine and prefer to have the main bed (the back bed) as the bed with the needle placement because this feels more like the main bed, then there would be no difference in methods or technique apart from switching the beds named in the instructions.

Needle Placement and Ottoman

Through this next section we will focus on the use of a needle placement on one side of the double bed to create a texture within the roll. This makes contrast in areas of the material of both density and openness due to the held stitches that create the Ottoman rolls. The held stitches will increase the texture by creating a closed section of material compared to the areas where needles are not being worked to create the Ottoman rolls. These areas will make the material expand more, emphasising the build-up of fabric and change of yarn.

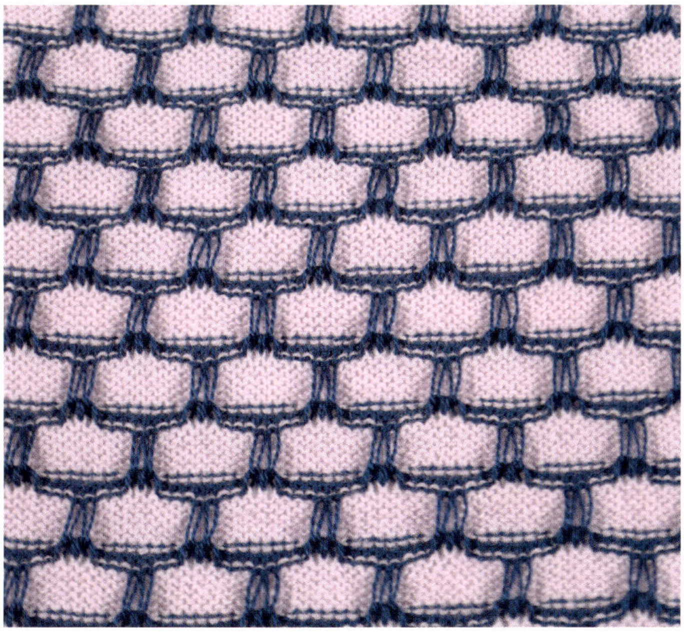

Using the V-bed machine, we are able to create very similar materials to lifted stitches by creating stitches and letting them rest on the needles. A close-up of the held stitches, which very closely resemble the lifted stitches visually and also structurally, despite being knitted very differently. The chart for this sample is on the next page. *Yarn A: Lilac 2/16NM worsted wool. Yarn B: Dark blue 2/16NE combed cotton.*

Ottoman for Lifted Stitches

Using a needle placement on the opposite bed to the one used to make the roll will create a similar texture to some of the lifted-stitches techniques covered previously in this chapter, especially the techniques in which we lift certain stitches back up onto the machine.

The technical process on the V-bed machines is the same as the lifted stitches on the domestic machines, but instead of working by hand to pick up stitches and rehang them back onto needles, we are creating a stitch on one bed in a needle placement, which is held whilst we work and create the Ottoman roll on the opposite bed. In some instances those formed stitches are then transferred over to secure the stitches and make the structure a single-jersey structure; but the formed stitch can also be worked with double jersey in between the Ottoman rolls to continue with a needle placement or pattern on the rear side of the material.

Creating a stitch on the non-working bed acts in the same way as a lifted stitch, by pulling the fabric made in the Ottoman roll upwards to create a roll or ripple. We will start with some examples of using this before moving on to create ripples with floats. Working with a very similar pattern to those first patterns with the hook-up stitches, we will explore the basics of the process before working towards more complicated patterns.

Cast on working all needles on both beds over the width of the desired sample in yarn A. Transfer all front-bed needles to the back bed as we will have the main material worked on the back bed and the needle placement on the front bed.

Knit a few rows only on the back bed to create a small border to the pattern. If you prefer to jump straight into the pattern, however, transfer to the back-bed only the needles in the pattern that are not in action on the front bed.

1. With yarn B, knit 2 rows working all needles (double jersey).
2. Change to yarn A, knit 6 rows back-bed only.
3. Change back to yarn B, transfer any needles within the pattern that now need to be placed out of action, remove the needles from work, and bring into action any needles that will now be worked. Knit 2 rows with all needles knitting. The new empty needles that have no stitches on them will build up full stitches over the two rows.
4. Repeat the last two steps for the entirety of the pattern, or for the length of the sample you wish to make.

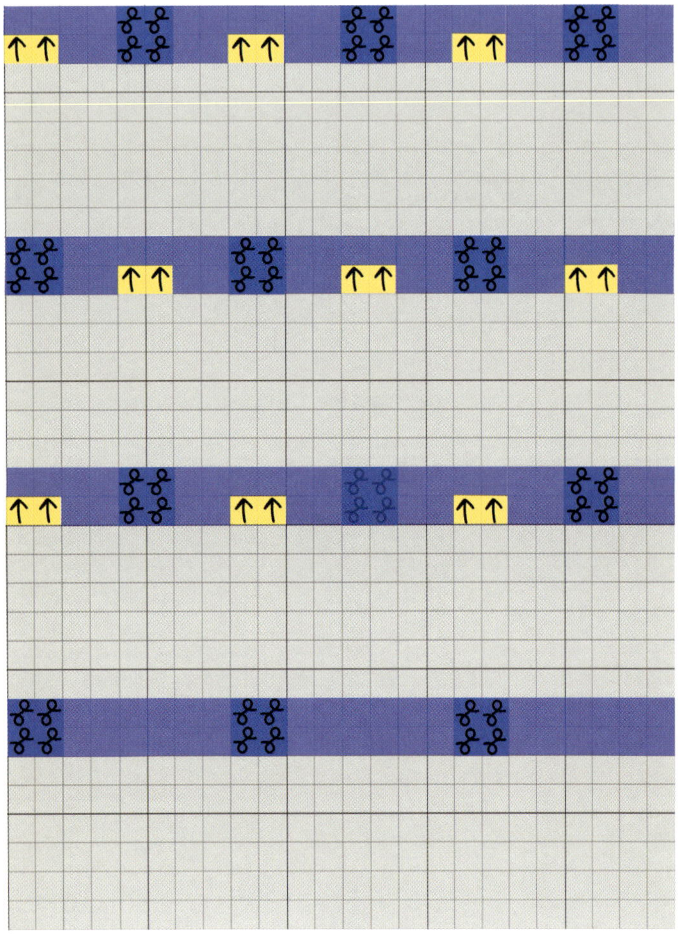

Yarn A – Back bed only

Yarn B – Double jersey. Placement of the working front-bed needles. All back bed needles working across these rows

Transfer front-bed stitches to back bed

A detailed diagram to show the technical elements of this sample, colour-coded to show each stitch and where they are transferred.

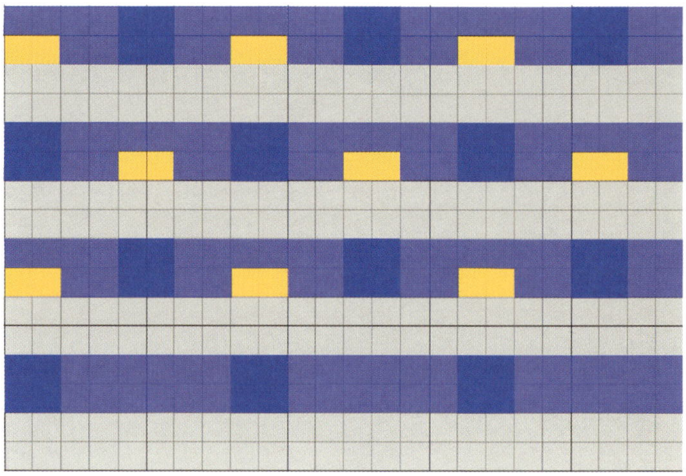

Yarn A – Back bed only

Yarn B – Double jersey, front-bed needle placement

Yarn B – Double jersey, all back-bed needles

Transfer the front-bed stitches to the back bed

This chart represents the pattern of the needle placement rather than the technical diagram. For the following samples, each will have a chart similar to this portraying where the front-bed needles should be, but not the stitch symbols.

WHEN TO CHANGE NEEDLE PLACEMENT

Transferring stitches for this method will happen after the Ottoman (single-jersey) row. Once you have changed colour for the double-jersey rows, or the row in which you have stitches on both beds, transfer stitches on the front bed that are no longer needed over to the back bed, or bring into action the needles on the front bed that you now want to have stitches built up over.

The Ottoman roll is knitted only on the back bed with yarn A. The stitches in the needle placement on the front bed are held.

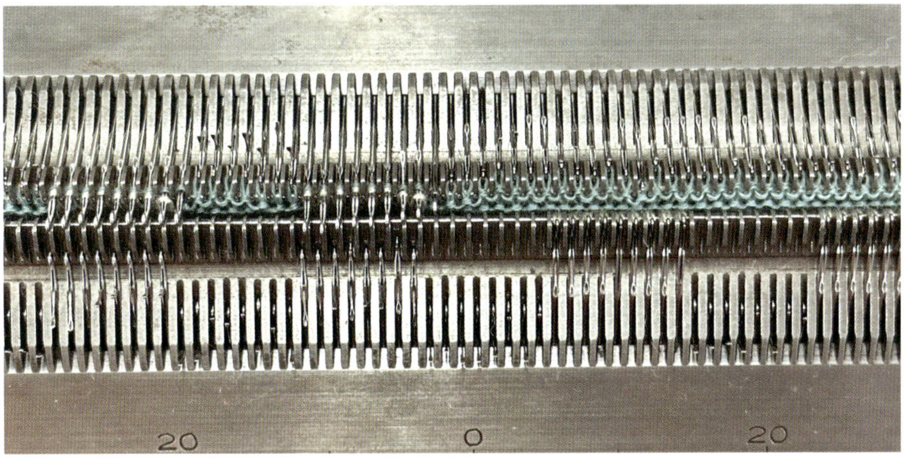

After the six rows made on the back bed only, the front-bed stitches are transferred to the back bed, the needles are taken out of action and the new needle placement is introduced.

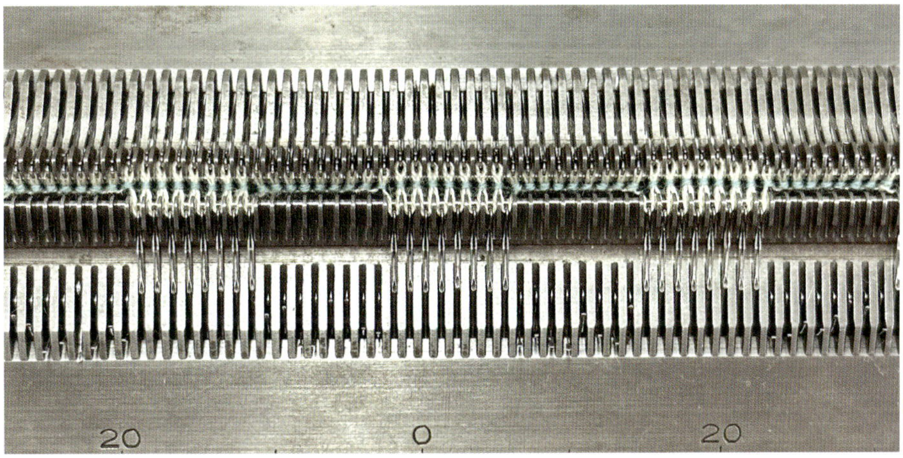

With yarn B, and working both beds, stitches are made on the front-bed needles and all needles on the back bed are knitted. Two rows are knitted in total.

Once off the machine, you will notice the stitches created on the front bed act very similarly to the lifted stitches in the samples earlier on in this chapter. They have a very similar structure.

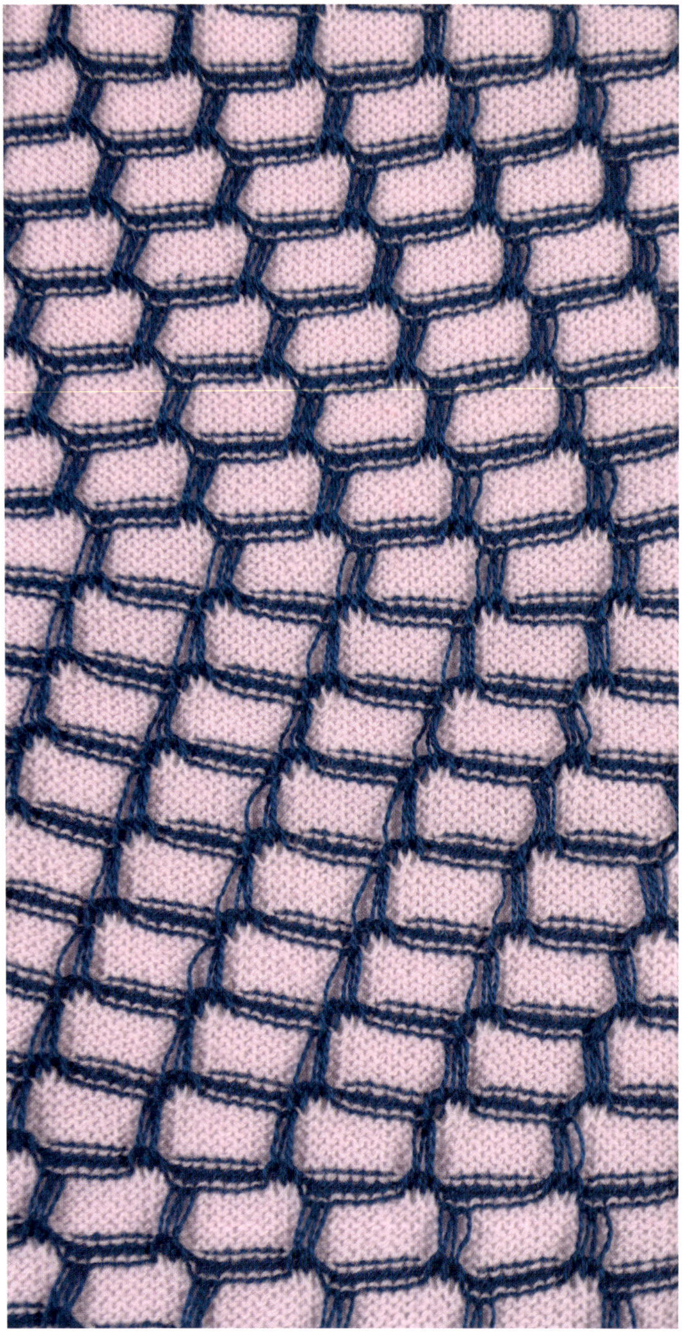

We can move the placement of the working needles to begin creating patterns on the front side. In this variation the stitches are moved to create a vertical chevron pattern, however, the front-bed stitches can be moved into whichever position you design. *Yarn A: Lilac 2/16NM worsted wool. Yarn B: Dark blue 2/16NE combed cotton.*

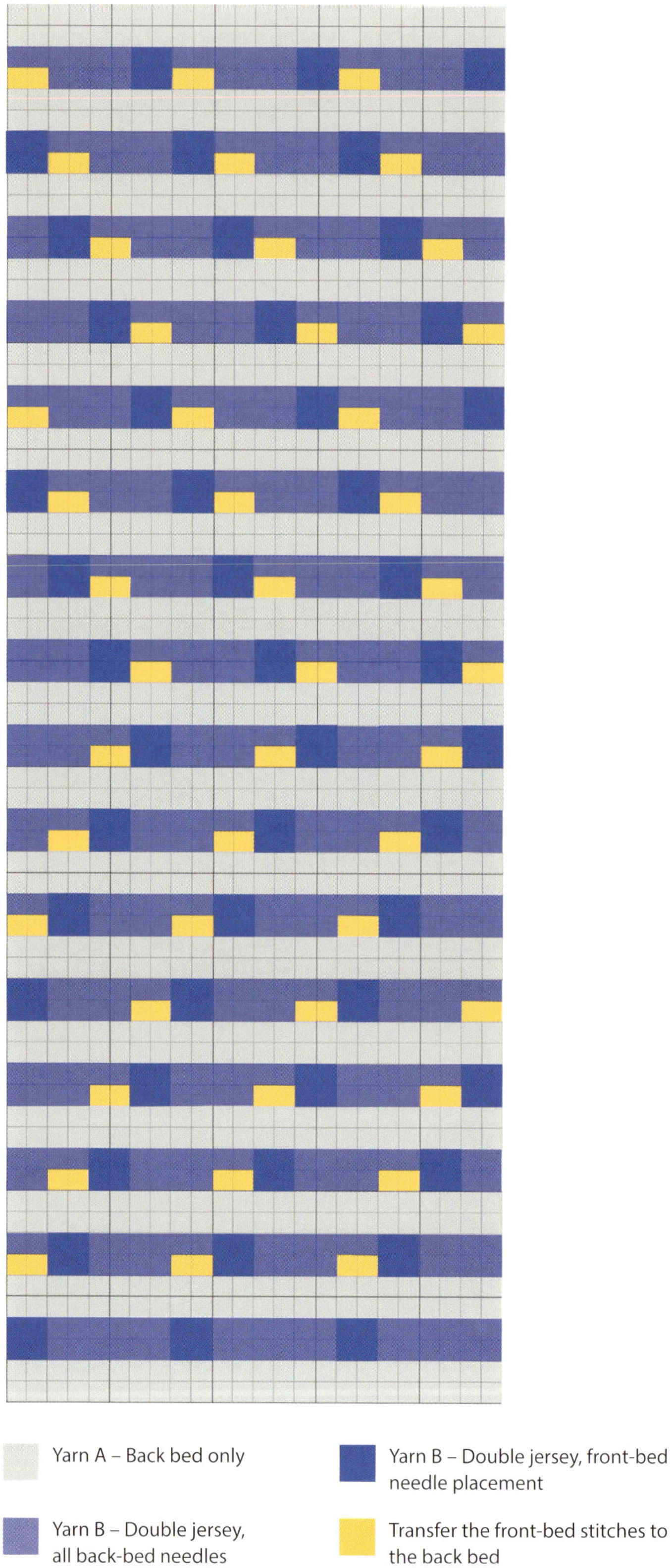

The pattern placement to show the movement of the held stitches to create the Ottoman.

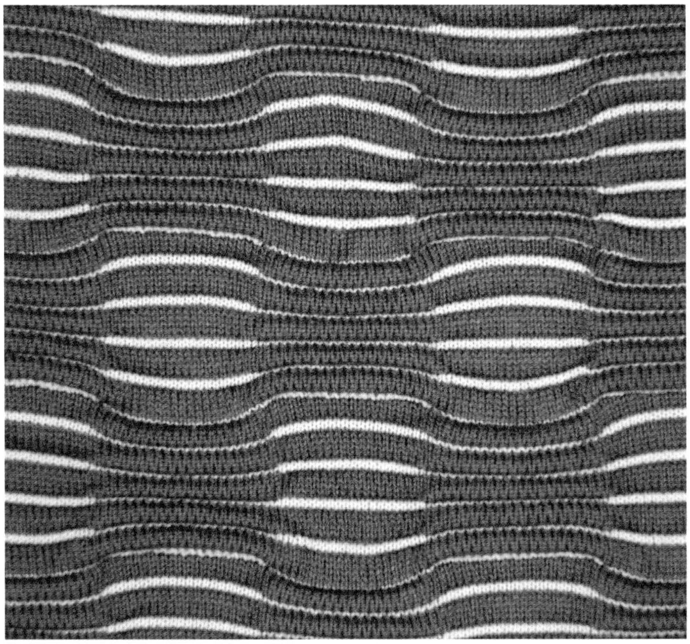

Working with blocks of front-bed needles, the ripples on the back bed become denser in areas compared to the adjacent sections where the rolls are more visible as they are spaced out. This not only creates pattern and shape on the back side (the side where the needle placement is seen) but also on the front side (the side where the ripples are visible). *Yarn A: Purple, one end 2/16NE cotton. Yarn B: One end nylon (count unknown).*

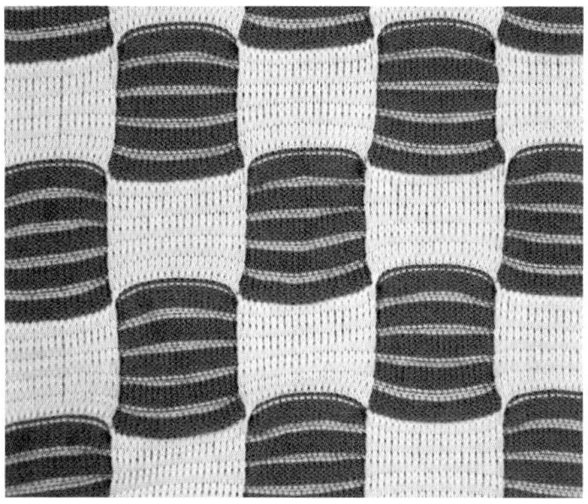

The rear of the sample shows the placement of the stitches that were held on the front bed.

Yarn choice for this technique can very much create different effects within the same sample. For example, using the same yarn for both the ripple material and the needle placement (or the all-needle knitting sections) will create tension within the knit, but only if the stitch size has been set appropriately. If you want to increase the tension when working with very similar yarns, you can alter the stitch tension between the single jersey and the full-rib rows. Working with an elastic yarn for yarn B will automatically introduce much more shrinkage into the sample, therefore much more structure.

You can begin to introduce your own patterns using this same structure to alter the effect and create areas of pattern and texture within your own designs, such as blocks of held stitches as seen here.

Identical in pattern to the previous sample, this sample was worked with an elastomeric yarn instead of the nylon in yarn B. The elastane has constricted the sample considerably, increasing the texture value of the ripples and the pattern. The elasticity of this sample allows the piece to stretch much more, revealing and concealing the pattern. The tightness of the material makes it feel much more suited for use as a technical fabric rather than a clothing material. *Yarn A: Green 2/16NE cotton. Yarn B: Pink, one end shirring elastic.*

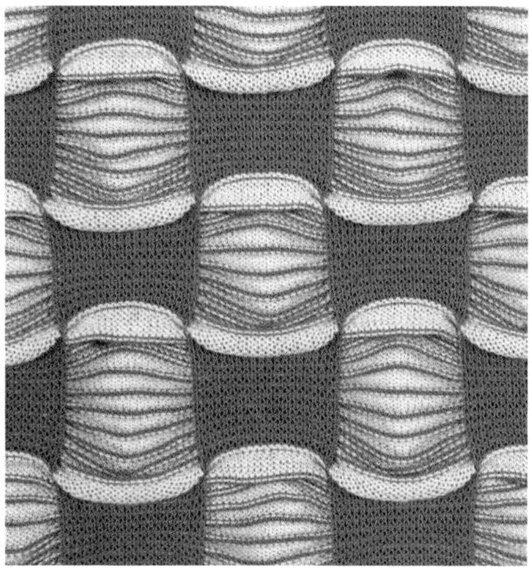

The back of the sample, showing the placement of the held stitches and the shrinkage of the elastomeric yarn.

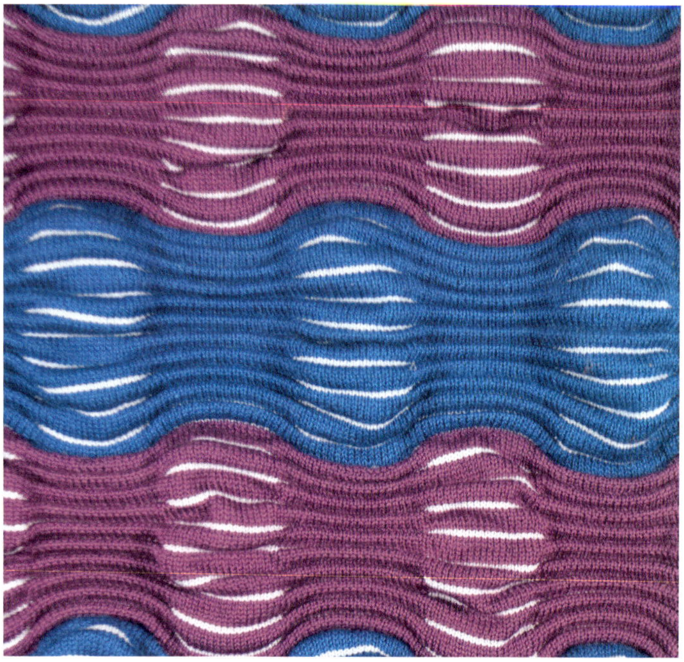

Changing colour after every block alters the visuals of the sample. This colour change is quite blocky; however, the colour can be changed much more often. Personally, I feel this sample emphasises the structure but also the main yarn, which is shown through the rolls.

The back side of the sample shows both the needle structure for the held stitches and also the change in colour.

We can explore how the same technique is used, where a pattern has been introduced into the placement of the held stitches on the second bed, and also by using a variation of yarns to provide an insight into the tactile elements they can add. For each sample, an elastic yarn has been used, whether this is a Lycra or a polyamide. This is to help slightly shrink the stitches that are held on one bed whilst the Ottoman is created on the other bed. It is this effect that gives the most dimension and form to the technique.

Yarn A – Back bed only

Yarn B – Double jersey, front-bed needle placement

Yarn B – Double jersey, all back-bed needles

Transfer the front-bed stitches to the back bed

The chart used for the above samples shows the placement of the working front needles.

FOUR-FEEDER V-BED MACHINES

Including colour into the Ottoman rolls is a method to elevate the technique further. Working with a four-feeder V-bed machine, all feeders can be threaded up with variations of coloured or textural yarns to work over the rolls. How often the colour is changed is a design element that can be incorporated.

An adjustment to the placement by shifting some of the blocks, which in turn creates full areas of front-bed stitches and full areas where only the ripples are shown. *Yarn A: Bright green, one end 2/16NE cotton. Yarn B: Dark green, one end nylon (count unknown).*

The front side of the Ottoman, to show how this adjustment affects the pattern.

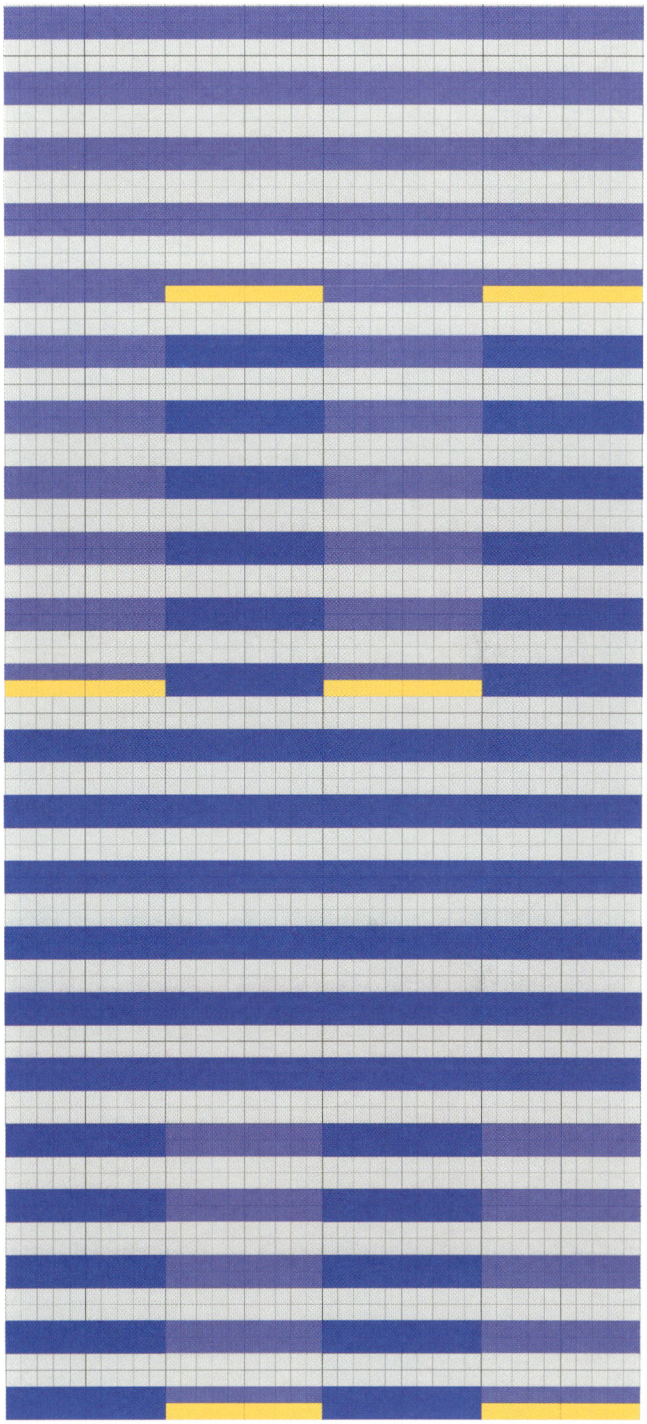

Yarn A – Back bed only

Yarn B – Double jersey, front-bed needle placement

Yarn B – Double jersey, all back-bed needles

Transfer the front bed stitches to the back-bed

The chart for the adjusted stitch placement.

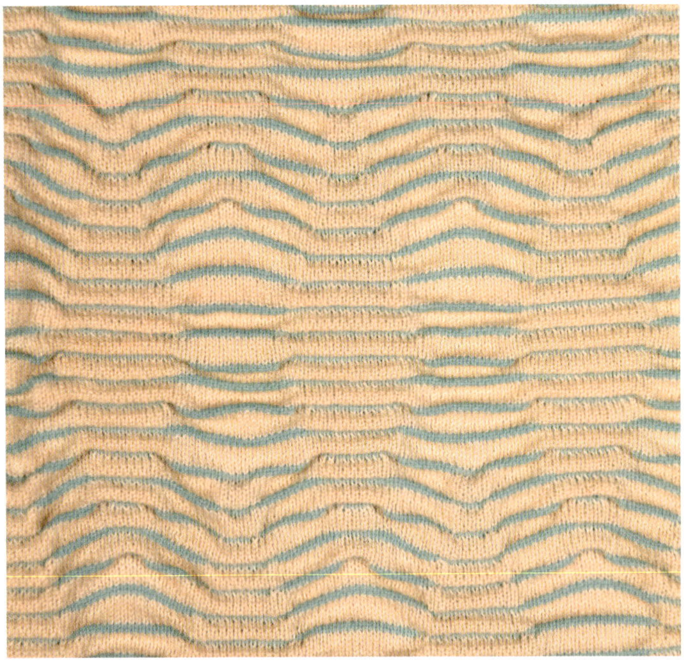

Altering the positioning of the held stitches can create more of a surface pattern and texture compared to when they are left in blocks. *Yarn A: White, one end 2/36NM wool. Yarn B: Blue, one end nylon (count unknown).*

The lifted stitches' placement on the rear side, this time in a diamond shape rather than worked in blocks.

This pattern that is created on the front bed is not limited to blocks. We can add in directional or geometric patterns to create interest. This first sample is again shown with two different material choices to showcase the difference and importance of yarn choice. The basic block has now been shaped into diamonds. The pattern on the back side (the side where the stitches in yarn B are more visible) is more graphic. However, if turned over, the pattern on the front side gives the most detail, particularly with a bit of colour reveal.

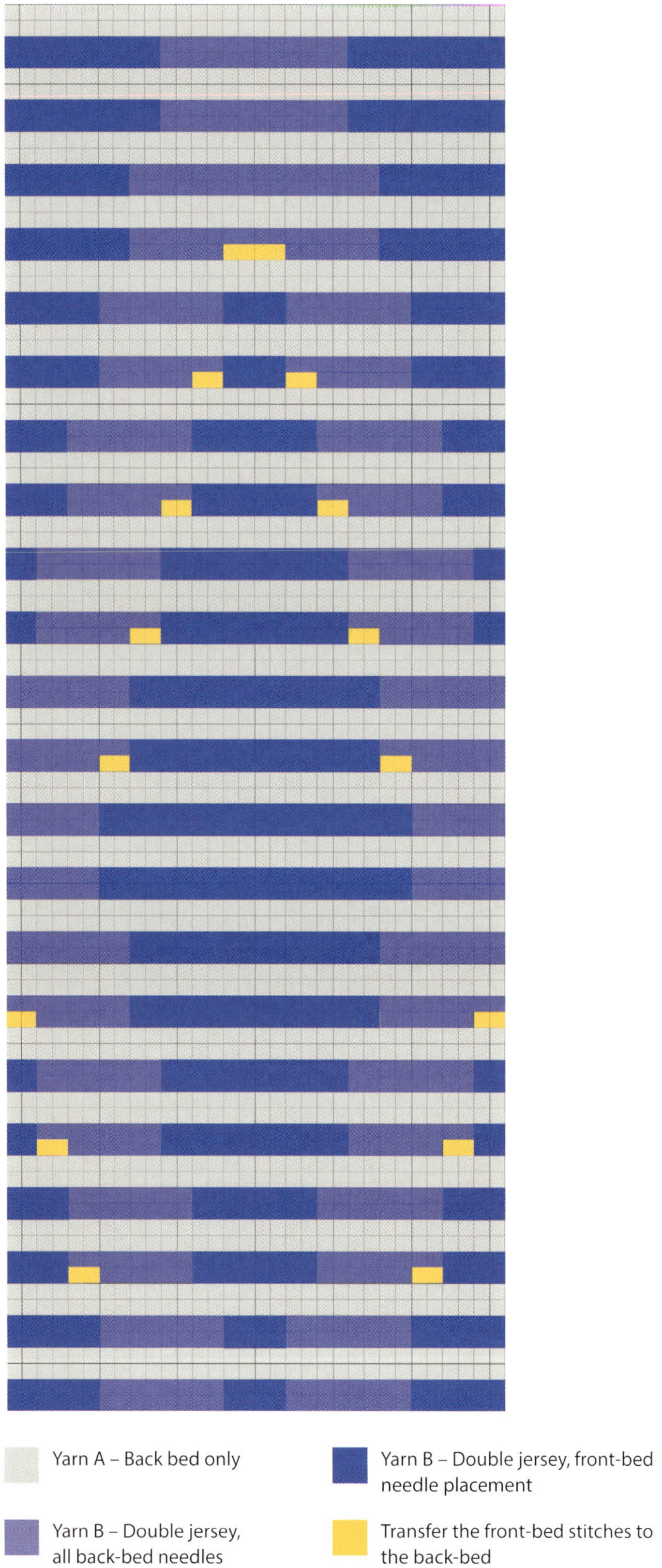

The pattern placement for the diamond-shaped held stitches.

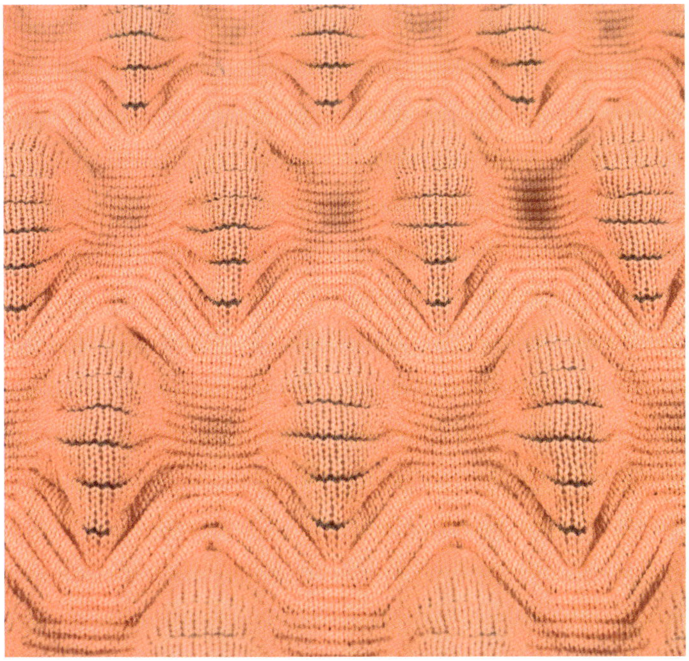

The same structure made with different yarns creates a completely different form. *Yarn A: Green, one end 2/16NE cotton. Yarn B: Pink, one end shirring elastic.*

The rear side of the sample with the held stitches worked in the shirring elastic.

The sample with the elastic provides a very tactile surface, enabling the areas with no held stitches to expand out, especially when tension is put into the piece.

Lastly to emphasise the difference that the gauge can make, these two samples were knitted on the domestic machine. The method for making the structure is identical but the change in gauge can alter the tactility and the density of the material.

Larger stitches make for a larger pattern, which can also increase the amount of structure there is in the sample. *Yarn A: Red 3-ply mixed yarns. Yarn B: Purple, two ends polyamide, count unknown.*

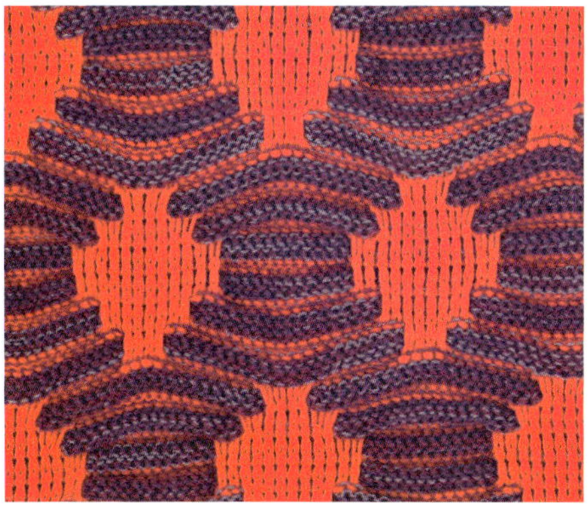

The back side to show the held stitches that were on the front bed.

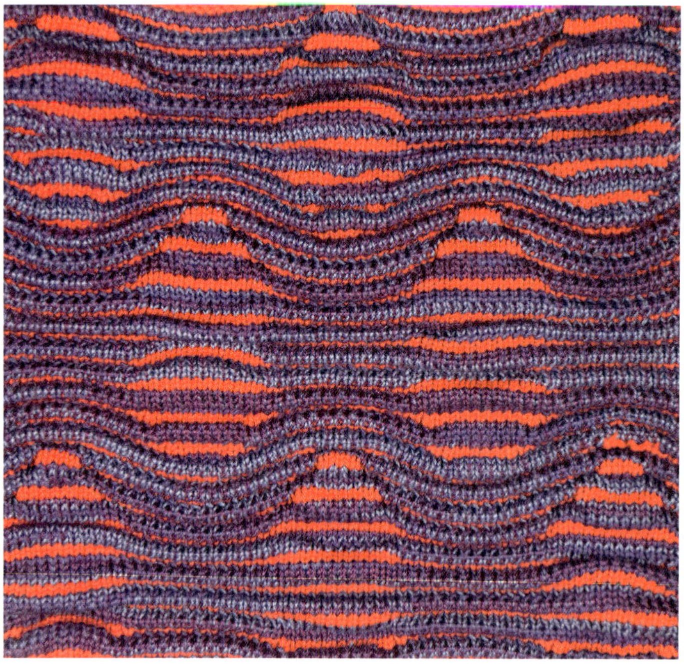

The exact same technique but with the pattern almost inverted.

The rear side showing the needle placement. This is the inverse of the diamond pattern used previously. Having more areas of held stitches on one bed creates more areas of denser material.

Working a more isolated placement of held stitches on one bed can give another effect to the pattern. As the Ottoman rolls are not held in place, the material flares out compared to the denser areas with the held stitches. *Yarn A: Red 3-ply mixed yarns. Yarn B: Purple, two ends polyamide, count unknown.*

These samples made on the domestic machine use a shrinking yarn over the double-jersey rows, meaning the shrinking yarn is used for the held stitches. The Ottoman-roll yarn is three ends of a wool in different colours. Similar to when using the V-bed machine, the effect of the shrinking yarn means that the held stitches bring a little more texture to the material.

More shape could be brought into the Ottoman by working more rows on the main bed before knitting the double jersey. It is easier to control the stitches on the domestic machines compared to the V-bed machines, therefore larger forms can be created. If you begin to see that the stitches are struggling to form for the Ottoman rolls, bring the needles into the forward working position to force the needles to knit; this cannot be done on the V-bed machines.

Ottoman and Floats

Now that we have explored the variation of creating material with a needle placement on the opposite bed to the roll, we can turn our attention to creating rolls on the same side as the needle placement, which in turn will create a material that has floats running across the rippled area.

Charts have been drawn out for the following samples which are to be tried and tested by yourself. Once you are comfortable with the technique it is suggested that you draw out your own pattern for your own design. We will, as always, start with some easier samples. Please note there is a different way to change the front-bed working stitches. This is highlighted in the 'Changing Needle Placement' box a little further on.

Cast on all needles on both beds with yarn A. As an option, you can knit a few rows of double jersey if you would like some material at the bottom of the sample; however, I tend to work straight into the ripple structure.

Transfer all the front-bed needles to the back bed and push the empty needles out of action on the front bed before knitting a few rows of back-bed only to create a small amount of single jersey.

Working on a fine gauge (such as a 10gg or 12gg Dubied, Universal or Stoll V-bed machine) to create a ripple with a needle placement. *Yarn A: Cream, one end 2/28NM combed cotton. Yarn B: Light blue, one end 1/13NE cotton.*

On the last row of yarn A before we change to yarn B to begin the ripple and float structure, bring up into work the needles in placement across the front bed. In this instance we have 2 working needles on the front bed with 6 out-of-action needles in between the working needles. Knit 1 row of double jersey to create the base of a new stitch on the previously empty needles on the front bed.

Change to yarn B; knit 4 rows on the front bed only. The needles in work will create a full stitch from the tuck stitch on the front bed and float across the empty needles.

Change to yarn A and knit 2 rows with all needles knitting on both beds.

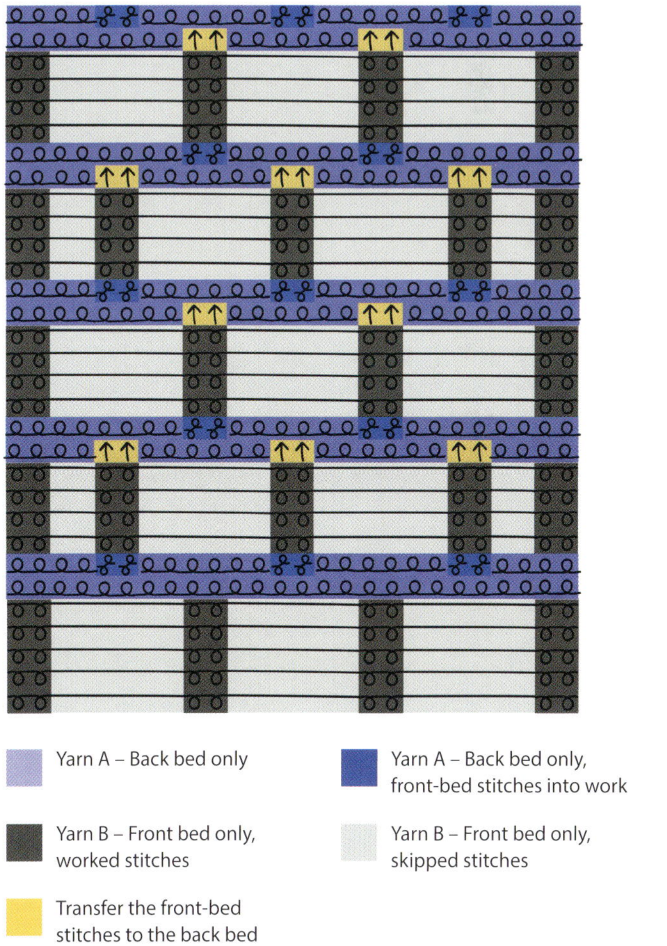

This chart shows the technical working of the stitches and the yarns over the needles. The colours used not only emphasise the technical elements, but also the differences in the yarns and when they should be changed. Note that the subsequent charts for this method have been simplified, but refer back to this chart if in doubt.

Before the second row of double jersey is knitted in yarn A, we need to change the needle position on the front bed. Transfer the stitches on the front bed that are no longer worked in the pattern to the back bed, push them out of action so they will not knit on the next row, and bring into action the new needles that will create stitches. Knit the second row of double jersey to establish the new stitches on the empty needles on the front bed. Change to yarn B and knit 4 rows front-bed only.

Repeat this whole process, following the chart for the structure.

The process of changing colours, knitting a ripple and altering the working needle placement will build up texture, colour placement and pattern over the working area. It can be a lengthy process, especially if transferring stitches is relatively new to you, but once you get into the swing of the transfers, the process becomes quicker. This pattern, being repetitive and predictable, means that soon you will not have to concentrate so much with the positioning of the transfers.

Using the same needle placement as the previous sample, a very quick adjustment to the pattern, such as altering the colour of the ripple between yarn A and yarn B, can give an additional surface pattern. It becomes almost similar to a basket-weave stitch in structure, with the floats mimicking the purl stitches, and the ripples the knit stitches.

CHANGING NEEDLE PLACEMENT

Unlike working with Ottoman to create the lifted stitch effect, when working with ripples and changing the needle placement, there is a specific time to transfer needles and introduce new needles into work in the pattern. We alter the needle placement before the last row of the double jersey, rather than as we change yarn to the ripple yarn, and deselect the back bed. This allows us to create a tuck stitch on the front-bed needles, so fully formed stitches can be made on the first row with the ripple yarn. If we do not bring in the new needles on the last row of the double jersey, we will be attempting to create front-bed stitches with no foundational stitch.

Creating new stitches on two adjacent empty needles is not possible as this essentially creates one oversized stitch and not individual stitches. Therefore, we need to ensure there is a fully formed working stitch on either side of the empty needle to correctly form a new stitch. When working on the double bed, formed stitches on the back bed work as the working stitches on either side of the empty needle to ensure new stitches are created on the front bed, regardless of how many empty needles there are. This is why we make sure to bring into work new needles on the last row of the double jersey.

Step 1: On the last row, transfer the front-bed stitches to the back-bed needles.

Step 2: Change the front-bed needle placement. Regardless of the machine, I bring the needles up into the forward working position to ensure the yarn will catch and the needles are worked.

Step 3: The first row with the new yarn will create tuck stitches on the empty needles. It does not matter if you have multiple empty needles because there is a back-bed needle with a stitch in between each empty needle on the front bed.

Step 4: Continue knitting the pattern, working on the correct bed for the sample. In this instance it is an Ottoman with floats structure.

To begin to add more structure to the sample, we can again incorporate blocks into the needle structure. Whilst this may potentially look more complex than the previous sample, it is actually easier to knit as there are fewer transfers overall.

This time we will work straight into the pattern so we do not need to transfer all needles, only the needles we want out of action. Cast on with all needles on both beds using yarn A before transferring some of the front-bed needles to the back bed. In this pattern we will work with groups of 10 needles: 10 needles working and 10 needles out of action.

Change to yarn B and knit 6 rows on the front bed only. Changing back to yarn A, knit 2 rows of all needles on both beds knitting. As you can see in the chart, we will keep the position of the needles for another 6 ripples, for a total of 7 ripples.

Switch between yarn B for the 6-row ripple and yarn A for all-needles knitting until this first section is complete.

Adding blocks into the needle structure rather than altering the placement continuously will build up a sample with more form and texture. *Yarn A: Light blue, one end 2/16NE cotton. Yarn B: Purple, two ends 2/48NM superwash merino.*

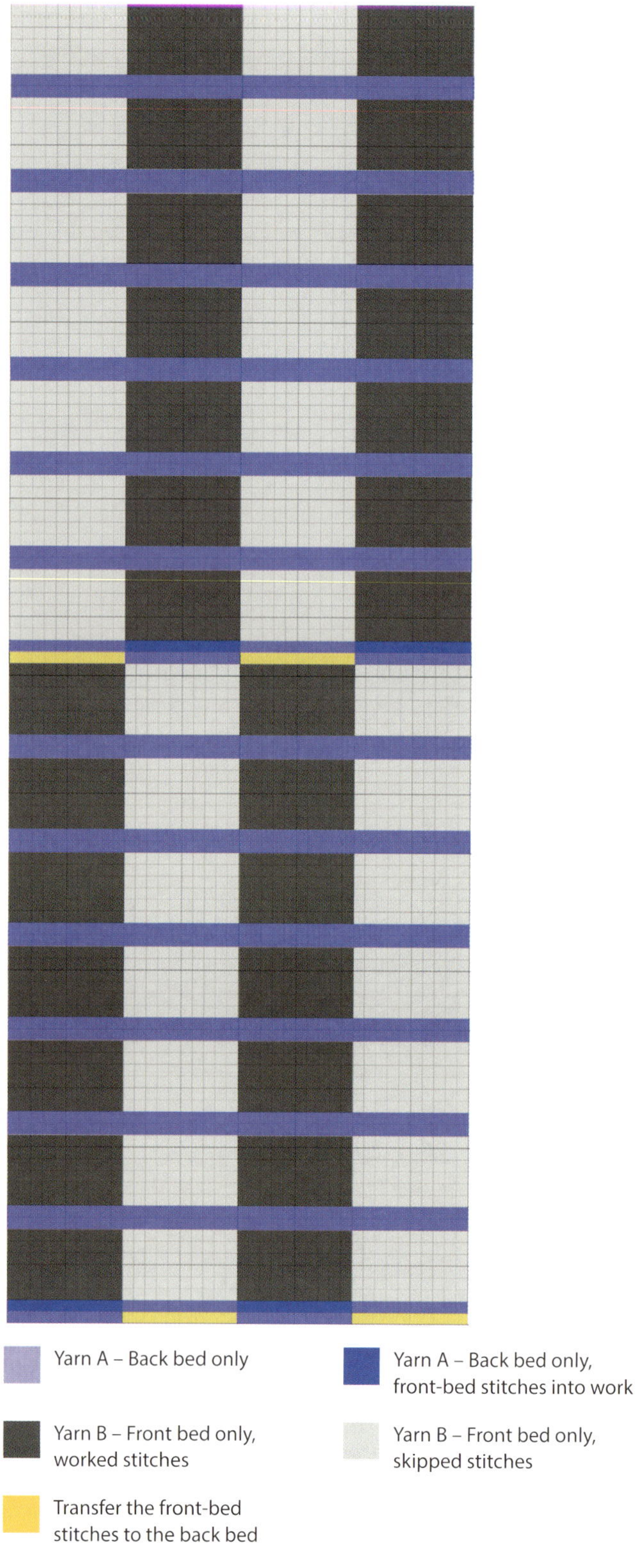

The pattern for the ripples needle placement. Note that it is a simplified chart compared to the previous one that has the stitch technical information. The rows are all included but the technical graphics are not. Refer to the key for more information.

We will next change the needle placement. Transfer all working front-bed needles to the back bed and reintroduce the previous out-of-action needles into work as these will create the ripples next. Remember to change the needle structure on the last row of the double jersey to ensure stitches can be built up on the empty needles on the front bed. Again, repeat this ripple structure for a total of 7 ripples before you change the needle structure again.

You can add more colour and texture into this sample by including more colour within the ripples or altering the number of rows within each ripple. It is up to you to incorporate your chosen variations into this basic sample.

Simply altering the position of the front-bed working needles, whether it is in blocks, as previously explained, or every couple of rows, the pattern can be shifted. In this next sample, a simple pattern of a horizontal chevron is worked into the front needles.

Moving the pattern into a vertical chevron, we can alter the positioning of the floats as we knit. *Yarn A: Light blue, one end 2/16NE cotton. Yarn B: Purple, two ends 2/48NM merino.*

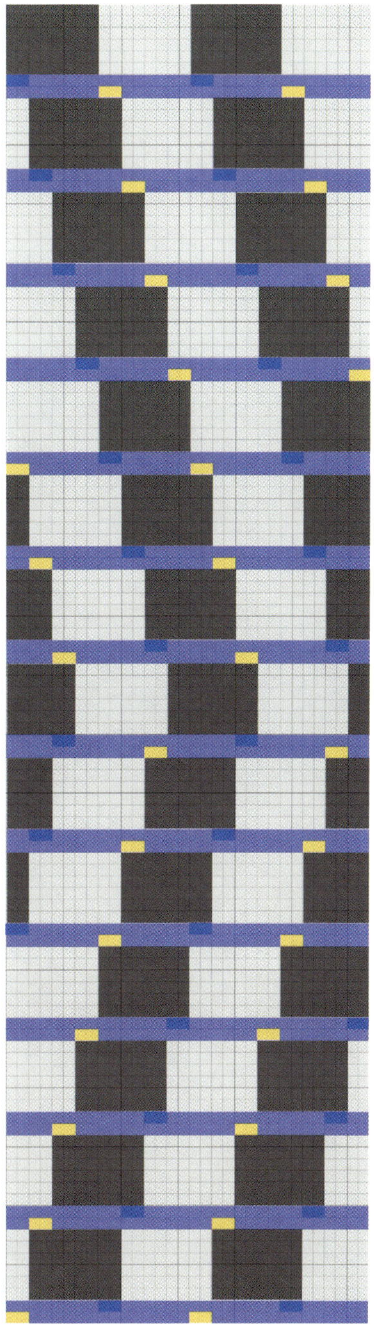

Yarn A – Back bed only

Yarn A – Back bed only, front-bed stitches into work

Yarn B – Front bed only, worked stitches

Yarn B – Front bed only, skipped stitches

Transfer the front-bed stitches to the back bed

The pattern for the ripples needle placement. Note that it is a simplified chart compared to the previous one that has the stitch technical information. The rows are all included but the technical graphics are not. Refer to the key for more information.

An altered scale of the vertical chevron ripple and float placement.

FLOATS AND NEEDLE PLACEMENT

A suggestion to bear in mind with this technique, which was previously mentioned when making pockets in Chapter 1: Partial Knit, is that whilst the needle placement is completely open to suggestion or design, I would not recommend floating across more needles than the gauge you are working on; or if you're unsure of your gauge, count the number of needles in an inch (roughly 2.5cm). There are some situations where you would be able to float across a larger number, and domestic machines tend to support this a bit more than V-bed machines. However, it is best to stick to this rule to begin with. For example, if I were working with a 10gg V-bed, I would not have more than ten needles out of action on the bed that the ripples were being created on.

This is all to achieve the yarn being fed correctly into the needle hook as the feeder passes it. The further the distance between working needles, the higher the yarn will sit as it enters the needle. When the yarn is placed into the needle and a stitch created, the yarn is drawn downwards and is held in a suitable position for the next needle to catch. When there is distance between the needles, the yarn will sit higher up towards the yarn feeder. If the distance between the last working needle is more than 2.5cm (1in), you run the risk that the yarn from the feeder will end up too high for the needle to catch it on the next working needle. This may not apply to all cases, but it is a good guide to begin with.

It is possible to very slightly lower the yarn-feeder tip with V-bed machines, which will help the insertion of yarn into the needle hook after a gap of out-of-action needles. However, do this with caution, and only if you know how. Lower the yarn feeder tip too much and you could cause the feeder tip to collide with the needles when they rise, which would certainly damage, if not break, the needles.

To follow on from these previous samples in which we have briefly explored the needle placement and patterns within that, it would be a good exercise to sample different yarns and their properties to understand further how these variations affect the textiles. I have knitted the same structure in a variety of yarn qualities, to begin understanding the differences the yarn choice makes to the overall structure.

I have worked with a needle placement within the front-bed needles to create a pattern in the shape of a repeating diamond. The staggered placement means there is never more than an inch (roughly 2.5cm) of floats across the work to ensure that the needles always catch the yarn to create the stitch.

Overleaf we have three examples of the same knit structure where an exploration into yarn choice has been worked to see the difference in appearance that changing the yarn can have. As we know from the previous section when working with Ottoman and a needle placement but without the floats, the choice in yarn can add and create an area of additional tension within the knit, emphasising the structure. This is best achieved using a yarn that shrinks slightly, whether this is a polyamide, a nylon or an elastic. In the next examples I have used nylon, which doesn't give the most elasticity and shrinkage, but there is a different effect that gives great results that I want to discuss. You are encouraged to swap the nylon for a yarn that shrinks further to create yet more dimension and depth to the piece.

To add further detail to the floats, in these samples a third colour has been included to emphasise the colour element. Six rows have been knitted for each ripple, meaning two rows in the first colour, two rows in the secondary colour and then two rows again in the first colour.

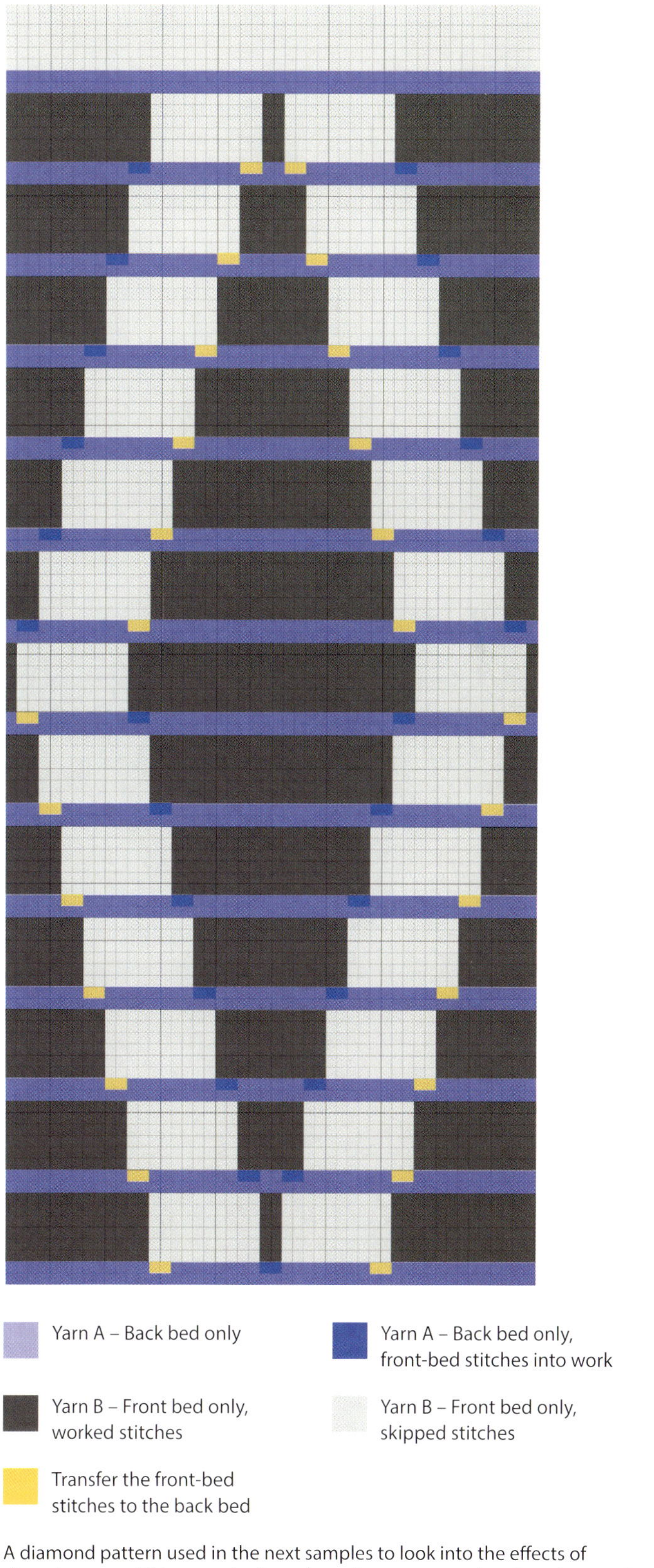

A diamond pattern used in the next samples to look into the effects of changing yarns. This not only shows how the pattern works when the needle placement is altered, but also what happens when it is worked over blocks of working needles.

The diamond form worked only with natural cotton-blend yarns over both beds. *Yarn A: Backing, one end 2/36NM cotton–wool blend. Yarn B and C: Ripples and floats, one end 2/36NM cotton–wool blend.*

The diamond pattern worked with a mix of synthetic and natural yarns. The backing is made in a synthetic yarn to slightly shrink and purposefully encourage the ripple and float pattern, to create more texture. *Yarn A: Backing, one end nylon, count unknown. Yarn B and C: Ripples and floats, 2/36NM cotton blend.*

The final yarn-exploration sample using the diamond pattern. This was worked with a natural yarn at the back and a synthetic yarn on the front with the ripples and the floats. *Yarn A: Backing, one end 2/36NM cotton–wool blend. Yarn B and C: Ripples and floats, one end nylon, count unknown.*

This first example has used only natural yarns. The backing material, or the knit made on the back bed, has a normal amount of stretch and openness that you would expect to find with a cotton. The front of the material with the needle placement also has the same open quality. There is no additional pull added to the sample from an elastic yarn. This means that the texture of the floats is not out of the ordinary.

If we were to compare this first sample to the second sample, in which a nylon was used for the main material and the natural yarns for the front-bed ottoman and floats, the main yarn has shrunk through heat, therefore it constricts the front bed marginally. As the natural yarn will not shrink at a similar rate, it is forced to bunch up slightly and become pulled together. The resulting effect, especially over the floats, creates a wavy texture and gives the floats a much more organic look. The backing material is much less visible because it has shrunk very slightly, meaning the rolls are closer together and increasing the textural element of the material. Personally, I very much like the way the floats react with the shrinking backing as it creates an additional texture, and one which is not typically associated with knit.

On an opposite note, with this third example where we have the shrinking yarn as the front-bed material which would be placed as the floats, this does not necessarily aid or hinder the texture of the material, but we are able to see the nylon yarn bloom in a much more interesting way as the yarn is not knitted. Over the floats, the yarn expands and almost disappears into an undefined area of fibre. Unlike the natural yarns over the floats, where the structure is quite visible, the floats become much looser in structure and have a fluffier texture. This contrast between the structured rolls and the floats is an interesting juxtaposition. The chart for these samples is on the previous page.

Further Development

The development of ripples and floats does not stop when they are completed on the machine. Once they are off the machine, we can treat them as elements to work with to increase the tactility within the textile or to add detail. For example, working a chain stitch through the floats to give an enlarged stitch effect on the vertical, or working beads into the floats manually. The area between the Ottoman rolls could act as channels to place additional material to offer support and stability, or areas that can join and fasten pieces together.

Lifting the floats onto an empty needle and knitting through on a back-bed-only row will hook up the floats and create additional tactility within the knit. This could be done every row or every other row, over each float or in a sequence. This was knitted on a domestic machine. The floats were lifted onto the centre needle every four rows. *Yarn A: Pink, three ends 2/36NM cotton–wool blend. Yarn B: Grey, one end nylon, count unknown.*

Additionally, hand knitting up the floats over a piece can introduce a further tactile element into the sample. Working the floats from the bottom up and then securing them at the top, enlarged stitches are formed. *Yarn A: Light green, one end 2/16NE cotton. Yarn B: Grey, one end nylon, count unknown.*

CHAPTER 3

TRANSFERS AND RIB STRUCTURES

I have to admit that the combination of transfers and rib stitches is one of my favourite techniques to work with. It is a relatively simple technique but one that creates incredibly versatile and tactile structures that have movement, form and shape retention. Throughout this chapter we will investigate the technicalities of the structure along with the basics of forming ribs on both the vertical and the horizontal, before delving into patterns using transfers. We will also touch upon yarn choice, colour use and plating.

After covering basic rib structures and how we can achieve them in either a horizontal or vertical direction, we will look at the process of transferring stitches between the beds in patterns that emphasises the knitted material and structures that create shape and form within themselves.

Unlike the previous chapters, in which we go into detail exploring several different methods and techniques under the umbrella of the chapter theme, within this chapter we are essentially dealing with one main method. We will explore different patterns that can be created with this method and the physical changes that are implemented through the patterns.

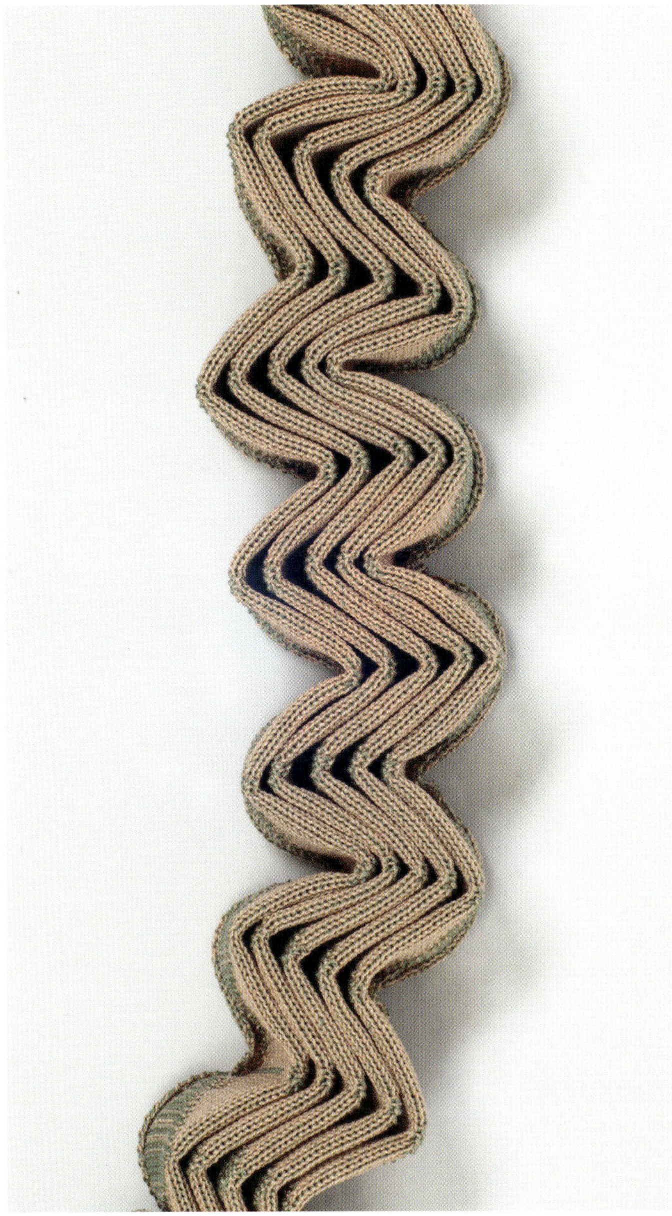

A chevron transfer structure folds up into a structured pleat after knitted. 1 end 2/16NE mercerised cotton in each colour.

OPPOSITE: A rib transfer that has been pinned into a new form to emphasise the plating and structure of the material.

MACHINE TYPE

Ribs can be worked with any double-bed machine in any gauge. It is merely the positioning of needles over the beds, in and out of action, that creates the structure. Therefore we can knit an extra chunky 6×6 rib on a 3gg with Aran-weight yarn to really amplify the rib structure, or we could create the daintiest subtle 1×1 rib with a 1-ply yarn on the 14gg. The techniques that we will look over in this section are probably the most versatile for working on either a V-bed machine or a domestic machine.

Regarding the humble domestic machines, their ribber attachments need to be in a good alignment to work smoothly. Because they are not directly attached to the main bed and can be removed relatively easily, this means that their alignment can get knocked out of place over time.

The placement of both the main bed and the ribber attachment is important as they have to be positioned a precise distance away from each other. Too far away and you will struggle to knit because the gap is too wide and the yarn will not stretch between the beds; too close and the needles may have trouble. Ensure that your ribber attachment is a good distance away from the main bed and that it feels easy to knit with both beds – check this by running the carriage across both beds with a needle selection when no yarn is placed in the yarn feeder. If the carriage runs smoothly, you have a good distance; however, if the carriage catches on any needles or is not smooth to pass, you may need to check the user manual to make some slight adjustments.

The gap between the beds on a domestic machine is, in my opinion, a little too wide. This fixed measurement cannot be adjusted to make it similar to that of the V-bed machine. A wide gap between the beds means that more yarn will be used when the stitches are formed, resulting in slightly larger stitches in comparison to the stitches made on V-bed machines. You will notice that a basic double jersey will be looser when knitted on the domestic machines rather than the V-bed, due to this slight difference. This is why the stitch size on a domestic machine is often very different for a double bed and a single bed, with the resulting material sometimes replicating a hand-knit finish rather than machine-knit, especially when working with all needles and a double jersey. Despite their drawbacks, ribber attachments are reliable and produce a good result for ribs for garments and other structures.

In contrast, the beds on a V-bed machine are much closer together resulting in a smaller gap between the beds. The beds are also secure in position and cannot come out of alignment over time. This immediately results in a much easier pass of the carriage, tighter stitches and an all-over smoother resulting material. Considering the V-beds are semi-industrial and have been used for garment-making for decades, and are still in use within industry, education and home knitting, this proves that they are very solid and durable machines.

Within this chapter, I have used a fine-gauge V-bed machine to produce the majority of the structures, because I find this gives a cleaner result. There are a couple of examples using the domestic machine to give a comparison, and also to demonstrate that the techniques can be worked on both machines. The yarns used are stated but, due to variations of machine, the stitch sizes are not stated.

YARN

Yarn choice for rib structures and transfers is like that for partial knit. Rather than using a yarn for ease of knitting, you can use a yarn for which you prefer the result. I prefer slightly harder yarns to work with because they help to enhance the structure. A mercerised cotton can be tough to get through the machine, especially if you want a plated tight knit; however, the result can be very clean and sophisticated. Shorter-filamented yarns can give a 'woolly' effect that can blur the structures of the knit. Mohair is also a yarn that can diffuse the structure rather than enhance it. This is, of course, my personal opinion, but I feel that if you put hours into manipulating a knit where the focus is the actual structure of the material, the structure should be the eye-catching element of the piece rather than the bloom of the yarn.

We will look into plating with contrasting-coloured yarns quite early on due to this technique's ability to offer a distinction between the front-facing stitches (knit stitches) and the rear-facing stitches (purl stitches). This adds a colour element along with the structure. To learn more about the basics of plating, please see the section on plating in Chapter 5: Tips and Tricks.

THE HUMBLE RIB

If we were to look at an item of knitted clothing, the chance of it having a rib on the cuff or the hem is pretty high. Ribs are used to create a natural elasticity within the material which will allow it to hug the body and keep those areas form-fitting rather than loose. There are many types of rib which have different appearances and uses due to their elasticity. Ribs in this chapter will be covered in both directions: on the vertical, which is the typical rib, but also on the horizontal, which is less common.

A garment from the author's 'The End is Coming' jumper collection, showcasing the cuff and neck ribs. All are 1×1 rib structures, with the neck being a folded sandwich-trim rib.

The traditional rib worked into garments is either a 1×1 or 2×2 rib structure, which means one needle is in action and one needle is out of action (1×1), or two needles are in action and two needles are out of action (2×2). As an approximation, these ribs have around a 50 per cent elasticity rate when allowed to relax into their form. Ribs can take any structure as long as there is a needle placement on both beds with needles in and out of action. The placement of said needles depends on the role of the rib that you are making, whether aesthetic or functional. Creating larger ribs, 6×6 or 8×8 ribs for example, highlights the structure much more, allowing the viewer to see the front-facing stitches and the natural pleating effect of the rear-facing stitches. Finer ribs, with a 1×1 structure or 2×1 structure, are used as a visual element but also as a structural enhancement to make a sleek but dense material with a lot of stretch.

PITCH POSITION AND V-BED MACHINES

Working in pitch position is not possible with V-bed machines due to the needle bed being fixed into position, compared to the domestic machines. We can slightly adjust the alignment of the domestic machine's needle position to place it into what is called pitch and half pitch. Pitch means that each needle is directly opposite a needle on the opposing bed; half pitch means that each needle has its own space regardless of which bed it is on. This is explained in more detail in the section on pitch position in Chapter 5: Tips and Tricks.

It should be noted that all of the charts for this chapter are drawn for the domestic machine working in pitch position, therefore having needles directly opposite each other on either bed. To work with the charts on the V-bed machines, the structure is still the same, but shifted slightly to accommodate for the half-pitch position. This may mean that, in some instances where you are using one bed on the V-bed machines, the instructions state four needles out of action but, due to the placement of the needles, there are in fact five needles out of action. This small difference will not disrupt the pattern. Use your discretion if needed where this arises.

The sample on page 125 using Pitch Position

The sample on page 125 using Half-Pitch Position

To emphasise, this will not have any effect on the overall structure that is being knitted apart from potentially a slight displacement of stitches where there is more of a gap because of the out-of-work needle where there could be a needle in work. Once the final knit is steamed and blocked, this will not be visible.

VERTICAL RIBS

Vertical ribs are what you could call the traditional rib structure. The structure is set into the needle bed just after the cast-on and remains for the length desired. The vertical rib is not a full double-jersey structure and works by alternating needles in and out of action across both beds. Generally, where you have working needles on one bed, directly opposite there will be out-of-action needles on the opposite bed. This then creates a vertical structure of front-facing and rear-facing stitches throughout the knitted area.

Ribs can be annotated according to their structure: for example, a 2×1 rib means there are 2 working stitches and then 1 out-of-work stitch across both the front and the back bed. A 2×2 rib translates as 2 working stitches and then 2 non-working stitches across the entire working area. This notation can continue through all rib structures to much wider examples, such as a 20×20 rib structure.

Reading the rib structure, you can also gauge whether the rib is set in half-pitch or pitch position. Generally speaking, all ribs with the same number of needles in and out of action (such as a 2×2 or a 4×4) will indicate that the needle position in pitch position; see chart A. When in pitch position, you can have the same number of needles in action and out of action directly opposite each other.

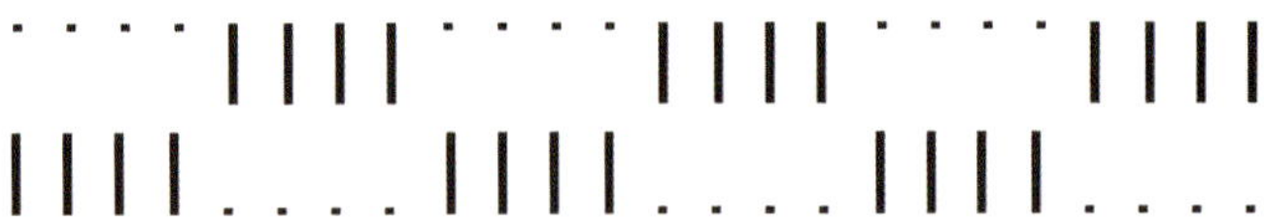

Chart A: a diagram of a 4×4 rib structure in pitch position.

If the rib annotation has an unequal number of needles, such as a 2×1 or a 3×2 rib structure, this would suggest that the rib is made on a needle bed that is set in the half-pitch position. This is due to the needles needing their own 'space' in order for the needles to move to create new stitches; see chart B. A 3x2 rib in the half-pitch position will mean that on both beds there are 3 needles working with a gap of 2 needles. If the needles are worked directly opposite each other, the risk of the needles clashing and becoming tangled with one another rises significantly as the needles are then working in the space 'owned' by the other working needle on the opposite bed.

Chart B: a diagram of a 3×2 rib structure in half-pitch position.

In this chart you can see that the front bed has 2 needles working but the back bed has 3 needles working. This is because, on the back bed, 3 needles are sitting in the open space made by the 2 needles on the front bed. If only 2 needles were working on the back bed, as shown by the next chart, there would be a small gap of one needle on one side of each vertical rib column. Once the knitted material is off the machine, washed and steamed, this small gap disappears and is relatively unnoticeable. A tighter stitch size will also help eradicate it.

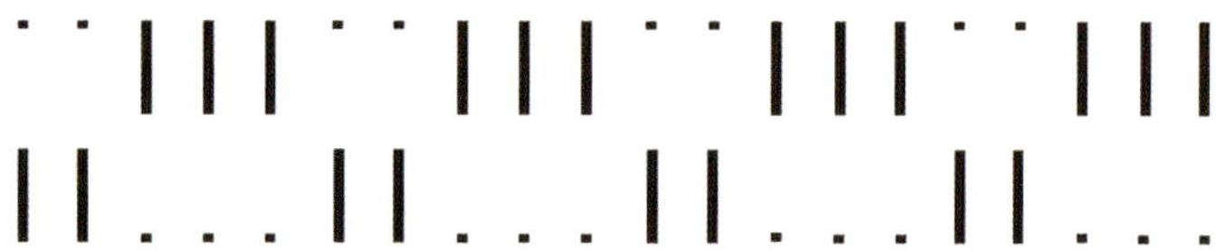

Chart C: the structure of a 3×2 rib in pitch position.

An added complication is that it is entirely possible to create any rib structure using both the half-pitch and pitch position: the reading of the rib set-up would have to change a little to accommodate for the pitch. With a 3x2 rib structure in pitch position, the set-up would change to have one bed with 3 needles working and on the opposite bed only 2 needles working – see chart C. This eradicates the potential for the needles to clash when working in pitch position. Both options produce a 3x2 rib structure, but approached slightly differently depending on the pitch placement.

In chart C you can see that the front bed has 2 needles working but the back bed has 3 needles working. This is because on the back bed, 3 needles are sitting in the open space made by the 2 needles on the front bed.

Lastly it is also possible to create an equal rib structure (such as a 2x2 or a 4x4) in half-pitch position. For this example a 2x2 rib structure is used – see chart D. If only 2 needles were working on the back be, as shown in chart D, there would be a small gap of one needle on one side of each vertical rib column. Once the knitted material is off

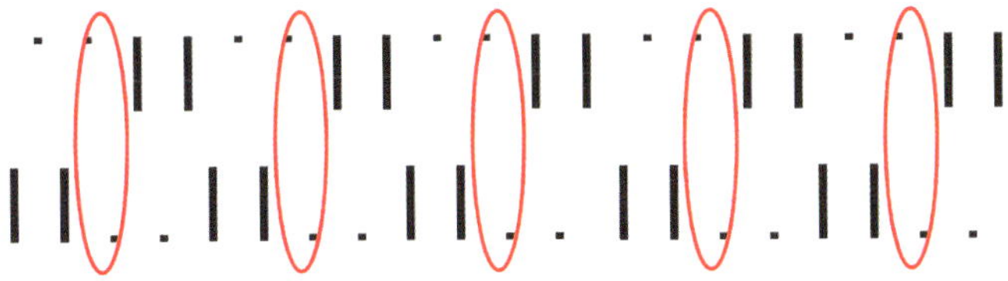

Chart D: a diagram of a 2×2 rib structure in half-pitch position. The small amount of empty space where there is no working needle or created stitch is highlighted.

the machine, washed and steamed, this small gap disappears and is relatively unnoticeable. A tighter stitch size will also help eradicate it.

It is always best to refer to any chart that has been given for the rib structure to clarify the needle set-up.

Continuing on with vertical ribs, the images below show a selection of rib structures that can be worked in both pitch and half pitch. All of these ribs are equal ribs, meaning there is an equal number of needles in and out of work. The following rib structures are shown: 1×1, 2×2, 4×4, 6×6, 12×12 and a 20×20. The numbers determine how many needles are working on the front bed and how many are working on the back bed.

A 1×1 rib is mainly used on cuffs and necklines due to the uniform structure and the elasticity that it provides. *Yarn A: One end 2/16NE cotton. Plating yarn B: One end 2/16NE cotton.*

A 2×2 rib is one of the most common rib structures used in hand knitting and also within garments. *Yarn A: One end 2/16NE cotton. Plating yarn B: One end 2/16NE cotton.*

The 4×4 rib. A very good all-round rib that offers structure and elasticity. A great rib for heavier yarns and chunkier garments. *Yarn A: One end 2/16NE cotton. Plating yarn B: One end 2/16NE cotton.*

Like the 4×4, the 6×6 rib is good for defining structure but also adding elasticity to a garment. When plated, it offers a great visual element also, with contrasting colours. *Yarn A: One end 2/16NE cotton. Plating yarn B: One end 2/16NE cotton.*

This large 12×12 rib is more useful as a visual element in the garment rather than as a structural element like the 1×1. It still has structure, but the vertical visuals seem to take precedence. *Yarn A: One end 2/16NE cotton. Plating yarn B: One end 2/16NE cotton.*

Much larger ribs, such as this 20×20, are mainly used for decorative fabric structures, and often used in the main material.

HORIZONTAL RIBS

Horizontal rib structures can be achieved by transferring the full working area between the front bed and the back bed. This alteration between the beds creates the front-facing and rear-facing stitches across the horizontal, which in turn mimics a rib structure. Instead of working in stitches, the rib size will be determined by rows. Bearing in mind that the shape of a stitch is not square, so more rows may need to be knitted to create a similar-sized 'rib' compared to the row count for a vertical rib, in which the needle placement creates the structure.

The visual aspect of the horizontal rib will also be different by replicating that of garter stitch rather than a rib structure; this is due to the tension of the stitches. When the rib is horizontal, the knit stitch is pushed in on itself, revealing more of the purl side of the stitch rather than the knit stitch. Therefore, the area that is the most visible will be the purl bump of the stitch. Due to changing needle beds regularly, especially within the smaller horizontal rib structures, the build-up of material will not replicate that of a purl side of single jersey, but rather it will create raised bumps that have similarities to garter stitch. It is for this reason that, depending on the visual effect you wish to create, you need to decide whether to use a vertical (standard) rib or the horizontal rib.

Horizontal ribs can sometimes be used as plackets in garments for a more seamless look, rather than knitting and grafting a separate rib for the placket. The horizontal rib is just a continuation of the main material but with the horizontal rib structure on the edge stitches. You still achieve the decorative and structural element but with one less element to calculate and knit.

Similarly to the vertical rib, you are not limited to working the same number of rows on either the front or the back bed to create the rib structure. You can alter and vary the number of rows knitted on either bed to create a different ribbed effect. Creating more material on one side of the bed before transferring the stitches across to the opposite bed to knit fewer rows will give an uneven effect to the rib, but this could be the effect you are looking for. It is best to test out all possibilities and variations.

Working two full rows on the front bed and then transferring all stitches to the back bed for two full rows. This is then repeated. *Yarn A: One end 2/16NE cotton. Plating yarn B: One end 2/16NE cotton.*

Working four full rows on the front bed and then transferring all stitches to the back bed for four full rows. This is then repeated. *Yarn A: One end 2/16 NE cotton. Plating yarn B: One end 2/16NE cotton.*

Working eight full rows on the front bed and then transferring all stitches to the back bed for eight full rows. This is then repeated. *Yarn A: One end 2/16NE cotton. Plating yarn B: One end 2/16NE cotton.*

Working sixteen full rows on the front bed and then transferring all stitches to the back bed for sixteen full rows. This is then repeated. *Yarn A: One end 2/16NE cotton. Plating yarn B: One end 2/16NE cotton.*

TRAVELLING RIBS

Rib structures do not have to follow only one axis: they can travel, giving a direction to the material. There are two ways in which you could have a rib structure leaning to a direction: firstly, by transferring all the needles and keeping the structure in a true rib position; or secondly, by transferring the edge stitches of each front- and back-bed block to the opposite needle bed.

The travelling rib will hold its structure and rib elasticity much more when working by transferring all needles. However, this is a lengthy process as all needles must be transferred, compared to only a few needles every row when only transferring the edge stitches of the rib structure.

The rib structure can vary to incorporate any needle placement you would like, including any of the previous structures touched upon earlier in the chapter. To make it simple to follow to begin with, the following samples use a 4×4 rib.

Stitch on the front bed

Stitch on the back bed

Transfer the back-bed stitch to the front bed

Transfer the front-bed stitch to the back bed

The chart to create a travelling rib by transferring the edge stitches.

Transferring One Stitch

For this first sample, cast on with all needles knitting on both beds and then transfer into a 4×4 rib structure after the circular rows within the cast-on. Knit a few rows to establish the rib.

To begin the direction of the rib, transfer the edge stitches of each rib column to the opposite bed in the direction you would like the rib to lean. The direction is determined by whichever needle is transferred to the front-bed rib group. So if the left-hand needle on the back bed is transferred to the front bed, you will have a left-leaning rib structure. Similarly, if the right-hand needle on the back bed is transferred to the front bed, you will have a right-leaning rib structure. At the same time, the other edge front-bed stitch needs to be transferred to the back bed to keep the 4×4 rib structure. If only one stitch is transferred to the front bed every row, eventually you will only have stitches on the front bed, rather than a needle placement.

As you knit up the piece, the direction will gradually move across to the left. If the direction were to be changed to head towards the right, then the right edge stitch of each group of 4 front- and back-bed stitches would be transferred.

As previously stated, this does not create a true rib structure as individual stitches are transferred each time, which constitutes a needle-transfer structure rather than a rib structure. With some steaming and a good yarn choice, you would be able to get some rib formation into the piece, but note that the elasticity will not be as strong as that of a true rib structure.

A 4×4 travelling rib structure made by transferring the edge stitches across to the opposite needle bed. *Yarn A: One end 2/16NE cotton. Plating yarn B: One end 2/16NE cotton.*

Transferring All Stitches

To create a rib in which the true rib structure moves and travels in a direction, all stitches need to be transferred across the bed, while keeping the needle placement of the rib.

For example, cast on and create a 4×4 rib structure and knit a few rows to establish the rib.

Next, working from the direction the rib is to travel towards (if left-leaning, start on the left-hand side), work in the groups of 4 stitches and transfer all the stitches of that group across to the left by 1 needle.

The original structure will need to remain: for example, move 4 front-bed stitches to the left by one needle, and also 4 back-bed stitches to the left by one needle. This will naturally consolidate the needles on the left-hand side by always ending with 2 stitches on one needle (decreasing by 1); and will naturally leave an empty needle on either the front or back bed, depending on where the last group is situated, on the far right-hand side where the needles have transferred from. This empty needle can either be left empty (as seen in these samples), or the needle can be filled in by using the heel from the adjacent stitch. This is a personal preference. If you are leaving the now-empty needle empty, a lace hole will be created, compared to filling in the empty needle with the heel of the adjacent stitch, in which case the knit will become more whole. Again, knit two rows before knitting the next transfer row. Repeat the transfers until the desired amount of direction has been achieved. This could be a small amount in a specific area of the material, or over the whole working area.

Multiple Directions

The travelling rib can be worked with any rib structure and travelling at any rate. You can also have travelling ribs working in different directions, or a base of a rib structure with a travelling section in the centre or in any part of the piece. It can be used as a decorative element as a pattern placement, or as a structural element. Depending on the direction of the transfers, the outer edges will also have a bit of a direction. This can either be emphasised or relaxed back into a more rectangular shape.

A travelling rib created by moving all stitches (apart from the edge stitches) one place to the right-hand side, keeping the formation of a 4×4 rib.

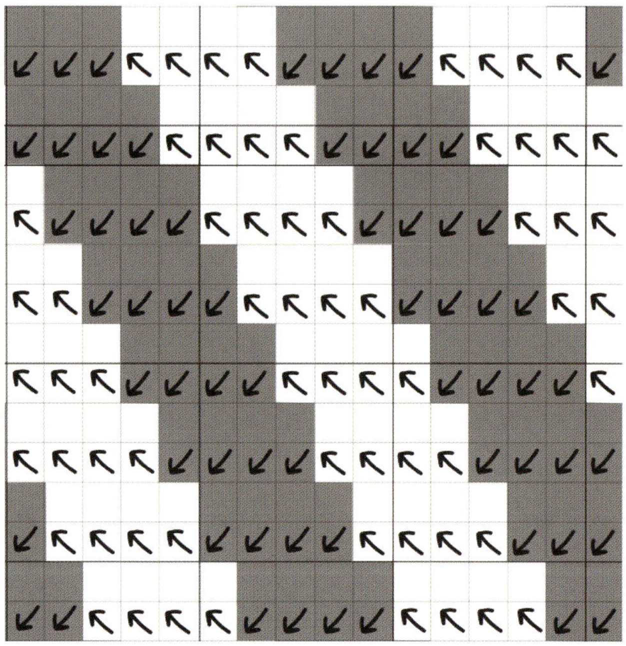

Transfer 1 stitch to the left on the front bed and knit

Transfer 1 stitch to the left on the back bed and knit

A diagram for the above transfers showing that all needles are transferred across the working area. Note that the very edge stitches are not included as this is a full repeat. The edge stitches on both sides are not moved.

With a definite divide down the centre, the 6×6 rib structure is transferred outwards and then, at the halfway point of the knit, back in again. This creates an outward direction with new rib structures made in the centre of the piece. *Yarn A: One end 2/48NM wool. Yarn B (plated): One end 2/48NM wool.*

Still with the divide down the centre, in this instance the rib is transferred inwards towards the centre point and then, at the halfway point, back out again. This creates an X-shape within the rib structures. *Yarn A: One end 2/48NM wool. Yarn B (plated): One end 2/48NM wool.*

An example whereby the main rib has been established and knitted with a separate section in the centre of the material that is transferred. By transferring only these middle needles in a direction, an area of pattern is created in an otherwise standard rib structure. *Yarn A: One end 2/48NM wool. Yarn B (plated): One end 2/48NM wool.*

Similarly, creating two areas with opposite directions of travel within the rib sections, this includes more pattern within the main knitted piece. Having a direction on both sides of the knit plus a shape forming in the central area creates a geometric pattern purely from the rib structure. *Yarn A: One end 2/48NM wool. Yarn B (plated): One end 2/48NM wool.*

COMBINATION OF STRUCTURES

Transferring stitches between each bed does not always need to create rib structures, and can in turn create structures with self-forming properties, elasticity, bounce and integrated form. This can be done by transferring stitches between the front and the back bed in either structured patterns and placements, or a more organic and unplanned method. There are infinite combinations to the structures as the transition between front and back bed can occur at any time. However, it seems that the more geometric and simplest patterns have the best effect in terms of giving additional structure to the knitted textile.

Moss stitch, a hand-knit technique, is probably the most commonplace structure that incorporates this idea of alternating knit and purl stitches, or in machine knitting the front- and rear-facing stitches. Although a hand-knit structure, the translation onto the machine is the same process: every two rows, change the knit stitch to be a purl stitch, and the purl stitch is changed to a knit stitch. The difference on the machine is that we are working with needle beds, therefore transferring stitches before the pass of the carriage to create the row.

We do not have to only integrate a standard rib structure. Some traditional hand-knitting techniques (moss stitch, basket-weave stitch) are based on the knit and purl formation similar to the basic rib stitch. This is not limited to basic structures, but can create patterns that are drawn images into the knit structure. The possibilities are endless in terms of pattern as there are no restrictions to this technique that could limit results.

Each of the following samples has been plated with two contrasting-coloured yarns to incorporate colour as well as texture. The plating emphasises the structure of the knit, enhancing the visual effect. You do not need to plate these samples if you do not want to, or do not have a plating feeder, as all samples can be worked with only one colour.

This first material to explore using transfers uses a basic square structure, alternating the stitches between the front and the back beds of the machine.

Moss-stitch knitting on the domestic knitting machine. *Yarn A: Two ends 2/36NM cotton–wool blend. Yarn B (plating): Two ends 2/36NM cotton–wool blend.*

HOW TO READ THESE CHARTS

The solid colour within the chart represents a front-bed stitch, and the non-coloured stitch represents a back-bed stitch. The charts work from the bottom up and where the box (or stitch) then changes colour, this indicates a transfer to the opposite bed.

Unless stated otherwise, assume one box is one stitch over one row. In some instances, one box will represent two or more stitches over two or more rows, but this will be stated in that specific chart.

Follow the charts for each of the structures to create a direct replica of the samples. Once you have followed the charts for a few samples, it would be good to draw out some patterns of your own on squared paper and work your own designs.

This first basic structure is a good foundation to begin exploring other structures and patterns within this rib transfer chapter. This is a face-on view of the relaxed material. *Yarn A (main): One end 2/16NE mercerised cotton. Yarn B (plating): One end 2/16NE mercerised cotton.*

1 square =
1 stitch and 1 row

Front-bed stitch

Back-bed stitch

The chart for this first sample. The two colours represent the needle beds on which the stitches are made, rather than yarn.

A side view of the same material, which shows the texture and dimensions of the structure.

Cast on in multiples of 10 with all needles on both beds. After the circular rows for the cast-on, transfer the stitches into the structure shown in the chart. There will be 10 stitches on the front bed then 10 stitches on the back bed across the full working area. Insert the plating yarn into the feeder and adjust the stitch size to accommodate for the secondary yarn if needed. Please see the plating section in Chapter 5: Tips and Tricks for more information.

Knit 10 rows with this first structure. Now we are at the first row to transfer stitches. All the current front-bed stitches will be transferred to the back bed, and all the back-bed stitches will be transferred to the front bed.

It is advisable to bring all the needles out into the forward working position after the transfers to ensure that the needles knit through that first row. This is because when the stitch is transferred, the tension on the needle increases slightly due the stitch now sitting in a slightly different position. By bringing the needles into the forward working position, we have done half of the work by moving the stitch past the latch, therefore forcing the needle to knit when the carriage is passed.

Working on a V-bed machine, there is no forward working position, therefore gently take the carriage across and, if necessary, manually increase the weight to ensure there is enough to hold the stitches down and away from the needle hooks. If you are still having problems with the stitches lifting in the needles when the carriage is slowly passed, use a transfer tool to gently press them back down the stem of the needle. This is a rarity, but it can occur if the stitch size is too small. If you notice this happening, increase the stitch size slightly for the next row. If you do bring the needles into the forward working position on the V-bed machine and pass the carriage, the stitches will drop off the needles. If you have brought the needles up into the forward working position by accident, then just rehang all the stitches back onto the needles' hooks with a transfer tool.

Now that the needles are in their new position, knit a further 10 rows for the next section of the pattern.

Repeat these two sections, transferring the stitches between the beds every 10 rows to build up the texture.

This second sample is identical to the first but with double the number of stitches and rows. This is again a face-on image but this time the material has been stretched to show the full structure. *Yarn A: One end 2/16NE mercerised cotton. Yarn B (plating): One end 2/16NE mercerised cotton.*

A side view of the sample to show the dimensions and texture of the enlarged structure.

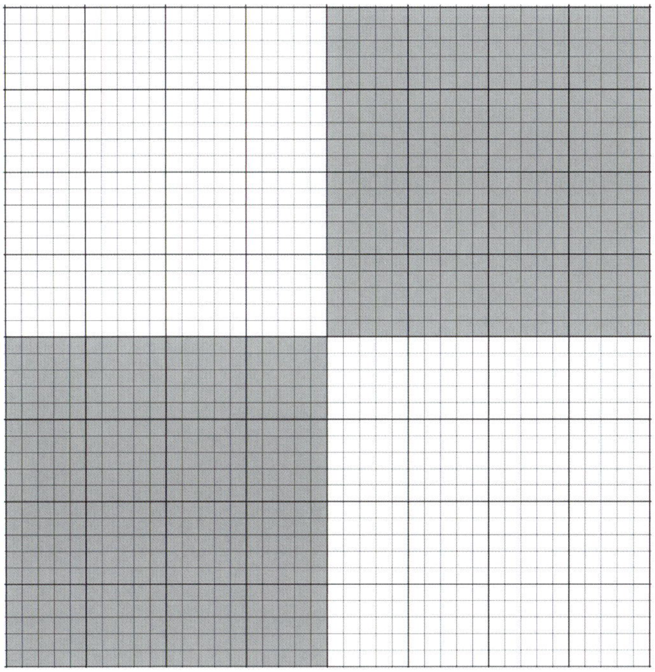

1 square =
1 stitch and 1 row

Front-bed stitch

Back-bed stitch

The chart for the doubled structure.

Doubling the number of stitches used over the number of rows knitted, the same structure can be built up but at a different scale. This sample is worked over multiples of 20 stitches worked over 20 rows before the transferring of the stitches to the opposite beds.

Depending on the final expression of the material, you can either pin and steam the knit out flat to have a flat surface with the decorative transfers as the pattern; or alternatively, if you allow the material to relax, the square structure can coil up, creating spiralled peaks and troughs in a diagonal direction over the knit. This texture is playful and elastic and could be integrated into many interesting garments or interior pieces.

A combination of larger and smaller areas can also create an interesting structure working with squared blocks. The possibilities of altering the structures are endless.

A combination of different-sized blocks worked on both the front and the back beds integrates a colour-block pattern and a tactile surface pattern. *Yarn A: Lilac 2/28NM worsted wool. Yarn B (plated): Two ends 2/48NM merino wool.*

Following on from these basic structures, we can begin to build further elastic structures solely through the pattern of the transfers. Not only can we integrate a vertical rib, but including a horizontal rib simultaneously will warp and alter the tension through the knit at different places.

This next sample has been knitted in blocks of vertical rib structures and horizontal rib structures which are then switched both across the working needle bed and vertically through the knitted rows.

Combining horizontal and vertical rib structures can create materials with even more expression and natural texture. *Yarn A: One end 2/16NE mercerised cotton. Yarn B (plating): One end 2/16NE mercerised cotton.*

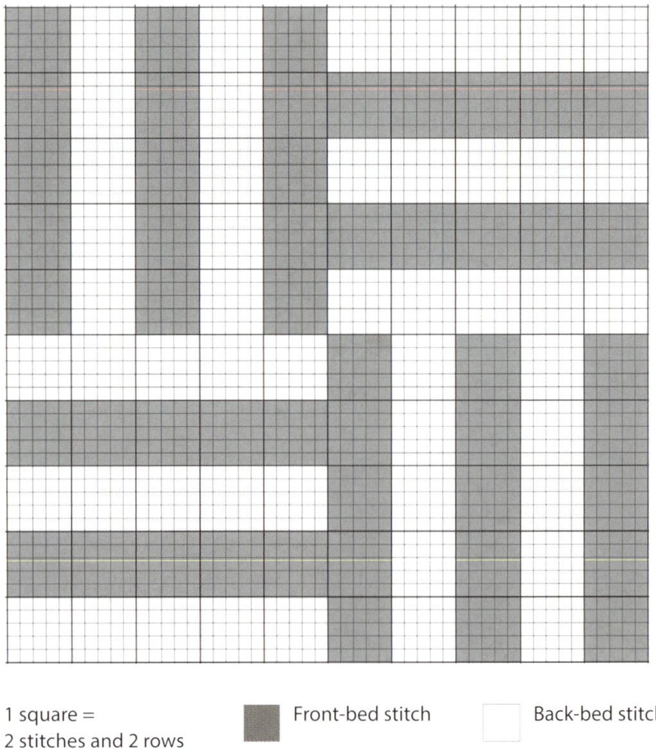

One repeat of the structure, in which both a vertical and a horizontal rib are used in blocks across the working area.

To find the correct number to cast on, work with one block of your preferred vertical rib structure as a base for the full structure. With this sample on the 12gg, a 10×10 rib has been used (10 needles on the front bed, 10 needles on the back bed). There are 5 sections alternating between the front bed and the back bed of this vertical rib within one block, equalling 50 needles. This means multiples of 50 needles have been cast on.

The first block of 50 needles will be worked as a 10×10 rib, and the second adjacent block of 50 needles will be worked as a horizontal rib, therefore to start all the needles will be on the front bed. These two blocks are repeated across the full working area.

Knitting up, after every 12 rows the horizontal rib structure is changed and transferred, therefore all the needles on the front bed over the horizontal rib will be moved to the back bed and another 12 rows are knitted. After this second group of 12 rows, the needles are transferred to the front bed. This is repeated for a total of 5 times until 60 rows have been completed.

After these 60 rows, we alter the whole structure of the material by swapping the vertical and horizontal ribs. Where we had a 10×10 vertical rib structure, all needles will be transferred to the front bed; and where we had a horizontal rib with all needles on the front bed, these needles will be transferred into a 10×10 rib structure. The knit is then repeated, altering the needle bed for the horizontal rib structure every 12 rows.

We can vary the size of the structure by altering both the vertical and horizontal rib structures, increasing or decreasing the number of needles in and out of action within the vertical structure, but also altering the number of rows knitted within the horizontal rib structure.

The blocks do not have to be square. The entire placement of the structure can be experimented with to produce different variations of this example. Working with a larger-gauge machine will also give different results as the tension from the heavier yarn weight will differ to that of the fine gauge. You would need fewer transfers to create a block the same size, but the pattern would be scaled up.

A variation of the same structure on a much smaller scale.

BROTHER GARTER CARRIAGES

For those lucky enough to possess a garter carriage (named for their ability to recreate the garter hand-knit stitch) for their Brother machine, the links (or transfer) process will be much easier and quicker as the carriage has the ability to create the same structures on the single bed, but automatically rather than by hand transfers.

The carriage works by re-forming the stitch on a single bed into a purl stitch whilst knitting across a row. It is an electronic carriage, meaning that you do not have to hand manipulate the stitch as it is worked automatically. For those who have any other machine, unfortunately you have to transfer stitches manually. There is a garter bar that can be manually used to turn multiple stitches; however, I personally find it easier and quicker to work by hand with the transfer tool because it is often only small groups of stitches that are being transferred to the opposite bed.

Continuing to explore with ribs and altering the basic structure, this next three-dimensional sample is worked with a basic rib structure across the full working area, which is then inverted, very similar to the first two samples that have been explored but with more knitted rows. In between the ribs, a section of single jersey can be inserted which adds a secondary element of form and structure, and allows the piece to make an accordion fold.

Cast on in multiples of 6 needles to establish the original 6×6 rib structure and knit 30 rows. After the 30 rows, all of the front-bed needles are transferred over to the front bed and 8 rows knitted front-bed only. Next, the 6×6 rib structure is established again but this time inverted, meaning where the front-bed needles originally were, the needles are now on the back bed, and similarly where once the needles for the rib were on the back bed, the needles are now on the front bed.

Again, 30 rows are knitted with the 6×6 rib structure. Once that has been completed, knit 8 rows of single jersey, but with all needles transferred onto the back bed. This alternation between the front and back beds works similarly to the horizontal rib structures covered earlier on in this chapter, which in turn folds and concertinas the knit sample up on itself.

A variation of the basic sample covered previously but with an additional single-jersey section that can create additional pattern and form in the material. This is the same structure as the cover image for this chapter. *Yarn A: Light green, one end 2/16NE combed cotton. Yarn B (plating): Dark turquoise, one end 2/16NE combed cotton. Yarn C: Bright peach, one end 2/16NE cotton.*

For an additional colour element, a third colour has been introduced over the single-jersey knitted sections. This not only adds a 'pop' of colour, but emphasises the natural corrugation of the stitches due to the alternating rib structure. The plating element used throughout highlights the rib structure and the front-facing and rear-facing stitches hidden within the collapsed rib.

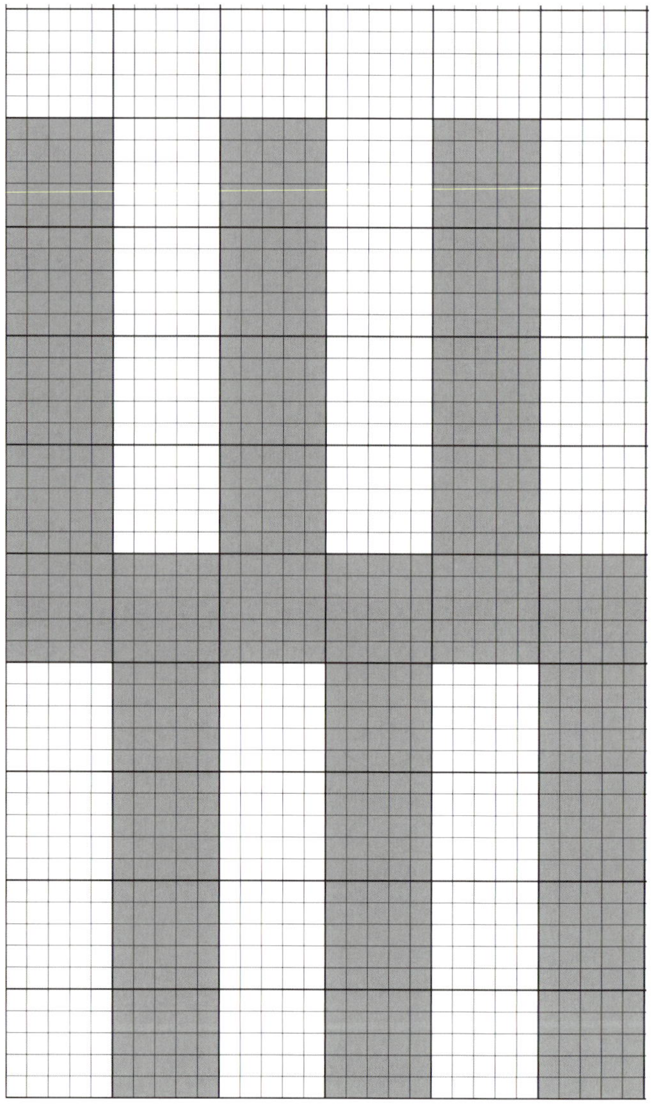

1 square = 2 stitches and 2 rows

Front-bed stitch

Back-bed stitch

Following the diagram, transfer the stitches between the needle beds after some rows of a single jersey that alternates between the beds. Change the yarn for the section of single jersey to help emphasise the structure.

These next few samples are variations of structure patterns from the previous samples, generally using a rib structure as a base and integrating either solid sections of single jersey into the pattern, or different-sized ribs. Due to the rib structures, the elasticity of the material will still encourage the sample to contract and create form naturally; however, the placement of the ribs and areas of single jersey will create contrast and alter the form from the typical rib.

This is a simple variation of the previous sample. By altering the size of the rib structure and the number of rows knitted before each transfer between beds, different expressions of the former accordion rib sample can be created. For example, this piece has been knitted in blocks of 16 needles on each bed over 20 rows before the transfer, with each single-jersey area being knitted over 4 rows.

Creating larger areas of rib structures but knitting fewer rows, the areas of ribs are blockier, therefore creating a different form overall in the rib structure. *Yarn A: One end 2/16NE cotton. Yarn B (plating): One end 2/16NE cotton.*

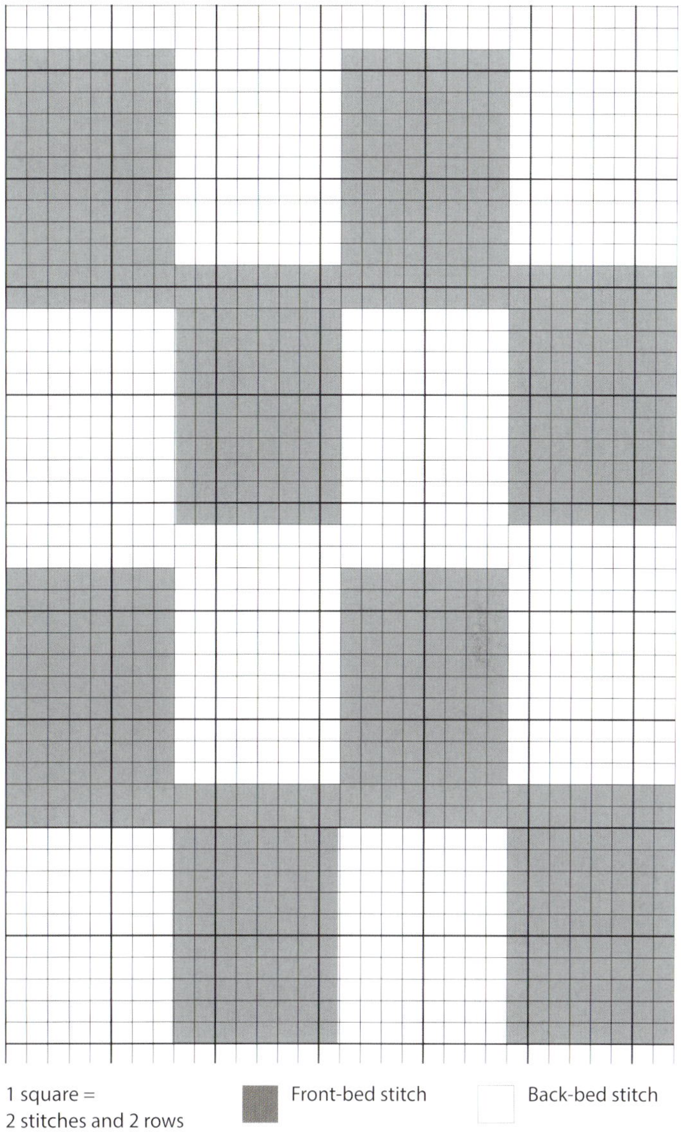

The graphic for the sample with the single-jersey stripe on the horizontal.

The same structure principle but shifted to be set on the vertical rather than the horizontal. This simple change gives a completely different, yet also similar, effect. This sample has been left to rest to showcase the natural gather, rather than being stretched out. *Yarn A: One end 2/16NE cotton. Yarn B (plating): One end 2/16NE cotton.*

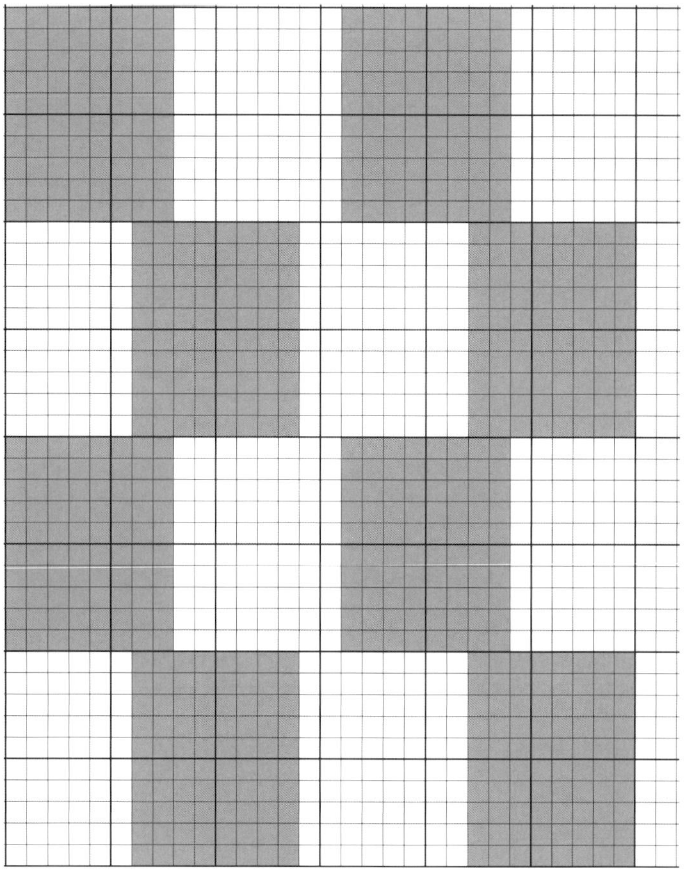

1 square =
2 stitches and 2 rows

Front-bed stitch

Back-bed stitch

The graphic for the sample with the single-jersey stripe on the vertical.

Altering this sample further, we can shift the horizontal-based single-jersey rows into vertical columns. If we look closely at the previous structure, we have areas within the knit where all the stitches will be on either the front or the back bed to knit several rows of single jersey, making it horizontal in structure direction. Instead, in this next sample we will have a few needles at certain points that will always knit on either the front or the back bed. This changes the structure and creates an accordion fold in the opposite direction, fundamentally making it more vertical.

Continuing with this exploration of basic rib structures and transfers, we can look into more detailed and more intricate structures which are all based on a rib, yet have transfers integrated to add detail and additional form.

A basic rib with a vertical detail running through the material emphasised by plating. This detail gives an almost hide-and-reveal detail as the sample can be opened up to reveal the rib structure. This has been worked with the base of a 6×6 rib with areas of four stitches on the front bed that create the additional structure. *Yarn A: One end 2/16NE mercerised cotton. Yarn B (plating): One end 2/16NE mercerised cotton.*

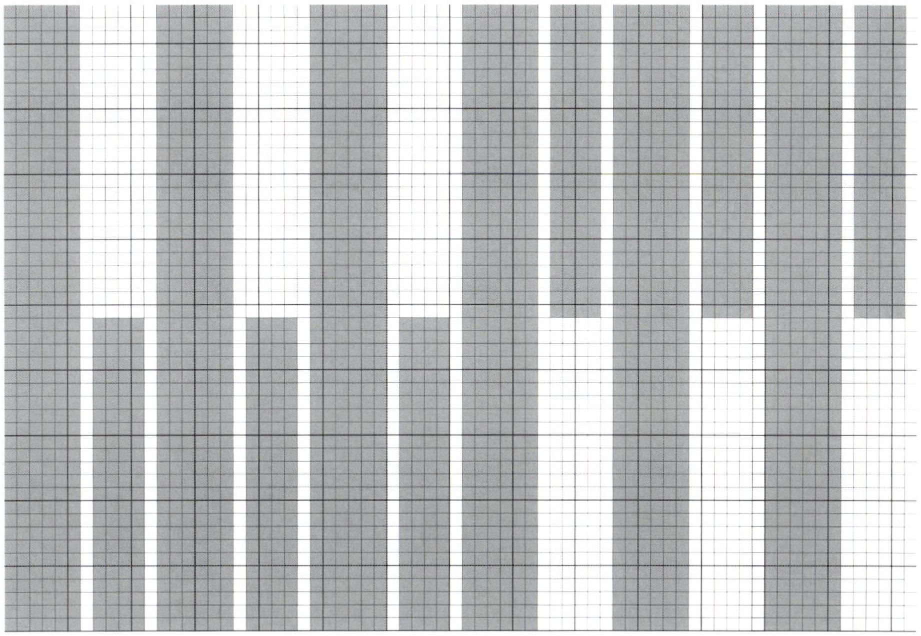

1 square = 1 stitch and 1 row   Front-bed stitch   Back-bed stitch

The chart for the detailed rib. This shows one repeat. One square in the chart also represents one stitch and one row.

Areas of rib are surrounded by sections of single jersey. These areas of single jersey create enough tension to push out the material, which in turn creates form and structure. Elasticity from the rib versus single-jersey material creates contrast within itself. *Yarn A: One end 2/16NE mercerised cotton. Yarn B (plated): One end 2/16NE mercerised cotton.*

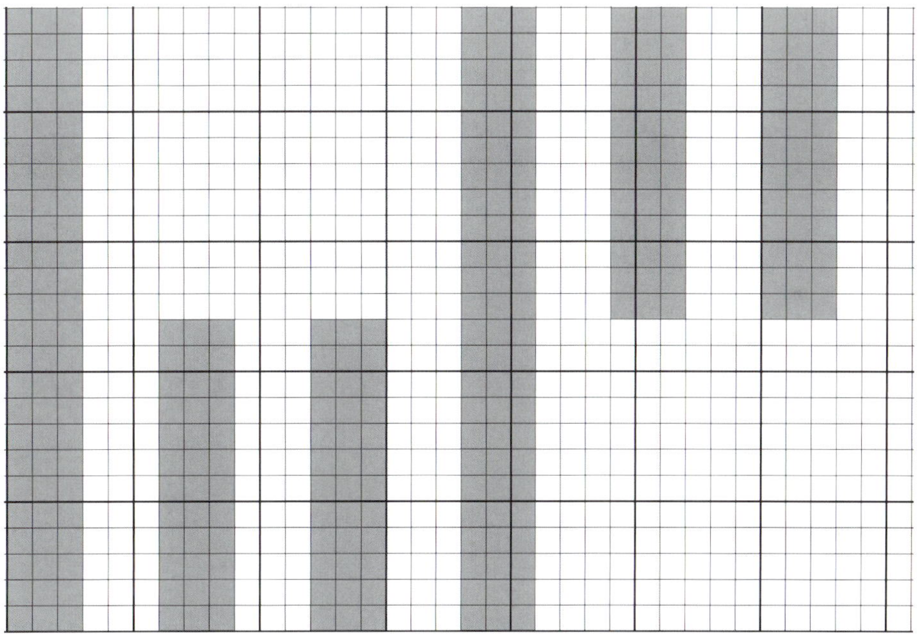

1 square = 2 stitches and 2 rows   Front-bed stitch   Back-bed stitch

The chart for this version of a rib structure. Note that each square in this chart represents two stitches and two rows. This is for one repeat.

A very similar technique to the previous sample, incorporating areas of a finer rib and others of single jersey. This incorporates more structural detail within the material. Again, the single-jersey areas within the structure push outwards compared to the areas of rib that are elasticated. *Yarn A: One end 2/16NE mercerised cotton. Yarn B (plated): One end 2/16NE mercerised cotton.*

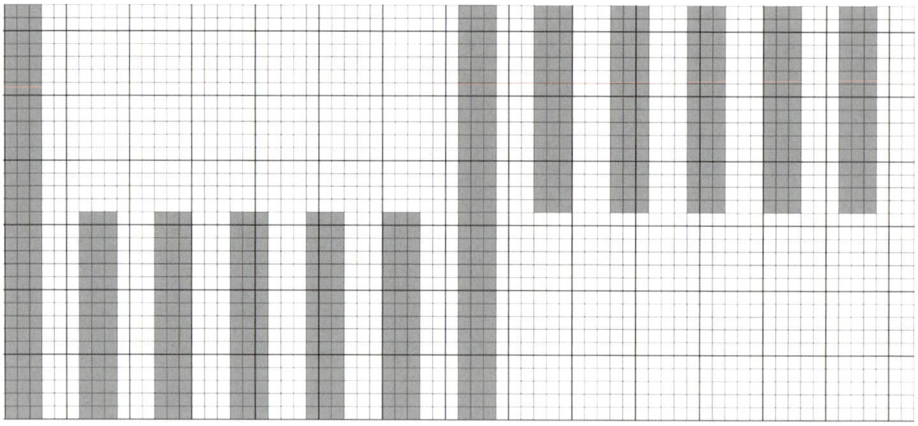

1 square = 1 stitch and 2 rows

Front-bed stitch

Back-bed stitch

The chart for the adjusted version with the smaller rib. This chart represents one stitch but two rows for each square.

This sample has a similar form to something like a broken rib structure. Areas within the front bed where we would have the rib structure have sections of back-bed stitches. This, as in the previous sample, allows the reverse stitches to push through into the front of the fabric, creating additional structure and form within the sample. Altering the position of these back-bed areas can alter the overall structure and can be experimented with. *Yarn A: One end 2/16NE mercerised cotton. Yarn B (plated): One end 2/16NE mercerised cotton.*

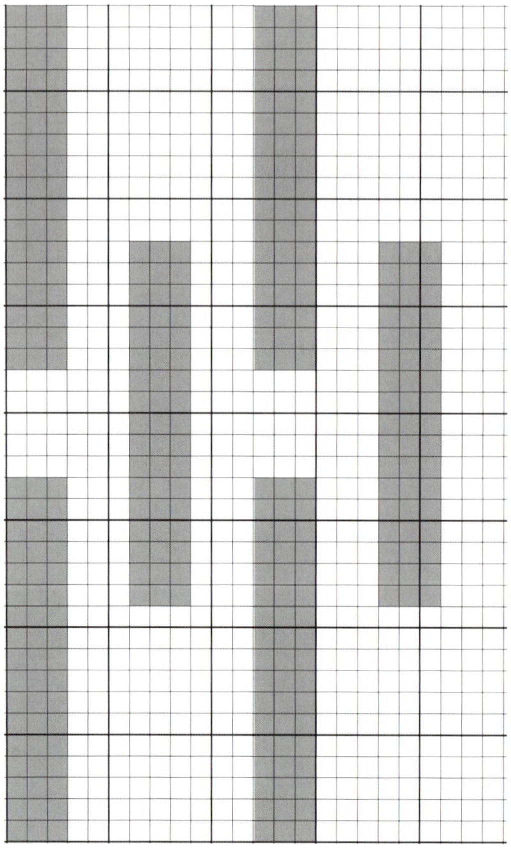

1 square = 2 stitches and 2 rows

Front-bed stitch

Back-bed stitch

The chart for the broken rib structure. One square represents two stitches and two rows.

Structures That Are Not Rib Structures

The following two samples will continue in a similar style to those previously explained, by transferring stitches between the needle beds over a pattern. However, they do not consist of a standard rib structure. A pattern will be made within the textile through transferring stitches one at a time to shape the needle-bed structure instead of transferring multiple stitches all at once. Singular stitches will generally be transferred every row or every other row, but please follow the chart for the pattern you are using.

These structures still hold a natural elasticity but potentially not in the presumed way. Instead of vertical folding, the material can also crease and fold on the horizontal. As you will notice from the range of examples, the samples with the most elasticity are based on rib structures. Structures with groups of transfers, or more solid areas on each bed, are most effective in creating form and structure compared to those with fewer solid areas and more details.

This structure focuses more on a vertical chevron rather than a rib structure. The pattern of the chevron enables the material to relax into a couple of forms. There is a flat fold in which the fold of the textile comes through the rib structure, but also a vertical fold in which the fabric can concertina up to create a slight chevron in form. *Yarn A: Two ends 2/16NE mercerised cotton. Yarn B (plating): One end 2/16NE mercerised cotton.*

Now working with triangles, this material folds similarly to a standard knife pleat but with more detail through the surface pattern. With the left-hand edge of the surface pattern shaping remaining in one position, the right-hand edge stitch is moved every row to create the triangular pattern. *Yarn A: Two ends 2/16NE mercerised cotton. Yarn B (plating): One end 2/16NE mercerised cotton.*

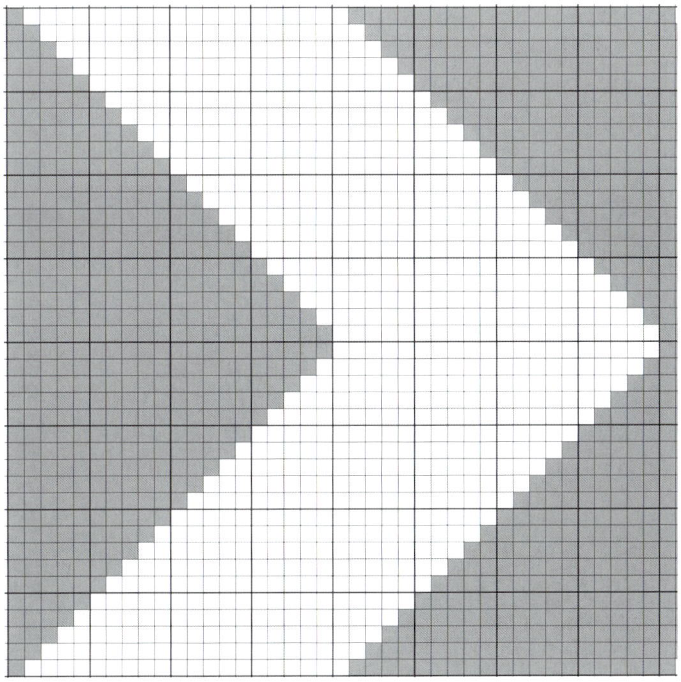

1 square = 1 stitch and 1 row; Front-bed stitch; Back-bed stitch

A vertical chevron will be knitted into the material to create a piece that can fold up in several ways. One square is equal to one stitch and one row.

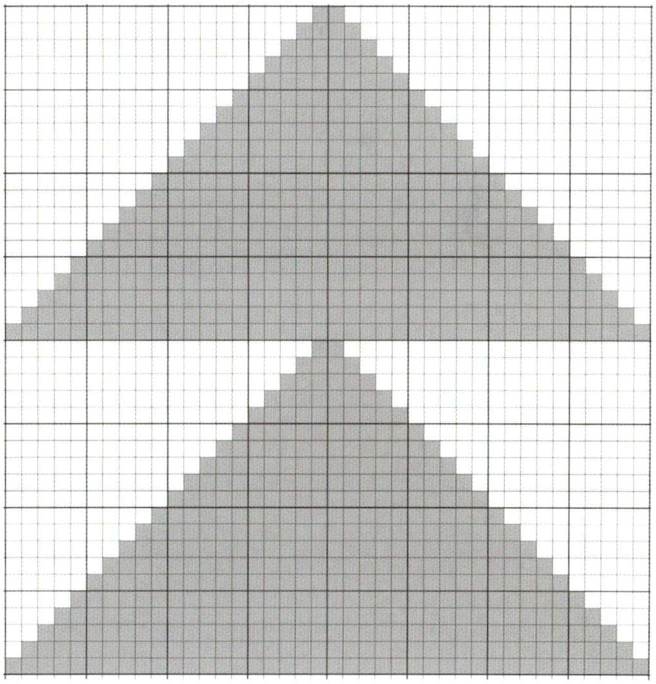

1 square = 1 stitch and 2 rows; Front-bed stitch; Back-bed stitch

A triangle repeated and knitted into the material creates a very bouncy and elastic fabric with a lot of movement. The triangle can be knitted on either the horizontal or the vertical. This chart is also represented by one stitch and one row to one square.

A Difference between Gauges

To showcase the difference between gauges, these next samples have been knitted on the standard-gauge domestic machine. You can see that the structures and the elastic effects are the same regardless of which machine has been used. The only difference is the stitch size in the resulting material, due to the weight of the yarn that has been used. All methods are the same as when working on the V-bed. You can also change the yarns at any point whilst knitting, to create more detail through colourwork from the plating. It is suggested that you place the domestic machine into pitch position after casting on and placing the stitches into the needle placement.

A simple structure worked with blocks that adjust and lean in position through the knit. *Yarn A: Light turquoise, one end 2/12NE cotton. Yarn B (plated): Deep green, one end 2/12NE cotton. Tension: Both front and back bed 5.*

The transfers do not necessarily have to stay in the same position. Within this sample the front-bed stitches travel and create an additional pattern. In this instance the moved stitches also have a directional lean to them. *Yarn A: Light pink, two ends 2/36NM cotton–wool blend. Yarn B (plating): Deep turquoise, one end 2/12NE cotton.*

The process of transferring stitches between the front and the back bed also does not necessarily have to be for structure and form within the knit material. We can effectively draw in the knit with the front and back bed using plating. Using contrasting colours within the plating, the structure is emphasised but also a pattern has been built up from the combination of front- and back-bed stitches and transfers.

This is the same method as previously used to transfer stitches, this time in fewer groups and working more with individual stitches. The patterns introduced can be the same as patterns found in a punch card or drawn up by hand using squared paper, and can be as intricate as 1-stitch detail. This first sample is an example of a standard optical illusion using two colours to make a three-dimensional effect. Instead of creating a form, we are focusing on the colour pattern. After being knitted, the piece is steamed flat rather than left to relax into a dimensional shape.

Working a previous sample but altering the colours of both the plating and the main yarn to add detail through colour blocking. *Yarns of various qualities and weights. Tension: Both front and back bed 5.*

Creating a pattern within the plating and using the rib transfers technique can be used to create pattern rather than structure through the use of the plated yarns. For example, this optical-illusion pattern. *Yarn A: Orange 2/16NE mercerised cotton. Yarn B (plating): Pink 2/16NE mercerised cotton.*

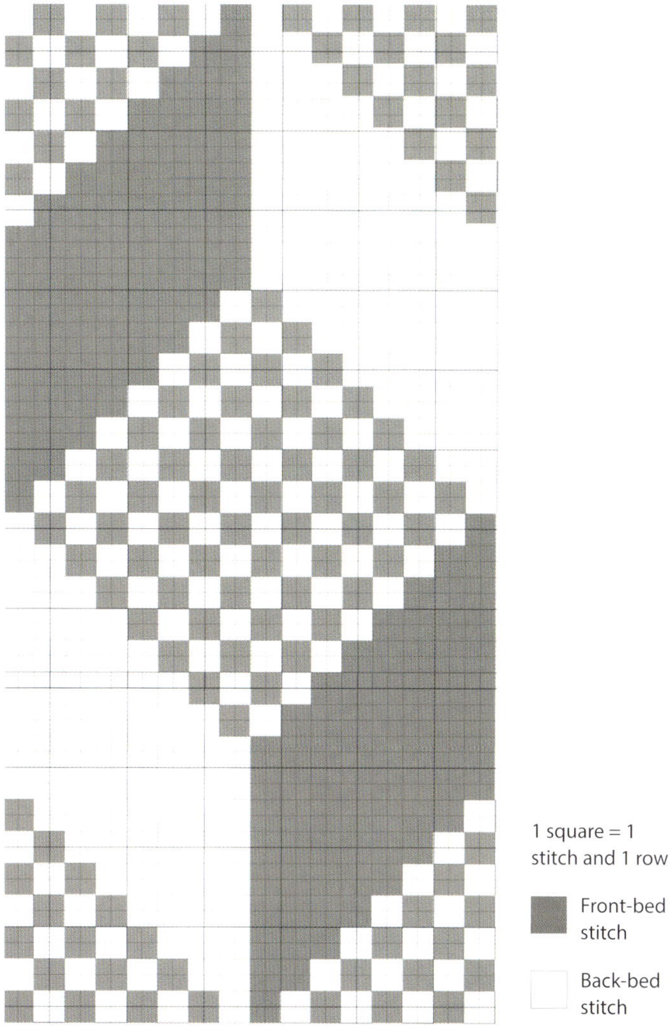

The chart which can be used for the optical-illusion knit. Blocks of front- and back-bed stitches with a block of moss stitch make up the whole pattern. One square represents one stitch and one row.

Similarly, it can be used for more fluid designs and motifs that can also replicate patterns from Fair Isle and Jacquard designs. By drawing up a pattern on squared paper prior to knitting, you can create any pattern you would like. You can also use this approach to create shading within an image to create depth. Think of it as a two-coloured Jacquard pattern but using needle transfer rather than different needles being selected for different yarns. This method allows for the pattern to be completely reversible with the colours inverting on either side, rather than having one side full of floats and only one usable side.

A single motif has been knitted into the sample. The larger the motif, the more detail that can be incorporated; however, this will mean more effort in the charting and the knitting of the piece. *Yarn A: Purple, one end 2/16NE mercerised cotton. Yarn B (plating): Cream, one end 2/16NE end mercerised cotton.*

I-PLATING

i-Plating, or inverse plating, is the ability to plate with more than two colours by working with separate yarn carriers rather than using a plating feeder where both yarns are inserted into one feeder. With industrial machines, the yarn carriers move independently and are not driven across by the carriage. This means that they are able to switch positions whilst the carriage is in motion, altering the leading and following yarn carrier(s). By switching the leading carrier, the colour on the front of the stitch can be changed, along with the colour of the back of the stitch. This can result in two or three different colours creating a reversible pattern in the material as well as a needle structure over both the beds.

It is worth noting that it is important to remember that each stitch is not square: it is wider than it is long. This means that any pattern drawn on squared paper should be scaled to fit to ensure that the design does not come out of the machine too short yet at the correct width. It is suggested that you make a tension sample first to determine how many stitches and rows there are in 10cm. Then you will know how many stitches and rows you need to make the knit the correct size for your pattern. Once the design is drawn on squared paper, this will create an area that is longer than it should be, but once knitted the piece will be the correct size.

Additional Techniques

Transfers and Lace Holes

Despite this technique including more than enough detail and structure through the basic transferring of stitches, we can add further detail into the single-jersey areas to incorporate yet more structure and form by implementing another method into the knit.

It is often through the inclusion of multiple techniques that we can achieve the most interesting effects within knit. It is best to keep each of the techniques included simple so we do not make the knit too complicated, which in turn can then either lead to mistakes within the knit or just make it generally hard to knit.

For example, including lace holes into the rib transfers is an easy enough technique to create an alternative structure, and one that is simple to keep track of and will not become complicated. In this first sample we have taken the basic form, but added some lace holes into the single-jersey area of the structure.

Once we have cast on and have placed the needles into the rib position and the plating yarn into the plating feeder, work 2 rows. This will knit through any double stitches on the needles from the transfers and establish the basic structure. Once this is done, start the transfers for the lace holes.

The basics of lace holes have not been covered within this book, but creating the effects that I have included is relatively simple. Instead of transferring every other stitch to the opposite bed, we will transfer every other stitch to the needle adjacent on the same bed. For this first row we will take each stitch to the left of the needle that it came from.

Pick up the stitch shown in the chart and transfer it to the needle to the left. Repeat this all across the single-jersey area, leaving two needles before the rib structure begins again. Work this across every single-jersey area to create the same sample shown.

Once that first row of transfers in the single jersey is complete, we will be left with areas where we have 2 stitches on one needle and an empty needle. These needles will alternate over the single-jersey sections as we will alternate which needle is transferred. Next, knit 2 full rows. The first row will knit over the needles with the 2 stitches combining them into 1 stitch, and will create a tuck stitch over the empty needle. The second row will knit across all needles forming full stitches over the tuck stitches.

The process of this tuck stitch being formed and then being knitted through on the second row is what creates the lace-hole effect. As there is no stitch for it to pass through and become tight, the tuck stitch can then expand outwards. The second time the carriage can be passed and yarn knitted through, an actual stitch is created at the correct tension. This does not tighten the original tuck stitch, which is what makes the lace hole.

Manipulating the stitches over the single-jersey areas of the knit will create an additional effect, adding structure and detail. The effect is different on both sides and complements the plating. *Yarn A: One end 2/36NM cotton–wool blend. Yarn B (plated): One end 2/36NM cotton–wool blend.*

After two rows have been knitted to build up stitches on the empty needles, we can now work another row of transfers to create more lace holes, but this time transferring the stitches to the needle on the right-hand side. Again, repeat this all the way across all blocked areas of single jersey. Once again, knit 2 rows to create the tuck stitches and then the fully formed stitches on the second row.

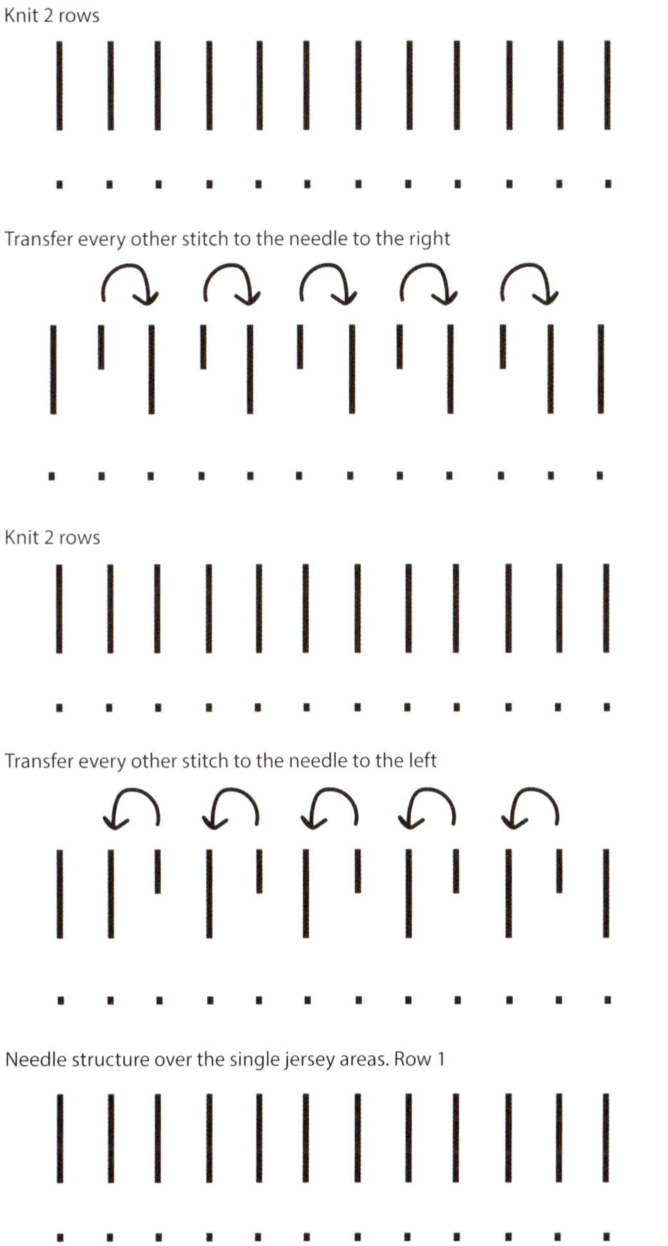

The transfers for the lace sections within this rib structure. It is to be repeated across the area, leaving one needle either side that is not transferred into the lace.

Repeat these 2 rows until there are 2 rows to knit before the whole structure changes and the ribs are repositioned to where the single-jersey blocks currently are. This is purely to create a small clean border around the single-jersey section. If you would like to continue the lace holes through the whole single-jersey area, then experiment with this.

The direction that we transfer the stitches in helps to give a direction to the knit over the lace-hole areas. By alternating the direction, a very slight zigzag is built up over the lace holes. If you wish for all stitches to transfer in the same direction to give a slight lean to the stitches, then this is another option to explore.

Experiment with different types of transfers and at different intervals to see how the transfers can affect the surface structure of the material. This technique is not necessarily limited to the areas of single jersey but can be incorporated into double jersey to give a relief pattern.

TRANSFERRING MORE THAN ONE STITCH

It is not possible to transfer two adjacent stitches away from each other and then build up full stitches over the two now-empty needles. Instead, one large tuck stitch will be formed over the two needles on the first pass, and then with the second pass of the carriage that large tuck stitch will be formed into a large stitch over two needles. This is because we will always need one full stitch on either side of the empty needle to help create a stitch on the empty needle.

If you find yourself in a position whereby you have two empty needles next to each other and you wish to build up stitches on them again, bring one needle into the working position and keep one out of work. It does not matter which needle works and which is left out of action. Create the tuck stitch on one needle and then you can bring the last remaining needle into work to create a tuck stitch and then full stitch.

This is the same for any open-needle work, whether you are working with larger areas of needles out of action and you wish to build them back up, or on a lace-hole structure similar to the one we have just gone through. Bringing needles into work needs a fully working stitch on either side of the empty needle for it to build up stitches again.

Transfers and Cables

A second approach to incorporate more detail into our rib transfers is to include cables into some of the single-jersey areas within the rib. Again, this manipulation is a simple twist of stitches but can elevate the texture and the sample further.

Again, I will not cover the process of cables aside from the basics, therefore for further explorations into cables over the suggested areas, I encourage you to experiment and see what happens when stitches are switched and twisted.

In this example we will work with a previous pattern created working with the areas of single jersey in between the standard rib structure. These areas have blocks of 4 stitches on the front bed surrounded by only one stitch on the back bed before the area of the rib, which is over 6 stitches on the front bed. We will create a small 2×2 cable within the 4 front-bed stitches.

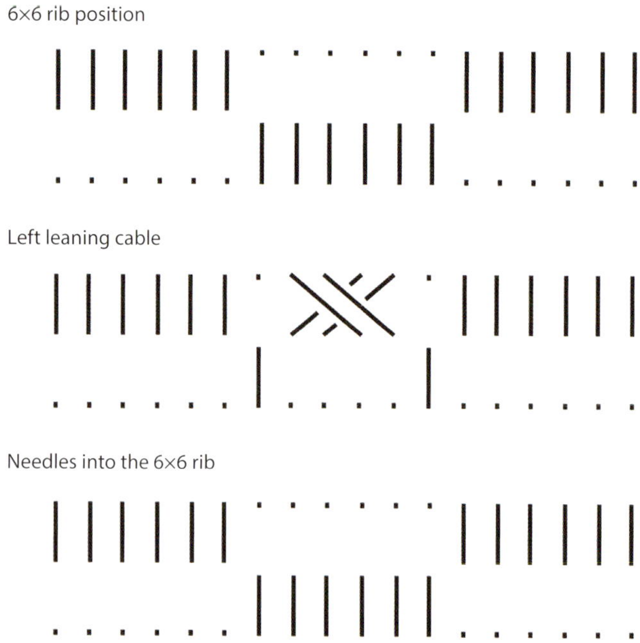

The positioning of the cable on the back bed when the needles are in position. A small 2×2 left-leaning cable is implemented.

We can work cables into the single-jersey areas as another method to create additional structure in the main piece. The sample has a 2×2 cable over some sections. *Yarn A: One end 2/36NM cotton–wool blend. Yarn B (plating): One end 2/36NM cotton–wool blend.*

Using 2 two-point transfer tools, pick up 2 stitches on each transfer tool. We will next rehang the 2 pairs of stitches but on the different needle pair. Take the right-hand transfer tool with the right-hand 2 stitches and place those 2 stitches on 2 two left-hand needles, holding the left-hand transfer tool with the left-hand 2 stitches out of the way. Make sure not to drop any of the stitches from the transfer tools. Next, take the left-hand transfer tool and place the 2 stitches onto the right-hand 2 needles. This will create a 2×2 cross cable.

For this sample, this cable has been repeated over all areas of single jersey with 4 stitches. This is not the main rib detail, but an additional area of structure within the original sample shown earlier on in this chapter.

After each cross has been made, 5 rows are knitted to space out the cable. Depending on the structure of the cable you wish to create, the number of rows knitted after the twist can be more or less. I would not suggest knitting fewer than 4 rows as this could create additional tension within the stitches, increasing the chance of the yarn breaking when the carriage is taken across. You can knit as many rows as desired if you wish to space the cables out further. It depends on the size of the cable and the type of yarn as there is tension built up within the yarn as you twist the stitches.

When working on a domestic machine, to help the needles knit, bring the needles up into the forward working position after the stitches have been transferred to create the cable. This helps to force the needles to knit as you have already moved the stitch past the latch. If you are working on a V-bed machine, knit carefully across. It might help to manually hold the knit down from the weight to ensure the stitches do not move up with the stem of the needle as the carriage moves.

Details with 2×2 Ribs

Lastly, we have worked over larger structures which create the general form of the knit. If we were to work on a smaller scale which is more suited to garments and rib elements of garments, we can introduce these stitch details and transfers into a much more common structure. These next few samples have been knitted with a basic 2×2 rib structure as this is one of the most commonplace rib structures. This means these subtle details can be incorporated into any garment on which there is a rib detail, such as over the cuff, hem or neckline.

Most of the previous structures have been made on the front bed as those samples were not originally for garment details, but for structure and form exploration. These next samples will be knitted with the detail made on the back bed. This is due to the positioning of the main bed with domestic machines and how the knit comes off the needles. This directs which bed knits the front of the material and which knits the back when working with a double bed. Generally the back side of the material will be facing us when working a single-jersey material. Therefore any details that we would like to place into the garment must be worked on the main bed (or when working with two beds, the back bed). If you continue to work on the front bed after working the rib details into garments, the details on the ribs will be on the wrong side. Be sure to note this before continuing with either a sample to see the structure, or working rib details into garments.

All of these structures are worked with the ribber bed in full pitch rather than half pitch. If working on a V-bed machine where you cannot alter the pitch of the needles because they are set in half pitch, ensure that you do not have any interlocking needles. This may mean that there is more space between needles on one side of the rib than the other, but this is okay, and once the material is washed and steamed the stitches will fill out any empty space. See the 'Pitch and Half Pitch' section in Chapter 5: Tips and Tricks for more information.

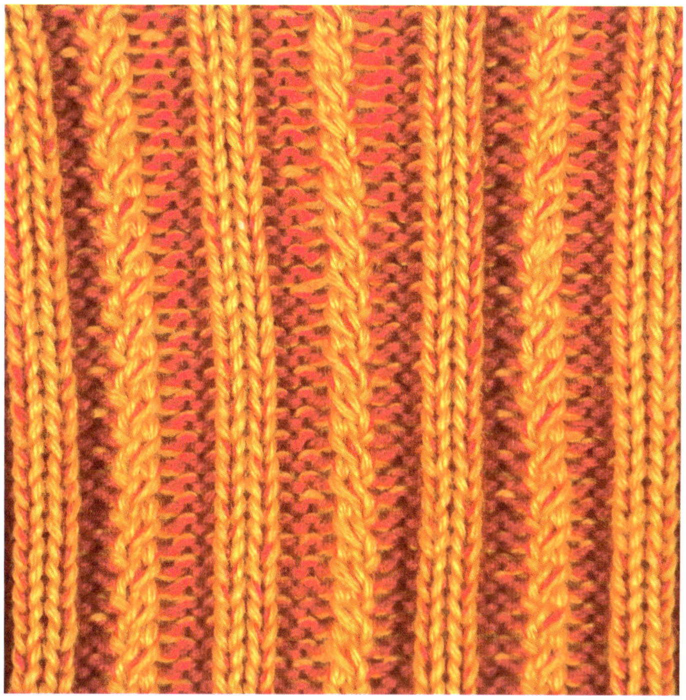

Continuing to work with plated rib transfers, these samples are much more suited for garment details and finishing. Small details, such as this twist in the rib areas, do not alter the functionality of the rib, but offer a visual and tactile element. *Yarn A: Yellow, two ends 2/30NM merino wool. Yarn B (plated): Pink, two ends 2/30NM merino wool.*

This first example works with every other front-bed rib detail to create a 1×1 twist within the rib structure. It has been called a twist because after each 1×1 cable, 2 rows have been knitted before repeating the cable twist, creating a dense repetitive structure. Due to the density of the cable, the resulting texture is much more like a twist than a cable. Technically it is a cable as we are switching the positions of the stitches onto different needles which in turn cable the stitch, but I prefer to call it a twist because the result is much tighter than a traditional cable.

Each twist is also worked in a different direction to give the sample additional structure and detail. This is a personal preference, and if you wish to work the twists in the same direction, then this is for you to explore. Each twist has also been placed on every other vertical pair. This is to keep some of the basic 2×2 rib detail. These twists can be worked on every vertical pair as desired – this is a personal preference and an element open for exploration and experimentation.

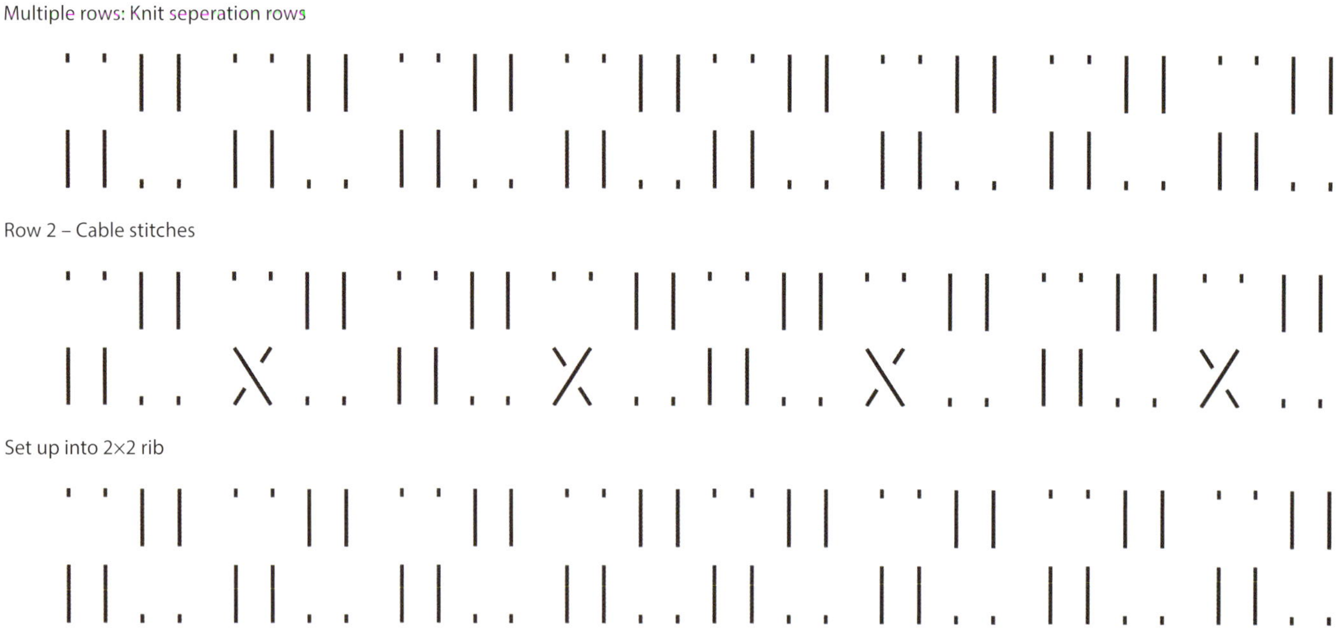

The transfer chart for the 2×2 rib detail with twists.

Additionally, to make the twists much more similar to a cable, 4 rows have been knitted in between each cable twist. No other adjustment has been made between this next sample and the previous one aside from additional rows to space out the cable transfers. Similarly, the twists have been made in opposing directions to create more interest and detail within the sample.

The placement of these twists has been made at regular intervals, but on the same row. However, you can stagger the cables to make them occur at different times on the vertical rib pairs. Also, giving them different directions can increase the detail within the cables.

Separating the twists with an additional couple of rows spaces out the cable twists more, enabling you to see the cable more easily. This has been achieved by knitting four rows between each twist rather than two. You can see this in the chart for this sample, comparing it to the previous sample's chart. *Yarn A: Yellow, two ends 2/30NM merino wool. Yarn B (plated): Pink, two ends 2/30NM merino wool.*

Moving away from twists and cables, introducing more lace-hole transfers into the equation of 2×2 rib details can give a really lovely delicate detail to the structure. We will still work with alternating vertical rib columns to create the detail.

For this structure, we will simply pick up 1 of the stitches of the front-bed pair and transfer it to the adjacent front-bed needle. Therefore if we pick up the right-hand stitch on the front-bed twin, we will transfer it across to the left needle to have 2 stitches on the left-hand needle and an empty right-hand needle. Similar to the previous technique, if we knit 2 rows, the empty needle that is left in the working position will pick up the yarn on the first row to create a tuck stitch, and then after the second row create a fully formed stitch.

When the stitch is fully formed after 2 rows, we will next transfer the opposite stitch from the twin front-bed needle arrangement to the adjacent needle. For example, if we previously took the right-hand stitch and transferred it over, we will now take the left-hand stitch and transfer it over to the right-hand needle to leave the left-hand needle empty, so we will have two stitches on the right-hand needle.

This alteration of stitches to be transferred creates the direction of the transfers. If we were to continuously transfer the same stitch across, we would only create a lace-hole detail on that side of the front-bed twin. By alternating them, we give a balance in lace-hole placement to the whole structure.

Repeat this transfer for the length of the rib, or only over the area where you wish to create the detail.

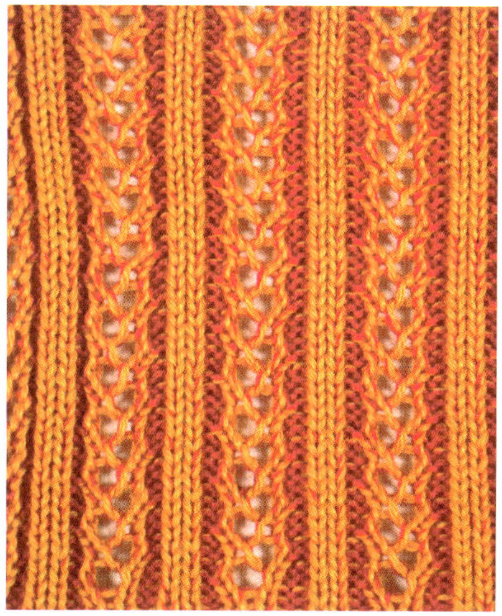

Working lace-hole details into the rib pairs to incorporate open-needle work into the rib structure. *Yarn A: Yellow, two ends 2/30NM merino wool. Yarn B (plated): Pink, two ends 2/30NM merino wool.*

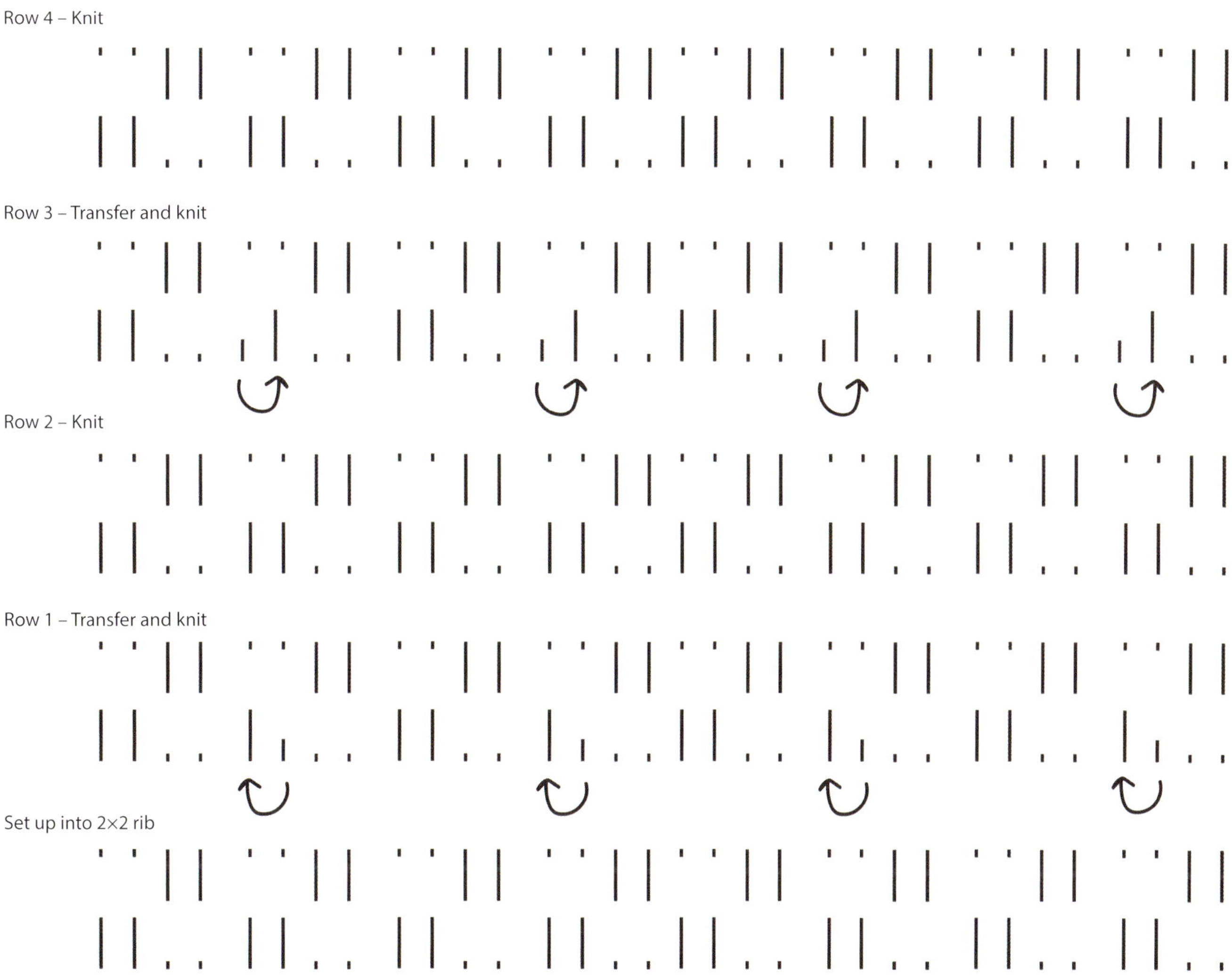

The diagram which shows not only the needle position, but also the transfers of the stitches. Repeat across the working area for the desired length.

Another lace-hole detail to be explored with this rib structure is to transfer one stitch at a time, but instead of moving it to the adjacent front-bed needle, we will transfer the stitch to the next needle on the opposite bed. Therefore, if picking up the right-hand stitch of the front-bed twin, this will be transferred to the left-hand needle on the back bed nearest the now-empty needle. Again, knit 2 rows before the next transfer, in which the left-hand stitch of that twin will be used and transferred to the right-hand needle of the back-bed twin nearest the now-empty needle.

Transferring the stitch to the opposite bed opens up the lace detail even more. The direction of the stitch transfer becomes more obvious with a much more open effect. Again, this transfer has been worked on every other front-bed pair of needles. *Yarn A: Yellow, two ends 2/30NM merino wool. Yarn B (plated): Pink, two ends 2/30NM merino wool.*

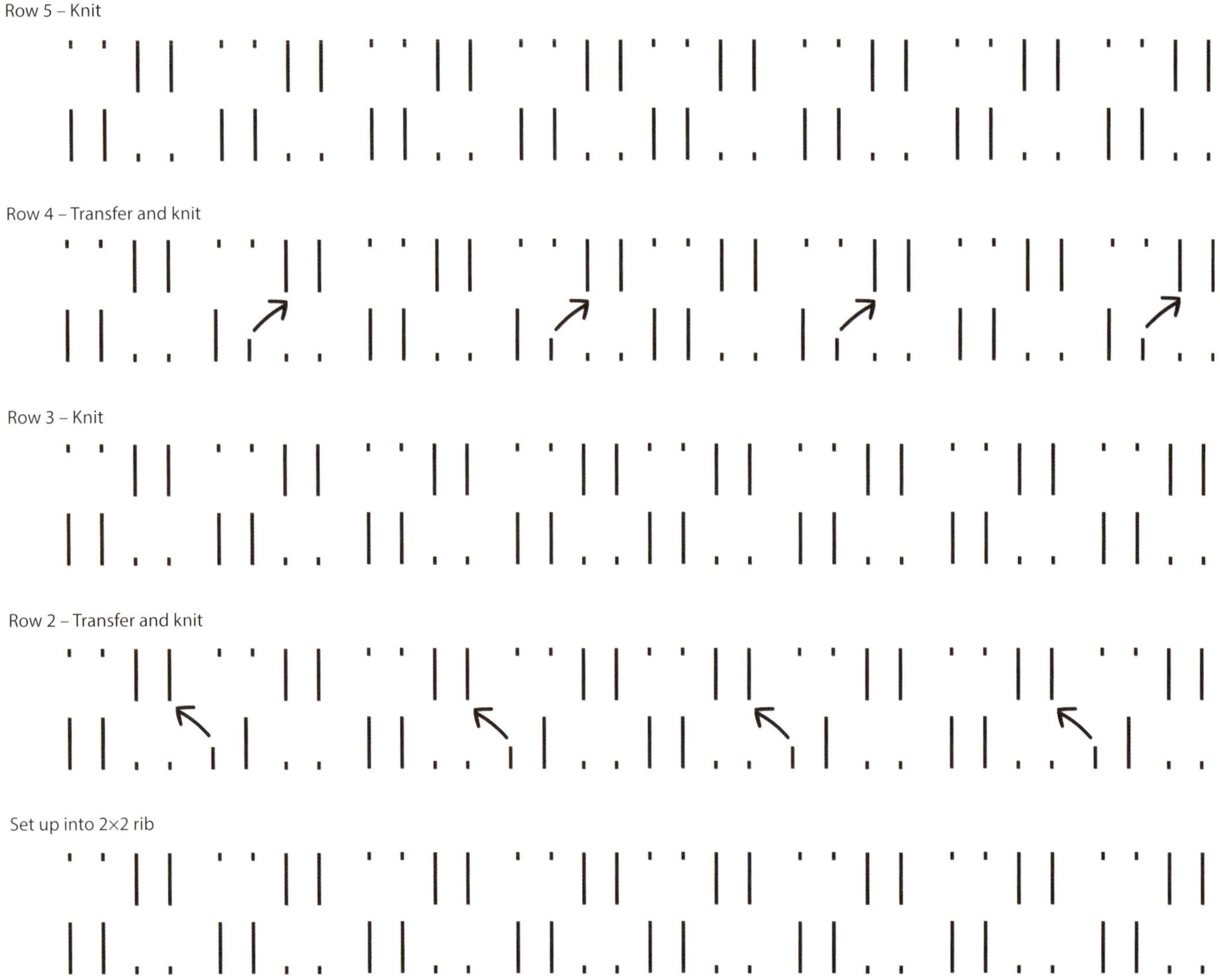

The diagram which shows not only the needle position, but also the transfers of the stitches. Repeat across the working area for the desired length.

Lastly, we do not have to stick with a 2×2 rib formation. To emphasise the possibilities of these structures and the infinite variations that can be incorporated into the structure, this last sample is based on a 2×2 rib but incorporates a moss-stitch detail, or transfer to the opposite bed.

We will be working with a 3×2 rib structure (3 needles in work, 2 needles out of work across the back bed, and 3 needles out of work with 2 needles in work on the front bed using the pitch position). To place the needles into the rib position, we can either cast on as a 3×3 rib with the needles interlocking and rack twice to get the needles into an actual 3×3 knitting position, then transfer 1 of the stitches over to the adjacent needle; or we can cast on with all needles and then transfer the stitches to create the 3×2 rib structure. It is up to you how you cast on but, for a neater cast-on edge, I prefer to cast on with all needles and then transfer. As you can only rack once in either direction before knitting a row, the former cast-on method will make a slightly larger cast-on than transferring the needles into position. See the chart for more definition of the needle structure on the machine.

This is mainly worked in the pitch position on the domestic machine. If working on the V-bed machine, where the pitch is set, there will naturally be more of a gap on one side of the rib due to the half-pitch placement. You can ignore this and knit as if the needles are in pitch position. Due to the moss-stitch transfer, a true 3×3 rib would need to be worked to ensure there is a needle in the centre that we can transfer to.

To create the detail within the rib, it will be the central needle within the set of 3 needles that we will transfer across to the opposite bed every 2 rows. This builds up a moss-stitch detail within the central section of the 3 needles, yet keeps the visual structure of a 2×2 rib. Similarly to the other samples, the transfers can occur at different intervals and you can build up a pattern of moss stitch. In this sample, the stitches are all transferred at the same time in the same direction.

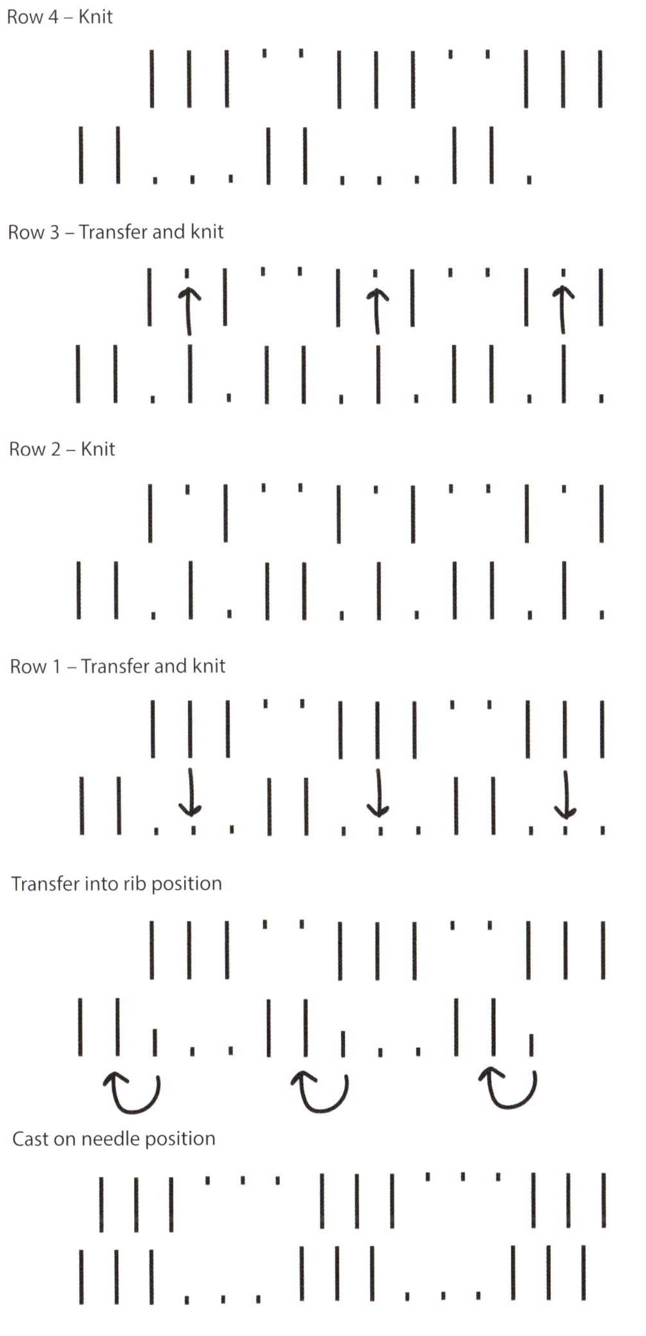

The graphic of the 3×2 rib structure with additional moss-stitch structure in the centre of each rib section.

Altering the basic needle structure slightly allows for details of the stitch transfer to be incorporated into the central part of the recessed stitches. *Yarn A: Yellow, two ends 2/30NM merino wool. Yarn B (plated): Pink, two ends 2/30NM merino wool.*

CHAPTER 4

PLEATS AND FOLDS

Within this chapter we will explore methods to incorporate pleats and folds into the knit samples. Folds are structures that can be as simple as vertical pleats – such as knife or box pleats – to much more complex folds including origami structures. The basic folds are much more suited to garments and accessories compared to the more complex fold structures, which are more suited for use in textile art. However, that is not to say that the complex structures are not suitable for garments.

There will be a yarn exploration within this chapter to understand further the types of yarn to use and which yarns, or combinations of yarns, are more suited to creating form and structure.

This chapter is structured similarly to Chapter 3: Transfers and Rib Structures in that there is only one main method to creating the folds. Once this has been covered, designs and tessellations are explored. Incorporating other techniques into the folds is not included within this chapter, but you will find that the fold skeletons, especially the more complicated processes, take time and patience to knit. It is best, as always, to start small and become comfortable with the process and the rules, and also with the yarns that you will be using.

OPPOSITE: A tessellated origami fold.

MACHINE TYPE

We are looking to create a textile that has structure and strength. Pleats and folds will work with any knit tension, but the best results are created through a denser material, therefore the V-bed machines are preferable unless you are working with a shrinking yarn on the domestic machines. This could be either a shrinking yarn on its own, or doubled with a main yarn.

Most of these techniques will include a double-jersey structure which, as previously mentioned, I have found the domestic machines can struggle with, especially if a dense double-jersey material is required. If you are using the ribber attachment for a domestic machine, ensure it is always set in half-pitch position when working these folds to ensure that the needles do not get caught together when the carriage passes during working the double-jersey areas.

ALTERING FOLDS BETWEEN GAUGES

As the majority of these next samples have been knitted on V-bed machines, you may find the patterns too large to work with on domestic machines due to the number of available needles.

To adjust the patterns to accommodate a domestic machine, half the number of stitches used in each section and half the number of rows knitted, but try to keep the number of needles out of action over the folds the same. The folds on domestic machines can be brought down to work over 3 needles, but I would not suggest going less than this.

The fold patterns can be used as a guide and can be adapted to work with any number of needles over any number of rows. Calculate before casting on and make notes either by each of the charts in this book, or using your own notebook.

YARN TYPE

It is not recommended to use a brittle yarn that breaks easily for these techniques, due to the double-jersey structure. Something that has some stretch in it would be preferable; something that shrinks would be even better. This is of course completely down to personal preference and dependent on the final material that you want to create. I prefer denser materials for pleats and folds as it really showcases the structures, and they become much more self-forming and folding.

Consider using an elastane yarn to knit with. It could be shirring elastic that is normally used for sewing. You do not need to place this simultaneously with another yarn; it can be used completely on its own, which works well and increases the foldability of the material. We will also plate with an elastane yarn, which will increase the shrinkage of the material but allow the main yarn (or the A yarn) to be highlighted. Despite plating being a technique that is normally used alongside a rib structure as a visual element in a rib structure, we can also use plating with a double-jersey material to incorporate more strength into the knit or to add another functional quality.

Also used here is a thermoplastic shrinking yarn. This is a yarn that shrinks and hardens when heat or steam is applied. This is a great yarn if you are looking for more stability within the knit. For example, if you want the knit to be self-supporting and even potentially support additional weight, the usability of the thermoplastic yarn could really benefit the knit. This is a plain white yarn with a very plastic touch once activated, therefore I would suggest that this is plated with a standard main yarn.

BASIC FOLDS

A fold within knitted material comes down to needle structure and essentially a negative space within the material. Working mainly with a double-jersey fabric, once needles are no longer used and placed out of action, an area of negative space within the structure is created that encourages the knit to naturally fold in the direction of the negative space. For example, if needles are out of action on the back bed, the material will want to fold in the direction of the back bed; and if needles are out of action on the front bed, the material will want to fold in the direction of the front bed.

The number of empty needles that are used to create the folds needs to be considered in relation to the yarn, as this will alter the sharpness of the fold. For example, only one needle out of action will create a gentle crease in the textile. Similarly, if we use a larger number of needles within the fold, for example five needles, the fold would still be implemented, but it would have less structure and potentially become a loose fold. The material would then take on an appearance similar to a rib structure with some double-jersey areas, rather than the precise folding skeleton we are aiming for.

Folds work best when three to four stitches are transferred to create the negative space. This is of course a guideline and something that should be tested before beginning a big pleat or origami folded project. It can differ slightly according to the gauge of the machine, the yarn type and the properties of the yarn used.

In all of the following examples the needle structure is stated along with the yarn choice. However, due to the differences in machines, the tension will not be stated.

Horizontal Folds

Horizontal Accordion

Relating back to the last chapter, where we explored the differences of rib structures, we can implement that knowledge directly in this chapter as we make basic folds. Working immediately on horizontal fold structures, we will begin to look at creating a basic accordion fold, with folds horizontal across the width of the cast-on area.

For this first sample, cast on approximately 10cm width of needles on the double bed with double jersey. We will work a smaller width whilst we become familiar with the processes. Establish the knit by knitting 20 rows. This will be the first section before the first fold.

Next, transfer all the stitches from the front bed to the back bed. Turn off the front bed, increase the stitch size slightly, and for this first row, if working on a domestic machine, bring all the needles out into the forward working position to help the needles to knit, as all needles will have two stitches on them. Knitting only with the back bed, knit 4 rows of single jersey. Sometimes you can get away with keeping the stitch size the same as the double jersey, but it is advisable to increase the weight of the knit by hand if you do not increase the stitch size, to ensure that the stitches are kept down on the needle stems.

We can next reintroduce the front bed into work and adjust the stitch size back to the double-jersey setting before knitting 20 rows of double jersey. Despite there not being any stitches on the front bed, the process of knitting the first row will create a tuck stitch on each empty needle on the front bed, and then a fully formed stitch on the second row. Even though all needles are empty, each empty needle is sitting between 2 working back-bed needles with fully formed stitches on them, therefore allowing the empty needles to build up stitches once again without having to transfer or cast on over those needles.

After the 20 rows of double jersey, we will transfer all the stitches once again but this time over to the front bed, and deactivate the back-bed carriage. Slightly adjust the stitch size again and knit 4 rows of single jersey on the front bed only.

Similarly, once the single jersey is complete, reactivate the back bed, decrease the stitch tension and knit 20 rows, building up stitches on the back bed to knit double jersey once again.

This process is repeated for the length of material that you want to achieve. The amount of double jersey knitted between each transfer will create the main material, and the single jersey sections will create the horizontal folds. You will notice that the knit will fold towards the front-facing stitches on the single-jersey areas, therefore having the purl bumps of the stitches visible. This example will give an even accordion fold for as long as the piece is knitted. There is no limit to the number of folds you place into the material because the length and number of folds are determined by the length knitted.

A basic horizontal fold is made by transferring all the stitches over to one bed and knitting a few rows. *Yarn: Two ends 2/36NM cotton–wool blend. All the basic folds will be knitted with this yarn.*

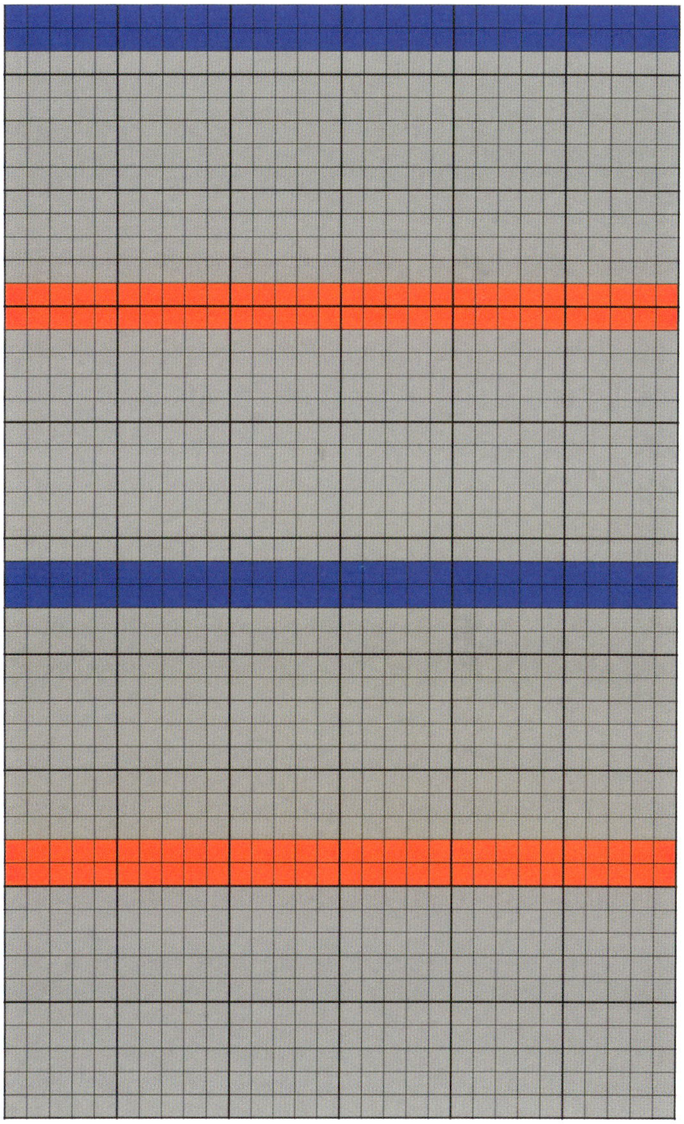

1 square = 1 stitch and 2 rows

Stitches on the front bed — Stitches on the back bed — Double Jersey

The basic chart that shows the positioning of the folds. The colours show which needles are being worked at each stage.

Working Ottoman into the structure can also build up folds within the material. However, these folds are not as sharp as the transferred fold.

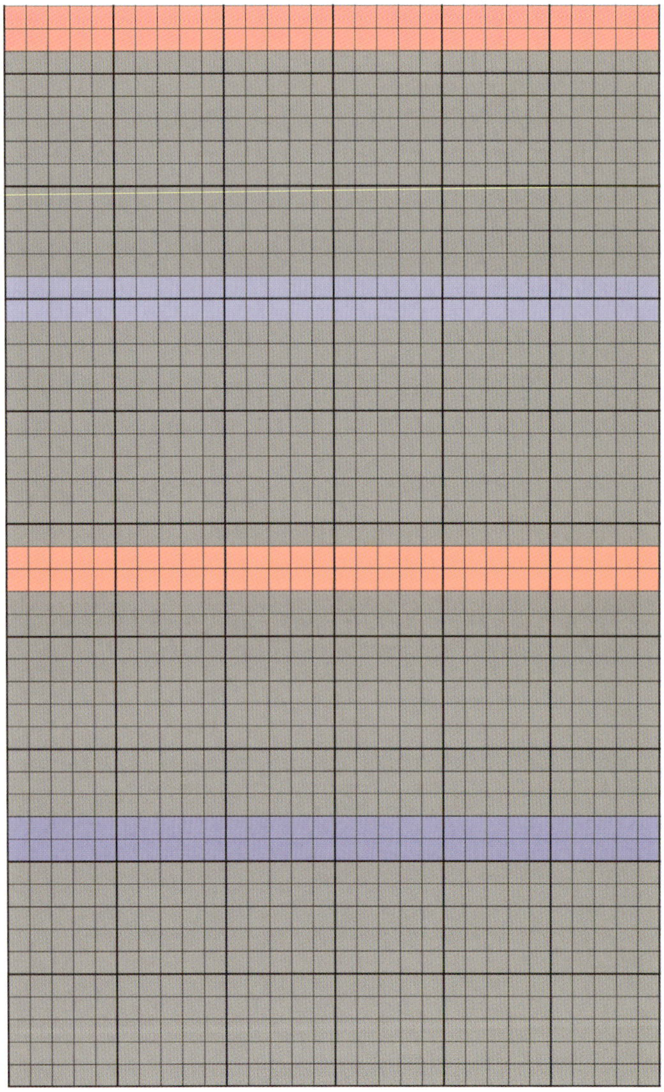

1 square = 1 stitch and 2 rows

Ottoman with the front bed | Ottoman with the back bed | Double Jersey

The chart to create Ottoman folds. Note that the change in colour also shows the change in needle bed.

You can alter the length of the sections in double jersey to create more form and structure in the knit if you wish. For example, where I have knitted 20 rows, you could start with 6 rows and build up to knitting 40 rows, and then decrease down again. This would alter the size of the accordion fold once it is off the machine.

There is also a secondary method in which we can knit the folds horizontally, whereby we use Ottoman technique by making a ripple. This ripple will build up more material on one side, therefore forcing the structure of the knit to fold over itself, creating the fold. The underneath of the ripple can also help to form the fold by creating additional tension with the held stitches.

Working Ottoman to create the fold will not make such a crisp fold compared to the transferred fold; however, after a good steam into place, the fold made with Ottoman is just as present. It could be argued that this is a more aesthetic fold compared to the transfer type, and also a much quicker method, therefore you could use Ottoman folds to test an idea and then use transferred folds to execute the final piece.

The Ottoman structure fold will fold in the opposite direction to the transferred fold. To create a fold using Ottoman in the same direction as the transfers, we would have to use the opposite bed. In other words, if our original fold was worked by transferring all the stitches over to the back bed, to recreate it with Ottoman, we would have to work 4 rows on the front bed.

For this example and to explore the technique, we will work the same number of needles and rows as in the previous sample.

Cast on the width of the sample you want to make with the double bed and establish the knit. Once 20 rows have been knitted, turn off the front bed to only work on the back bed. Knit 4 rows with the back bed only, which will hold the front bed, and then reintroduce the front bed back into work and continue knitting with both beds to make double jersey.

After 20 rows of double jersey are knitted, create the opposite fold by deactivating the back bed and only knitting on the front bed. Again, knit 4 rows on the one bed to create the ripple of Ottoman to make the fold. Repeat the steps for the length of the sample needed.

Similarly to the previous sample in which the stitches were transferred, the size of the knit between the folds can be altered, therefore altering the size of the fold.

The positioning of the folds can also change. For example, we do not have to only alternate between using the front and the back bed, but can build up different structures by repeating a fold on either bed.

All lengths or numbers of rows are variables that can be altered and explored to create samples of different shapes and sizes.

Repeating folds can build up alternative shapes rather than a consistent mountain-and-valley fold

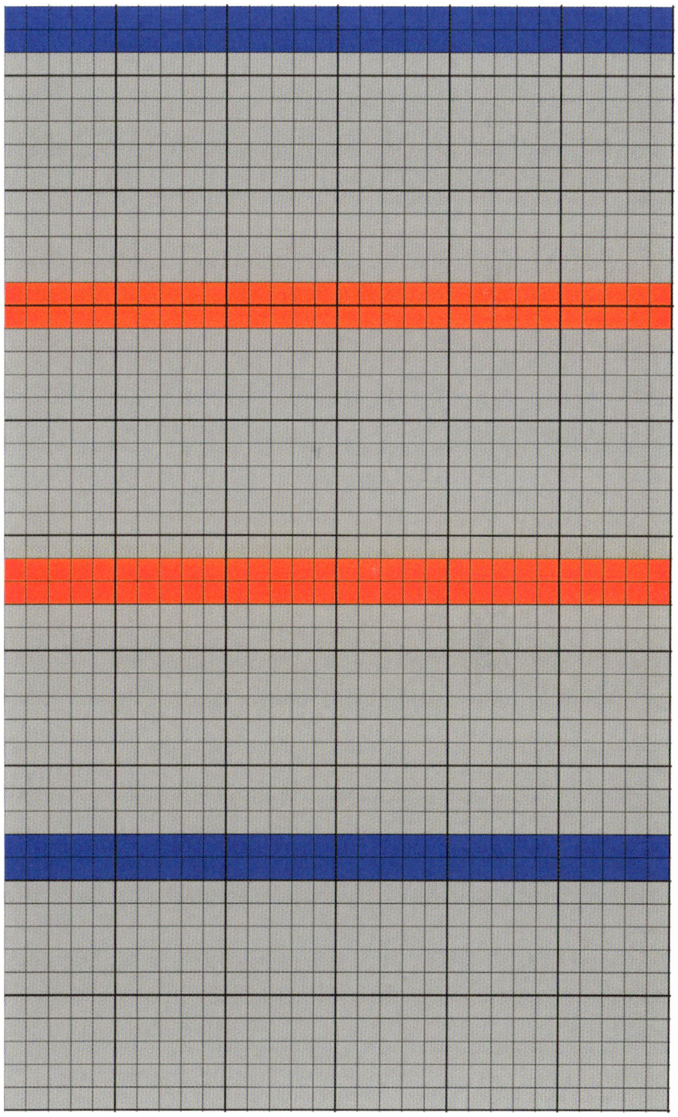

1 square = 1 stitch and 2 rows

Stitches on the front bed

Stitches on the back bed

Double Jersey

An additional folding structure which utilises the basic horizontal form.

Also working an Ottoman structure to create the build-up of folds in the same structure as the transferred repeated fold.

Colour elements can be added into the folds, incorporating a secondary colour into the folding areas by changing colour. This can be over the transferred stitches, or by working a second colour when working the Ottoman.

Working a different colour over the horizontal folds when the stitches were transferred.

Similarly, a separate colour worked over the repeated folds when transferring gives an edge detail.

Working a different colour over the Ottoman roll to create the fold.

And again with the Ottoman folds.

Vertical Folds

This is the process whereby folds are integrated into the structure of the material from the beginning of the knit and stay throughout the length knitted. Placed into the needle structure typically just after the cast-on, we can only work vertical folds with one method: transferring stitches.

To keep the folds vertical, nothing needs to change after the structure has been set unless we decide to move the folds; this will be covered further on in this chapter.

Unlike horizontal folds, we are unable to place colour elements into the folds unless horizontal stripes are incorporated. Vertical stripes can only be implemented with a type of Jacquard or intarsia which is not possible with a V-bed machine, but may be possible with a domestic machine. Plating with two contrasting colours can add a colour element, but only over the folds. Due to working mainly with a double-jersey structure, the plated yarn will be sitting on the inside of the knit rather than becoming visible on the purl side.

Vertical Accordion

This first sample is identical to the horizontal accordion with regard to shape but with the folds turned 90 degrees and placed on the vertical. Due to the folds reducing the width of the piece, a much larger number of stitches will need to be cast on. However, once the fold structure is integrated into the needle beds, the length to be knitted is very quickly built up as there is no alteration of needle structure, unlike the process for horizontal folds.

Cast on in multiples of 24 plus 20. There will be 20 needles working in double jersey with areas of 4 needles for the folds. Each side of the working area should be a section of 20 needles so neither side is worked as a fold. There is nothing more to this than aesthetic reasons, and if you would like to have the edges of the fold worked in a single jersey, then this is a design feature you can decide upon.

Once the final row of the cast-on is complete, set the fold structure into the needle bed. In this instance there is a section of 20 needles for the double jersey, then 4 needles

A vertical accordion pleat whereby there is an equal distance between both the mountain and the valley folds. The folds are implemented into the needle structure and do not need to be changed.

have been transferred to the front bed. A second section of 20 needles is left for the double-jersey section with the 4 needles being transferred to the back bed. This structure is repeated across the whole working area.

Knife Pleats

Knife pleats are a typical sewing method to integrate more fabric into a garment to create a flared look or to give more movement to the material. Similar to a gathering, yet more structured, the amount of material overall is often around a third more than the actual measurement of a pattern piece without the pleat. This is a guide as this will depend on the amount of additional material that is to be incorporated into the structure.

Knife pleats are given their name due to their structure: straight, narrow folds of material that resemble a knife edge. Technically, you can fold any form of material into a knife pleat and secure the folded edge with a row of stitches; however, we can go one step further with knitted

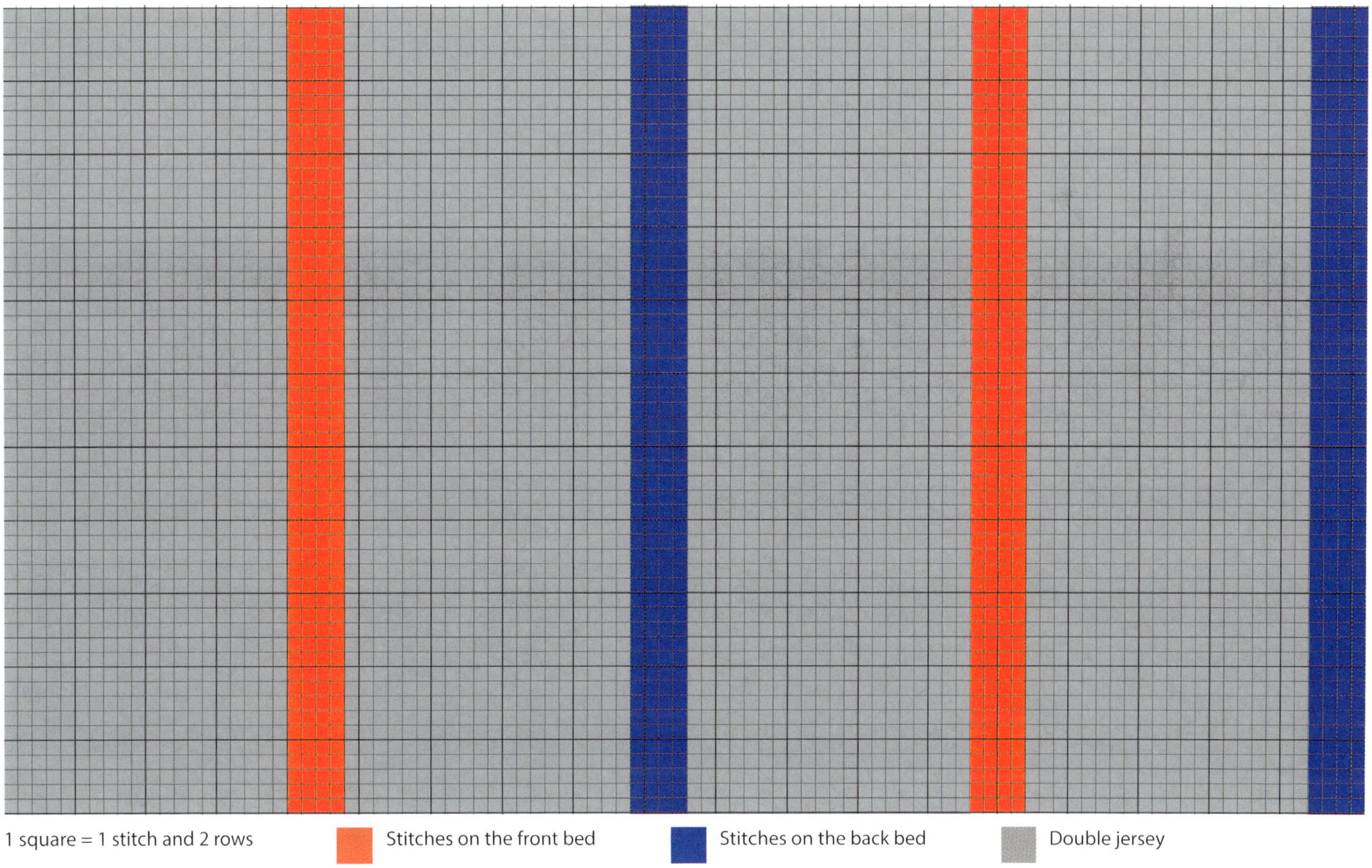

1 square = 1 stitch and 2 rows | Stitches on the front bed | Stitches on the back bed | Double jersey

The placement of the vertical folds to create an accordion fold.

material and integrate the knife pleats into the structure of the material. This will mean that the pleat will never drop out of the material as the fold is within the skeleton of the material. If we were to fold up a piece of knitted material into a knife pleat, the pleat might struggle to hold due to the natural weight of the knit and its elasticity. Even with a strong steam and press, the natural bulkiness of knit will hinder the pleating. This is why it is suggested to incorporate the pleat into the structure of the material through the needle placement.

Technically, the vertical pleat we have just covered is a knife pleat, although it cannot lie flat as a knife pleat characteristically does. To help the material to lie flat, we need to arrange the folds in a specific arrangement.

To calculate the basic knife pleat, we will need two widths of stitches: one double the width of the other. This creates a longer section and a shorter section of double jersey. This shorter section will fold up either on top of or underneath the longer section, depending on the needle bed used for the pleat. If the front bed is used, the pleat will sit behind; and if the back bed is used, the pleat will sit in front.

For this first piece, section A is 20 needles wide and section B is 10 needles wide. Each of the vertical folds are 4 stitches wide. Therefore cast on 158 needles in a double jersey for three full pleats in the material. After the cast-on, transfer the needles into the folding structure as shown in the chart. Work 20 stitches in double jersey then work the following as a repeat: 4 stitches transferred to the front bed, 10 stitches in double jersey, transfer 4 needles to the back bed, 20 stitches in double jersey. Work these repeats three times over; this should leave 20 stitches in the double jersey.

The needle placement for the knife pleat is now in place, so knit the length desired for the material before casting off.

To alter the size of the pleats, we adjust the number of needles in work between the folds. To increase the size of the pleat (make the pleat size larger), increase the number of needles in section A in the chart or decrease the number of needles in section B. Alternatively, to decrease the size of the pleat (make the pleat size smaller), work the opposite; decrease the number of working needles in section A or increase the number of needles in section B.

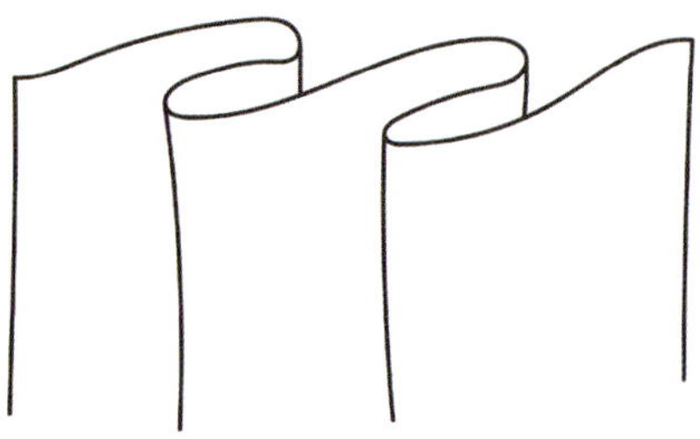

A basic illustration of a knife pleat.

A basic knife pleat using the rule of section A being twice the needle width of section B.

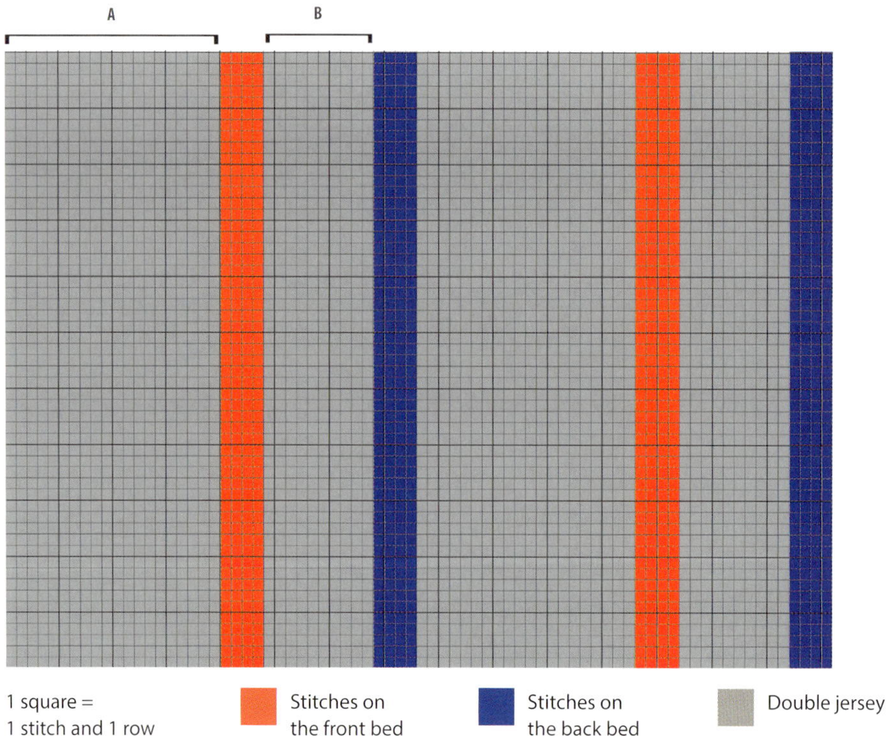

The technical chart for the standard knife pleat.

A pleat with an increased amount of material. For this structure, section A has fourteen double-jersey stitches and section B worked with ten double-jersey needles.

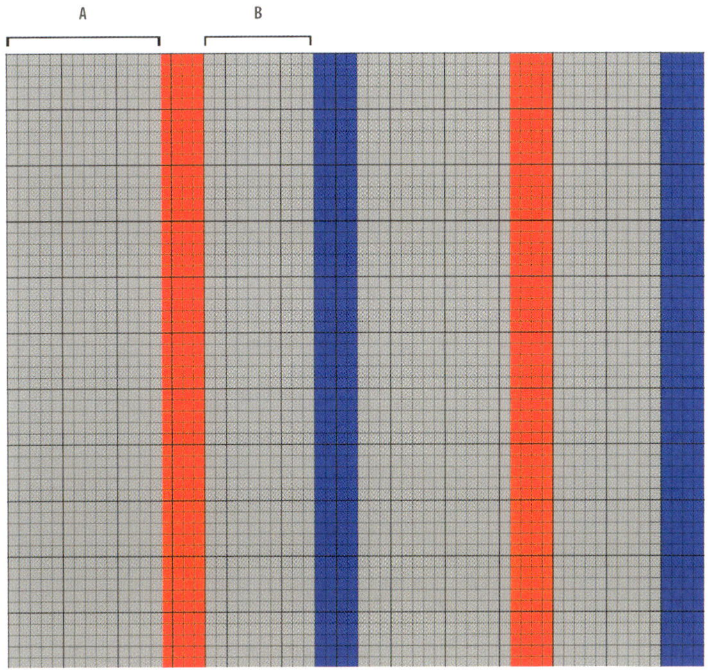

1 square = 1 stitch and 1 row | Stitches on the front bed | Stitches on the back bed | Double jersey

The first chart to create an increased knife pleat.

A second method to increase the amount of material within a pleat. Here, section B has an increase in the number of stitches to fourteen. Section A has stayed the same as the original, which is twenty stitches.

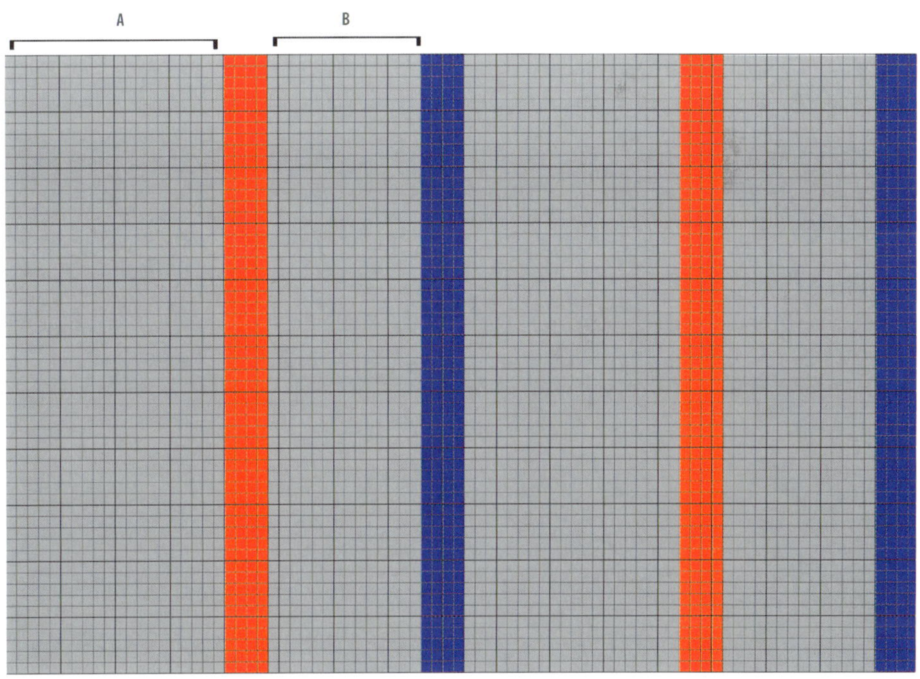

1 square = 1 stitch and 1 row | Stitches on the front bed | Stitches on the back bed | Double jersey

The chart for the secondary method to create an increased knife pleat.

An example of a pleat with a decreased amount of material, or a decreased pleat size. Section B has fewer working needles than the original: in this sample only six compared to the original, which has ten. Section A has stayed the same.

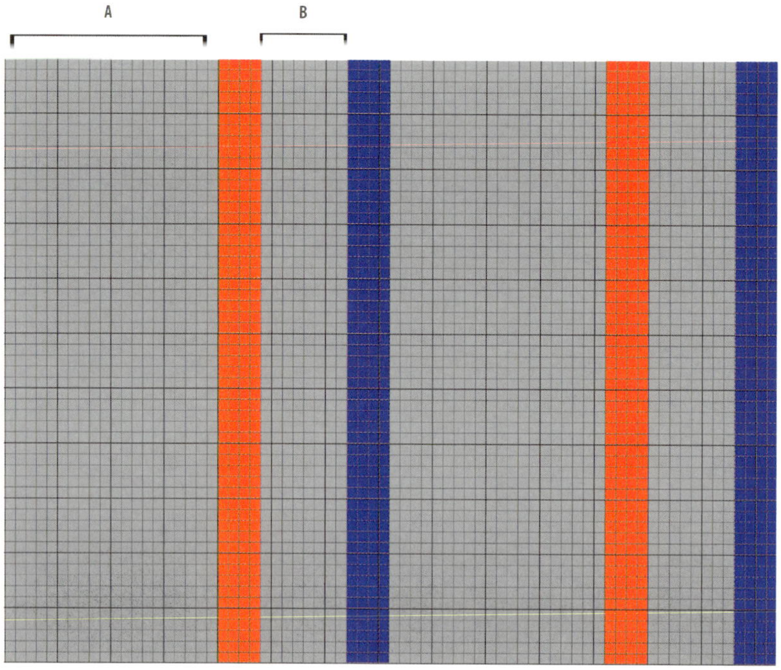

1 square = 1 stitch and 1 row | Stitches on the front bed | Stitches on the back bed | Double jersey

The first method to make a decreased knife pleat.

Another method to decrease the pleat size is to increase the number of working stitches in section A. In this sample, section A has 26 double-jersey needles compared to the original, which has 20. Section B has stayed the same.

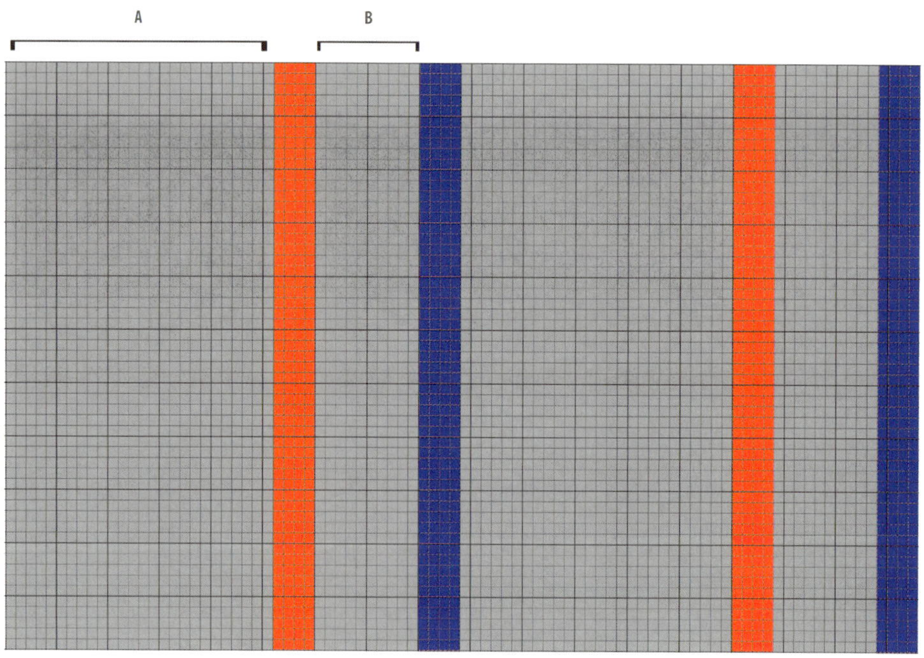

1 square = 1 stitch and 1 row | Stitches on the front bed | Stitches on the back bed | Double jersey

A secondary method to decrease the knife pleat size.

Box Pleats

Box pleats work in a very similar way to knife pleats, but instead of alternating between mountain and valley folds, we repeat a pleat to create two folds in the same direction. This creates two knife pleats but in opposing directions to each other, which then fold and gather in the material. Whereas knife pleats alternate mountain and valley folds, box pleats work with a mountain fold, then two valley folds, then a mountain fold, and so on across the working area before ending in a single mountain fold.

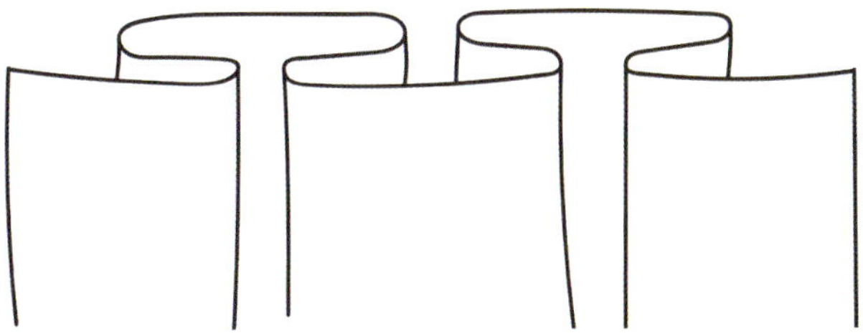

A basic illustration of a box pleat.

Again, to create a simple pleat we will work with 2 sections, section A and section B. Similarly to the knife pleat, section A will be 20 needles working double jersey and section B will be 10 needles of double jersey. The folds in between are worked over 4 needles on either the front or the back bed, depending on the fold needed.

In this first sample we have cast on a total of 248 needles on the double bed for three repeats of the pleat. If working on a domestic machine, work two repeats, which would be a total of 172 stitches. Leaving 20 needles at each end, the first fold is on the back bed for 4 needles. The front-bed stitches over this fold have been transferred to the back bed. We then position the following: 10 double-jersey stitches, 4 stitches on the front bed, 20 double-jersey stitches, 4 stitches on the front bed, 10 double-jersey stitches, 4 stitches on the back bed, 20 double-jersey stitches. This is one repeat of the box pleat, and therefore should be repeated another two times over.

The box pleat is another method to gather up the knitted material using the structure of the material, rather than a post-knit process; you work two identical vertical folds next to each other rather than alternating between mountain and valley folds.

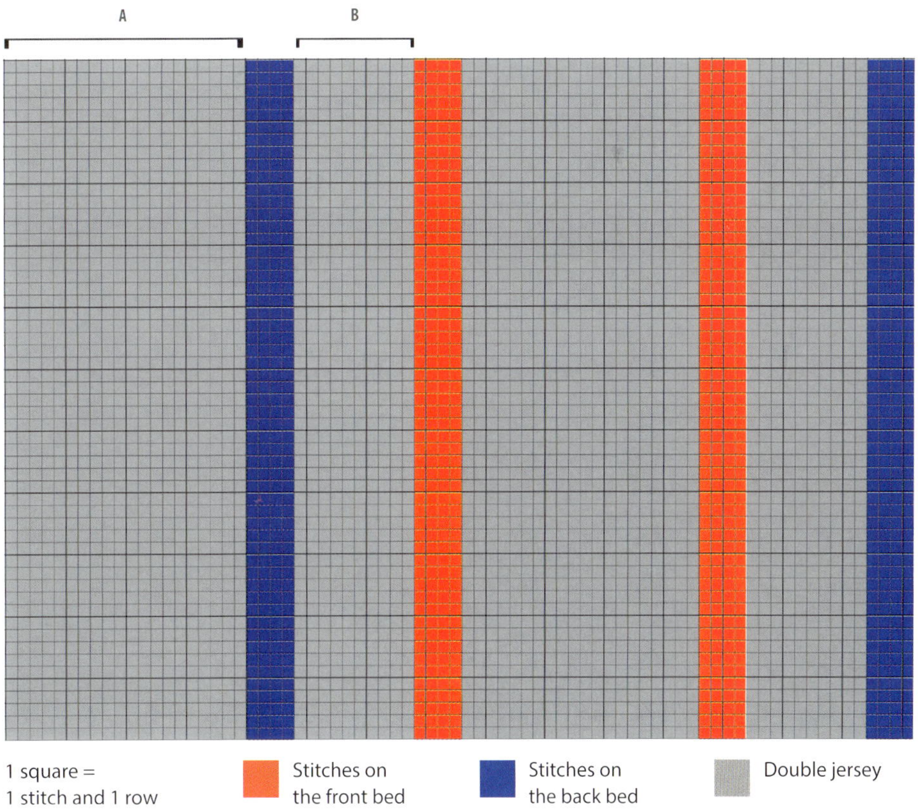

The chart shows a basic box-pleat structure.

Unlike the knife pleat, alterations to the box pleat can only really be made to decrease the pleat size as, otherwise, we would have two sections overlapping each other. Whilst this could be a design detail, it will create additional bulk. Decreasing the pleat size is done by decreasing section B. This means less material is folded up in the pleat, making the box smaller.

Decreasing the number of double-jersey stitches in section B to six will create a smaller pleat that gives the effect that it is more drawn out.

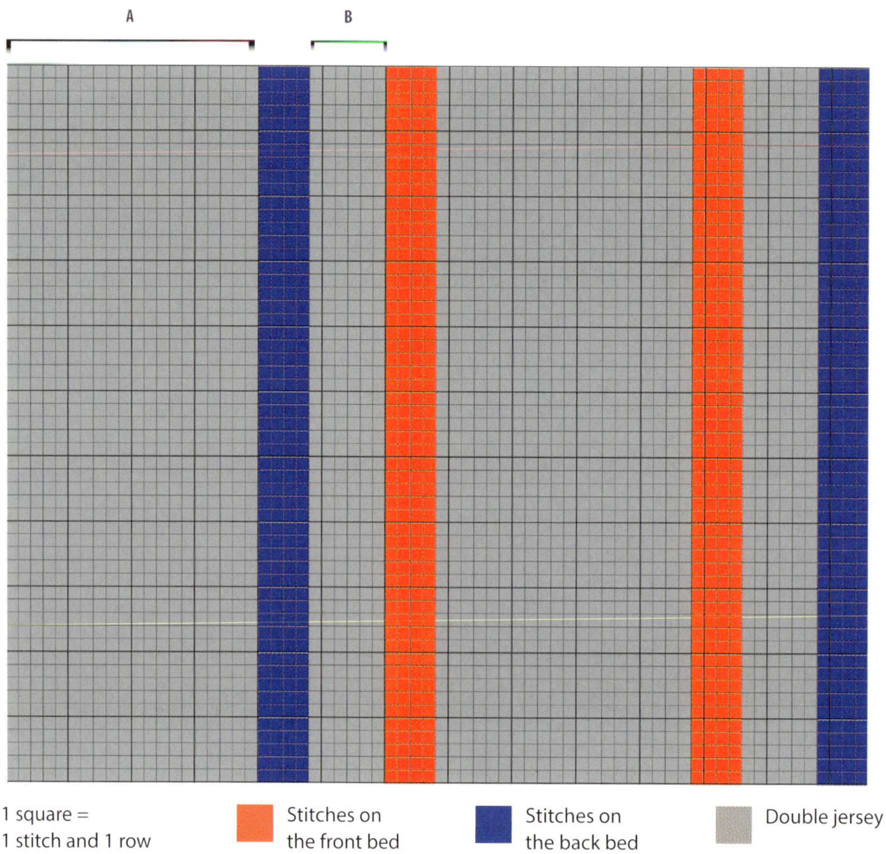

The chart for a decreased box pleat.

If an increased box pleat were to be trialled, the result would be more like a three-dimensional pleat which has similarities to some of the horizontal pleats. The pleat stands up on its edges, giving dimension and form. In this instance the part that lies flat is too short, therefore pulling the pleat upwards.

An increased box pleat is no longer a box pleat but more of a three-dimensional folding form.

MOVING PLEATS

It should be noted that when making moving pleats (diagonal pleats, moving box pleats or any other origami knitted structures further on in this chapter) that any needle that is currently empty, because the stitch has been transferred to either the front or the back bed, must be placed out of action. If the needle is left in action, with the pass of the carriage a stitch will be built back up onto the needle, thus eliminating the structure that we are placing into the knit.

When moving the pleats, eventually the needle that was out of action will need to be placed into action once again. Simply introduce the needle and knit over the empty needle. We do not need to fill in the empty needle with a part of the adjacent stitch.

Remember to keep an eye on the needles that need to be brought back into action to save you from getting folds that are too large in areas of single jersey.

DIAGONAL PLEATS

Working on the diagonal to create pleats and folds enables us to incorporate further folding structures and shapes. Creating a fold on the diagonal is also one of the basic folds with paper origami, therefore it is a must in order to recreate origami shapes.

Folding on the diagonal can only be achieved by transferring stitches rather than through Ottoman ripples. Depending on the angle of the diagonal fold that is to be created, the number of stitches transferred to rows knitted needs to be determined.

Remembering that each fold needs to have three to four stitches transferred onto either the front or the back bed to encourage the material to fold, the easiest diagonal fold would be to transfer one stitch to the same needle bed as the fold for every two rows knitted.

We also need to remember that if we were to transfer a stitch every two rows, we then need to reintroduce a stitch every two rows to keep the four-stitch fold, otherwise we would end up transferring all stitches to one bed and not keeping the base material that should be double jersey. This is the simplest fold as we do not need to remember a specific transfer rate: we always transfer when the carriage is back on the same side.

The actual angle of this fold will be determined by the tension of the material. Whilst we could expect the fold to be slightly more than 45 degrees due to the rate at which the stitches are transferred (we have not transferred one stitch every row), the shape of the stitch, the shrinking of the material or the looseness of the double jersey will affect the angle.

For example, if we were to knit with an elastic, as I have done for some of the samples further on in this chapter, the shrinkage once the material is off the machine and the sample is steamed will be quite significant, meaning the vertical height of the material is reduced. Compare this to a double-jersey knit with a looser tension which would create a piece that is much longer. The details within both of these knits, such as the fold lines, would then be very different to one another. The elastic piece, being reduced in height, will have a more horizontal fold compared to the loose double-jersey sample, which will be more vertical, when they have both been knitted at the same transfer rate.

The most basic fold on the diagonal, whereby one stitch is transferred into the fold in every knitted row. The angle of this fold is undetermined as the tension of the material is what will determine the density of the material. This was knitted with an elastic simultaneously with the main yarn.

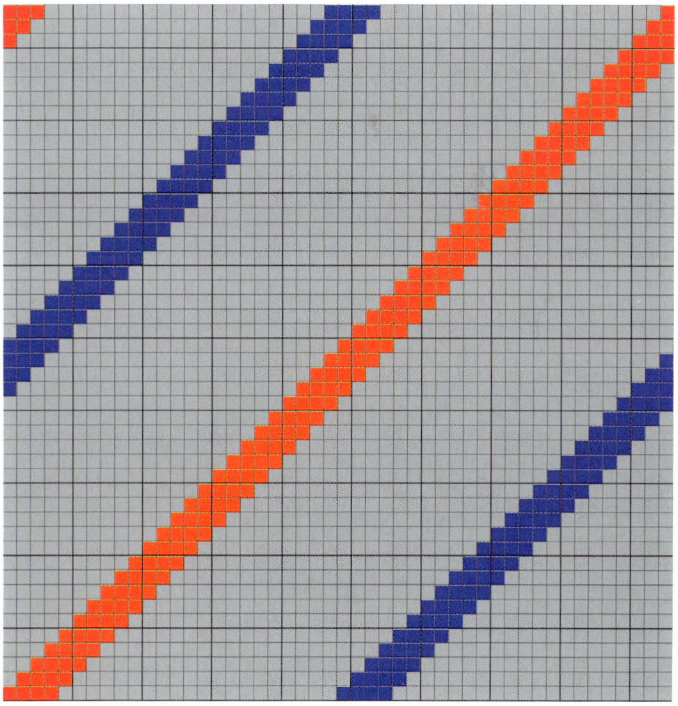

1 square = 1 stitch and 2 rows

Stitches on the front bed | Stitches on the back bed | Double jersey

A standard diagonal fold implemented into the knit structure.

To be more specific about the angle of the fold, the transfer rate will help to determine the angle of the fold. If we transfer more stitches than there are rows knitted, the angle of the fold will generally be less than 45 degrees; whereas if we knit more rows than there are transferred stitches, this would mean the angle of the fold will generally be more than 45 degrees. It must be emphasised that the true angle of the fold that is created will be adjusted by the density of the material, which is affected by the tension of the yarn and any post-knit processes: washing, felting or steaming. The only method to ensure the angle of the fold is exactly what we want it to be is to create a tension sample first, to get a stitch density.

Worked with only the natural yarn and no shrinking yarn, the folds are much more vertical. These folds were transferred at a rate of one stitch per row, therefore already relatively horizontal once the shape of the stitch is taken into account. *Yarn: Two ends 2/36NM cotton–wool blend.*

A thermoplastic yarn has been plated with the natural yarn. Compared to the other image of this fold, the size is much smaller and much more horizontal. This yarn naturally alters the angle of the diagonal fold.

The Rule for Diagonal Folds

There is a rule when working diagonal folds that relates to the previous information about tension and angle. This rule determines which needle bed the fold is knitted onto. When implementing vertical folds into the structure of the knit, stitches transferred onto the front bed will create a mountain fold and stitches transferred onto the back bed will create a valley fold. We work the opposite for horizontal folds, therefore a mountain fold will be knitted on the back bed, and for a valley fold the stitches are transferred onto the front bed.

When we work with diagonal folds, we keep the same rule but use the angle of the fold. If the fold is less than 45 degrees, we will work this as a horizontal fold, meaning a mountain fold would have the stitches transferred over to the back bed. If the angle of the fold is more than 45 degrees, this is worked as a vertical fold and the stitches for a mountain fold are transferred to the front bed.

It must be stated that this rule applies when the fabric is relaxed and off the machine. If a shrinking yarn is being used, such as a thermoplastic, the angle knitted may be different to the angle after shrinking. Therefore ensure that you have done a tension sample first to know the stitch-size ratio.

A diagonal fold that is less than 45 degrees. This means the folds are treated as horizontal folds. A mountain fold has the stitches transferred to the back bed and a valley fold has all the stitches transferred to the front bed.

Diagonal folds which are more than 45 degrees are treated as vertical folds. A mountain fold is made by transferring stitches to the front bed and a valley fold is made by transferring stitches to the back bed.

A paper origami crane was the starting point for a long-standing development of knitted origami, which finally resulted in a knitted origami crane.

Through yarn tests, tension samples and calculations using ratios, any origami shape, such as this crane, can be knitted.

There are many fold patterns that do not require a specific angle of fold, and generally speaking you will be able to knit most patterns with a basic diagonal fold, such as transferring one stitch to the appropriate bed every two rows. This will produce a diagonal fold that is most suited to the herringbone folds and is a good place to begin.

Putting This into a Design Context

To explain this a little further, I will use an example of a knitted origami crane and explain the process that I undertook to develop this shape. After some simple material explorations, I decided that I needed to work with an exact square of material. Once folded, the wings need to align, meaning the folds needed to be in the correct position from the start when I was implementing the folds into the structure of the material. I knitted out a basic tension sample in the yarn to be used, then activated the shrinking yarn through steam to get a count of rows and stitches within 10cm to enable me to work an exact square. I then knitted out an exact square to test the tension and the yarns. Bear in mind that the piece will not be square when it comes off the machine, but much more rectangular, and only becomes a square after it is shrunk.

Once I had an exact square, I could then translate the folds of the origami crane onto the knit sample.

Using a paper origami crane as the base, I measured each point and the distance between the folds and then calculated where they needed to be on the knit, using the stitch ratio as a guide.

Using the rule for the angle of the folds, I then marked which folds need to be on either the front or the back bed and knitted out a crane, making sure I knew exactly which row I was knitting and the folds that were to be worked within that row.

After several attempts, finally I was able to knit out a working, folding crane from the double-bed machine.

If I were to then change the plating yarn for the structure, or the outer yarn for the main material, I would have to work a new tension sample and slightly adjust the fold skeleton to the new tension. This is why it is most important to decide on the working yarns prior to developing the fold skeleton.

Sample 1: Knitted only with natural yarns.

Sample 2: Knitted with an elastic alongside the natural yarn.

Sample 3: The elastic has been plated rather than running through the feeder at the same time as the main yarn.

AN EXPLORATION OF YARN COMBINATIONS

Throughout this section, I will introduce different yarn combinations which can enhance the folding abilities of the material to help create the shapes and structure. All of the yarns are purchasable through online shops so are therefore available to the domestic knitter rather than only available to industry. There is a short list at the end of the book of online sources from which to purchase these yarns that is correct at the time of publishing.

For this exploration, a basic herringbone fold has been used for each of the structures. This is to show the abilities of the folds in a more structured sense, rather than a basic knife or box pleat, and to show the self-forming and self-folding capabilities. The instructions for how to knit the herringbone fold are further along in the chapter.

Each of these samples was knitted on the fine gauge apart from one which was made on a domestic machine to show the difference in gauge and double-jersey structure. All yarns are transferable between machines. Each of these samples has been made with the same number of needles and repeats of the structure apart from the domestic-knitted sample where fewer needles were used (but not for the fold itself). This is to show the difference in size of the end piece that will be made, depending on the yarns used. The fold structure is also the same for each of the samples, to show the difference that the materials can make to the resulting structure.

Sample 1

Worked only with a natural material, this was knitted with two ends of 2/36NM wool and cotton blend. The cotton helps add some structure into the knit, but the density of the material is quite loose. The structure is formed well but easily falls out of place if the sample is played with. Despite having the fold structure integrated into the structure of the material, the folds may not form or, if formed, may not stay structured.

The material has a natural drape and handle and out of this set of samples it is the most similar to a typical knit we might wear. If you are looking to have the material as a folded structure whereby the folds are emphasised and are the main element of the textiles, it would be advisable to work with either a supporting yarn, as suggested in the samples below, or to work with an elastic yarn that will shrink and create a much denser textile.

Sample 4: A thermoplastic yarn is used instead of the elastic to create more shrinkage and support.

Sample 5: Only the elastic yarn has been used.

Sample 6: Only the thermoplastic yarn was used to create a plastic herringbone fold.

Sample 2

This sample has used an elastic within the main yarn to help the final structure to fold. The elastic has been put into the yarn feeder simultaneously with the main yarn, which will add elasticity and shrinkage to the main material once it comes off the machine.

As the yarn is not spun together, a pattern element may become present on the surface of the knit, similar to when two different colours are knitted at the same time without being twisted. This will be more visible if a contrasting-colour elastic is used compared to the main yarn (in this instance to give effect), but generally the elastic will shrink enough to be hidden by the main yarn. If you do not have a plating feeder, this is a good method to use to create a dense and structured material for the folding process, providing the structure yarn and the main yarn are similar colours.

If you are working with an elastic yarn, it is recommended to increase the take-down, or the weight, on the machine. This helps the stitches to stay at the bottom of the needle stem as the needles are moved by the carriage.

Sample 3

Working also with the 2/36NM wool and cotton blend, an elastic has been used to plate with it. Normally we use plating in the structure to incorporate a colour element that allows us to view the front-facing stitches and the rear-facing stitches as two different colours. Working plating in a double jersey, the plated yarn will just sit on the inside of the stitches at all times. This will result in the plating yarn not being visible apart from the areas on the fold where we are using a single jersey. This allows us to use plating within knitted material to incorporate structural yarns to aid the structure rather than for the colour element.

With elastic, the folds will form much more naturally and will hold their shape. The base material becomes stiffer and denser.

Plating with elastic will naturally give a shrinkage to the sample once it is off the machine, similar to Sample 2 where elastic was used alongside the main yarn. This shrinkage will compact the stitches and also the folds. The density of the knit increases, emphasising the folds and the structure.

Sample 7: Two ends of a viscose and nylon yarn knitted together using different colours.

Sample 8: Two ends of a polyamide yarn used to create a strong, dense knit.

Sample 9: Worked on a domestic machine with natural and elastic yarn to help the density.

Sample 4

Instead of working with an elastic, we can introduce a thermoplastic into the combination to give an even stronger and denser material. This thermoplastic is a heat-activated yarn that shrinks up to 40 per cent into a hard plastic when either steamed or set in an oven. Plating with the thermoplastic will place the heat activated yarn right into the centre of the material. This will allow for the main yarn to sit on the outside of the stitches, meaning the overall colour and texture of the material is not compromised by a hard plastic.

After knitting, the piece can be steamed and folded into shape. When the thermoplastic is hot, it is malleable and formable. Once the piece has cooled, the folds are harder to form, but this also means that the likelihood of the folds loosening or becoming soft is pretty low.

The piece can be heated and moulded until the correct shape is made, which means heating and cooling can be repeated. The inner yarn is effectively a plastic which can break, so bending and moving the structure once it is set will, over time, create a softness in the folds, but it is still very effective at keeping the overall form.

Sometimes, due to the shrinkage of the thermoplastic, the main yarn, being a wool–cotton blend, can get a very slight pile. The folds are also not as sharp as the sample plated with the elastic, due to the amount of shrinkage, therefore making a denser material. This means that the structure of the folds can become a little depleted due to the density. If working with this material for folds, it is suggested to increase the size of the fold slightly to account for the shrinkage.

Sample 5

Instead of working with a main yarn and a secondary yarn to help with the structure, in this sample only the structural yarn has been worked: in this case, the elastic. This naturally creates a solid double-jersey structure with tight folds over the folding skeleton, which aids the material to self-form into the desired shapes.

As there is not a main yarn to work with, there is no extra bulk to fill out the folds which is why such a sharp fold can be produced. This piece has extra elasticity when stretched and handled, and will always return to the shape and folds placed into the piece when it was knitted.

Knitting with elastic only can sometimes prove a little problematic because of the stretch of the yarn: when it is sitting on the needles it forms a natural grip. When the needles are raised with the movement of the carriage, sometimes it becomes harder to slide down the stem of the needle, meaning that you may need to apply additional take-down or weight, or the stitch size needs to be increased. In this sample, I held the weight down with my hand whilst carefully moving the carriage to ensure that the stitches were worked with each row. You will begin to feel through the carriage if the needles are not knitted properly. If this is the case, bring the needles into the forward working position for a couple of rows with a slightly larger stitch size to help the tension over the needles to become correct. If, like myself, you are working on a V-bed machine, just work the rows slowly with extra weight and an increased stitch size. You should only need to do this for a couple of rows.

In terms of wearability and comfort, this would not be the best yarn choice as the elastic is cold to touch and quite rough. It does not have the main yarn covering to give a comfortable feel to the material. If the purpose of the knit is purely for structure, then this yarn would be a good choice.

Sample 6

Similarly, only the supporting yarn has been used to create the material for this sample, in this case the thermoplastic yarn. As you can see, the piece has shrunk considerably and has essentially now been turned into a plastic rather than a textile.

This means that the general material will be completely stiff and set once the material is shrunk through steam or heat. It would be advisable to set the folds as much as possible before steam or heat is applied to ensure the right shape, and to wear protective heatproof gloves to help shape the piece whilst it is hot through steaming or oven heating.

Thermoplastic is a very fine yarn and the appearance of it when off the machine is a very light material. Take care when knitting with it on its own due to its delicate nature, and try not to apply too much weight or resistance through the needles. This yarn is much better suited to the fine-gauge machines if worked on its own, rather than a domestic machine and ribber attachment.

Sample 7

Two ends of a similar-coloured viscose and nylon yarn have been plied together to create this folded piece. The yarn has 2 per cent elastane which aids the shrinking slightly and helps to form the folds. However, the material is still loose and will potentially fall out of position. The yarn, being lightweight and the equivalent of a 1-ply yarn, may not necessarily work as a secondary yarn to give structure to a natural yarn, but could give more structure if three or more ends are plied together. In this instance only two ends have been plied.

Sample 8

Polyamide was worked previously in Chapter 3: Transfers and Rib Structures but is also a good choice for folds. Two ends of this yarn have been used, which not only creates quite a heavyweight yarn but also, once steamed, reduces the size and increases the density of the knit.

This is similar, in a sense, to working only with elastic as it gives quite a hard finish to the textile, but the folds are sharp and formed with not much additional help.

This yarn is also quite strong which means a slightly smaller stitch size can be used. The yarn has some natural stretch which allows for it to stretch into the needles as the carriage passes, and then the smaller stitch size will help to create a denser material. These aspects, along with shrinkage with heat, make this a great yarn for technical applications and form-making.

Sample 9

Lastly in this yarn exploration, a 4-ply yarn has been worked on a domestic machine and plated with a single elastic yarn. This sample is just to show the difference in machine and gauge. The yarn used has been plied to make a 4-ply out of 2/36NM cotton and wool. As mentioned previously, due to the gap between the machine beds, the stitches on the domestic machine using double jersey are naturally slightly larger, meaning the textile is a little looser. The elastic in this sample helps give more density to the shaping, enabling the form to become more structured and stable rather than soft and free-flowing despite the folds.

A full sample of the herringbone structure knitted in two ends of a polyamide yarn to give structure and to aid the self-forming properties.

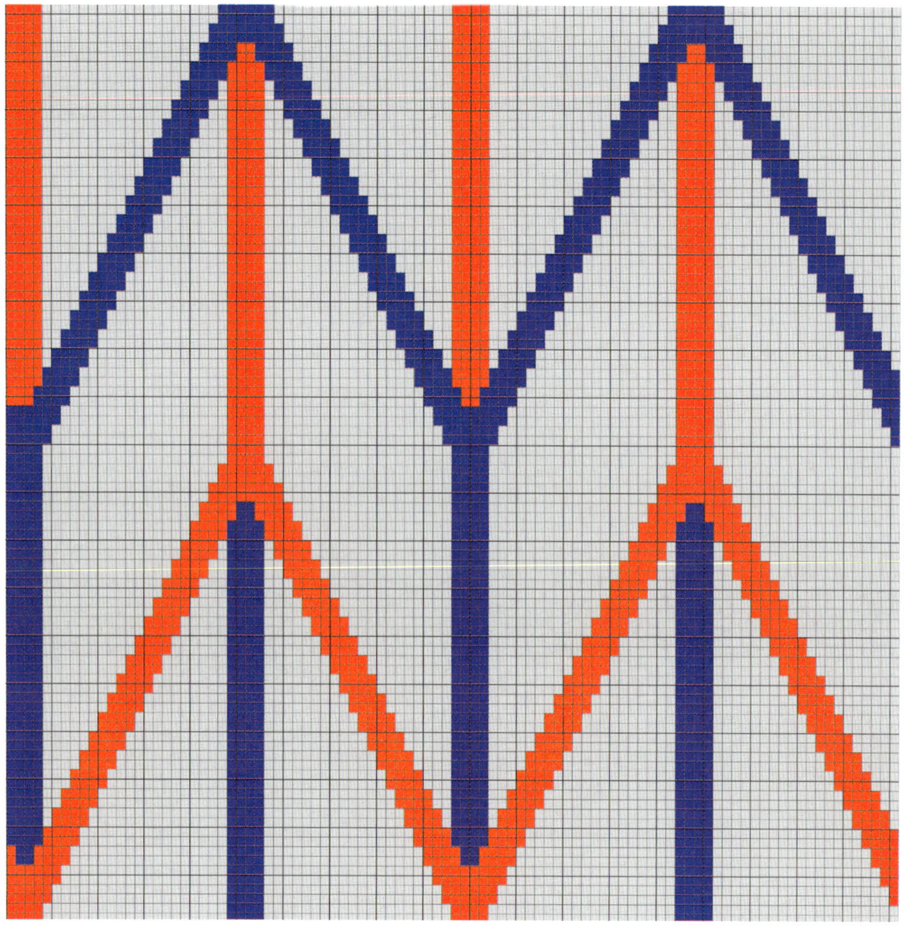

A standard diagonal fold implemented into the knit structure.

MAKING KNITTED ORIGAMI

Now that we have explored the basic folds, we can implement the folds and the rules into any shape of folding knit that we require. There are several examples and fold skeletons included within this chapter. If you would like to explore outside these folds, it is recommended to begin with folding paper to establish the folds and work out the positions of them, and then work your way through into knit by drawing out the patterns and calculating the fold positions for the machine.

Herringbone Fold

The herringbone fold is one of the most basic folding structures to make in origami, but also in knit. A base of alternating mountain and valley vertical folds are worked with diagonal folds that create a horizontal chevron across all vertical folds. These diagonal folds also alternate between mountain and valley folds. This alteration between vertical folds and the chevron allows the piece to very simply fold up into an intricate chevron within an accordion pleat.

The angle of the chevron is not critical to the structure, and the herringbone structure will fold whatever the angle. This is a great starting point for knitting folds as the rate of shaping can be chosen to suit you, rather than being specific to the material and the tension.

The general fold skeleton is also well suited for beginners, given that the structure is repetitive. The diagonal folds will always start from the same vertical fold and travel across the knit to meet the adjacent vertical point. When the diagonal fold meets the vertical fold, the whole process is repeated but using the opposite bed to create the folds.

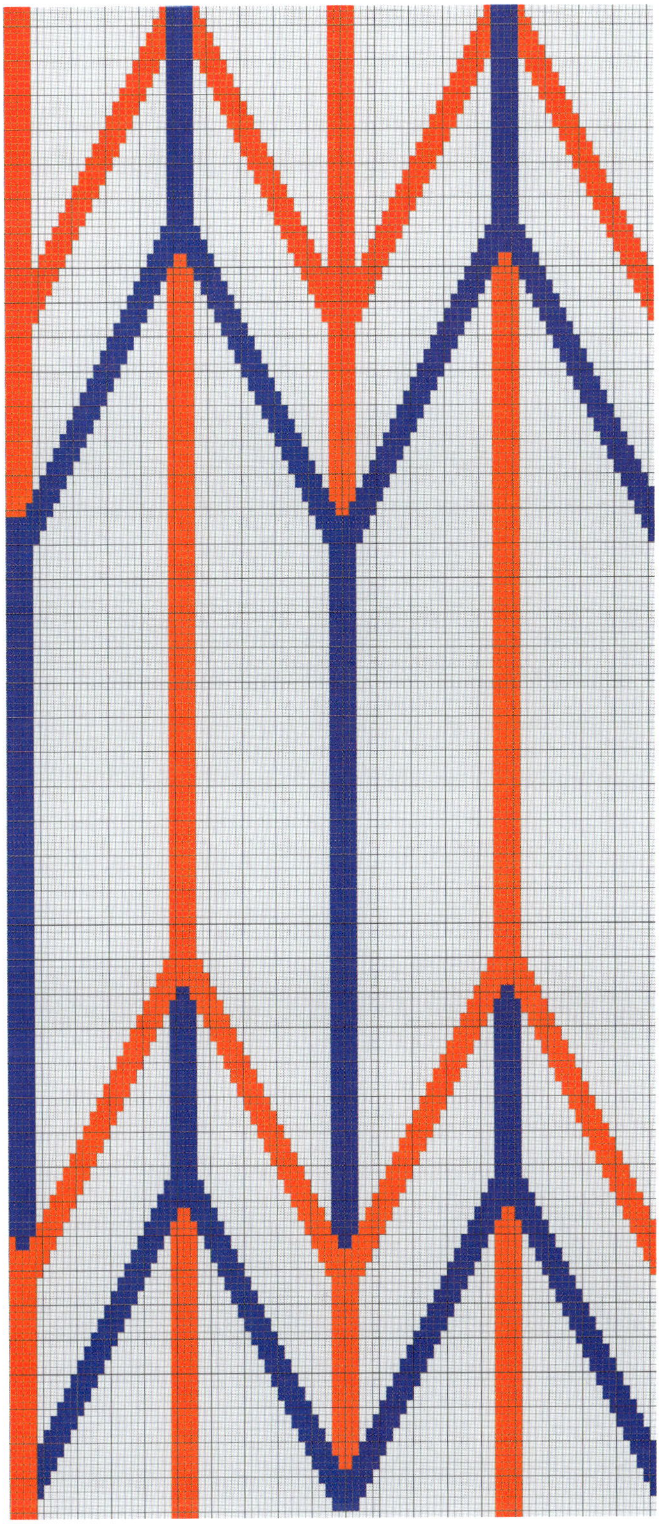

1 square = 1 stitch and 1 row

Stitches on the front bed

Stitches on the back bed

Double jersey

The chart for the adjusted herringbone fold.

Variations of the Herringbone Pleat

Once the general structure of the herringbone has been understood, the shape can be developed, for example by elongating areas in between the folds or mirroring some of the folds to create more complex and intricate forms.

This first example has had one area in between the V-pleats lengthened, and one area in between the V-pleats shortened. This creates a stepped effect with the herringbone pleat. Once one V-pleat has been made, 40 rows have been knitted where a standard accordion fold is implemented into the material structure before the next V-fold is made.

Adjusting the lengths knitted in between the V-folds alters the general shape of the herringbone. *Yarn: One end 2/36NM wool–cotton blend plated with elastomeric yarn.*

Mirroring the folds within the V-pleat is also an option. For example, if the V-pleat was worked as a valley fold and then a mountain fold, it is then mirrored and knitted upside down, first as a mountain fold and then as a valley fold. This incorporates yet more complexity into the structure using a method which is no different to what we have already explored.

The charting for this is also relatively simple as, once one fold is complete, you flip the fold back up on itself.

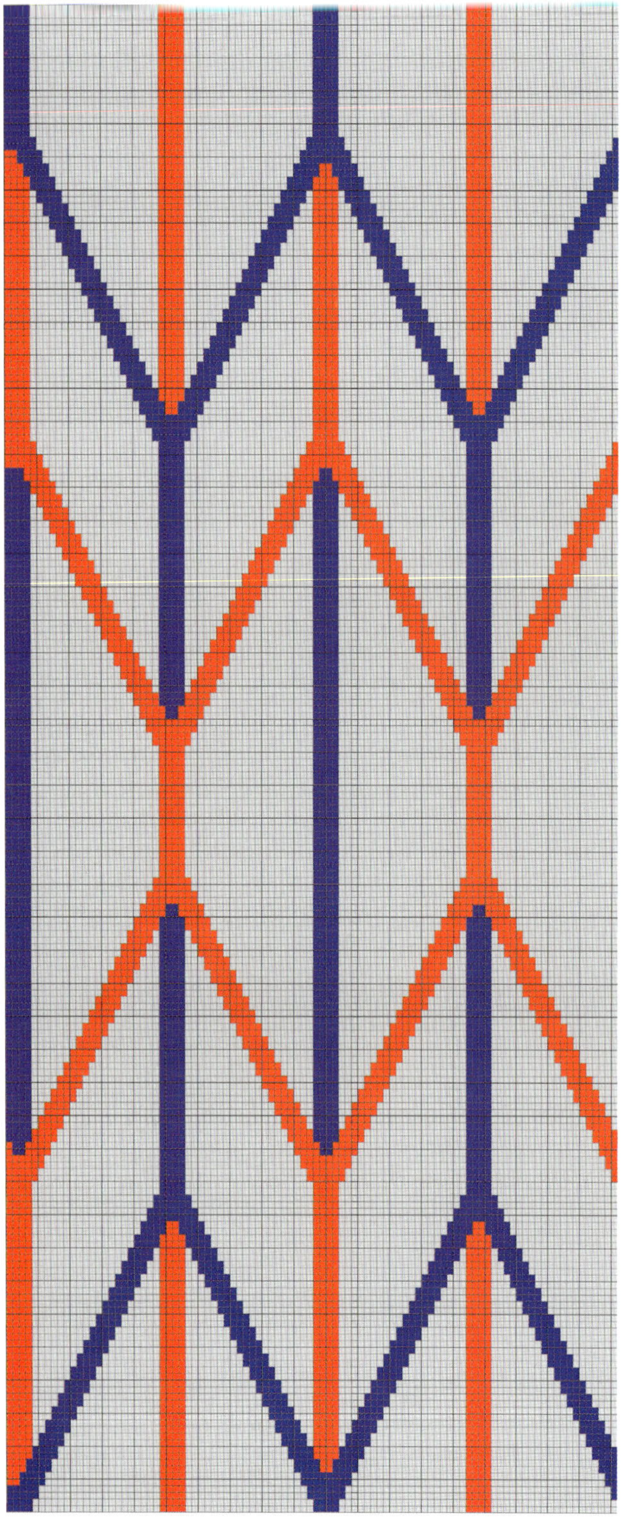

1 square = 1 stitch and 1 row

Stitches on the front bed | Stitches on the back bed | Double jersey

The mirrored V-pleat structure as a chart.

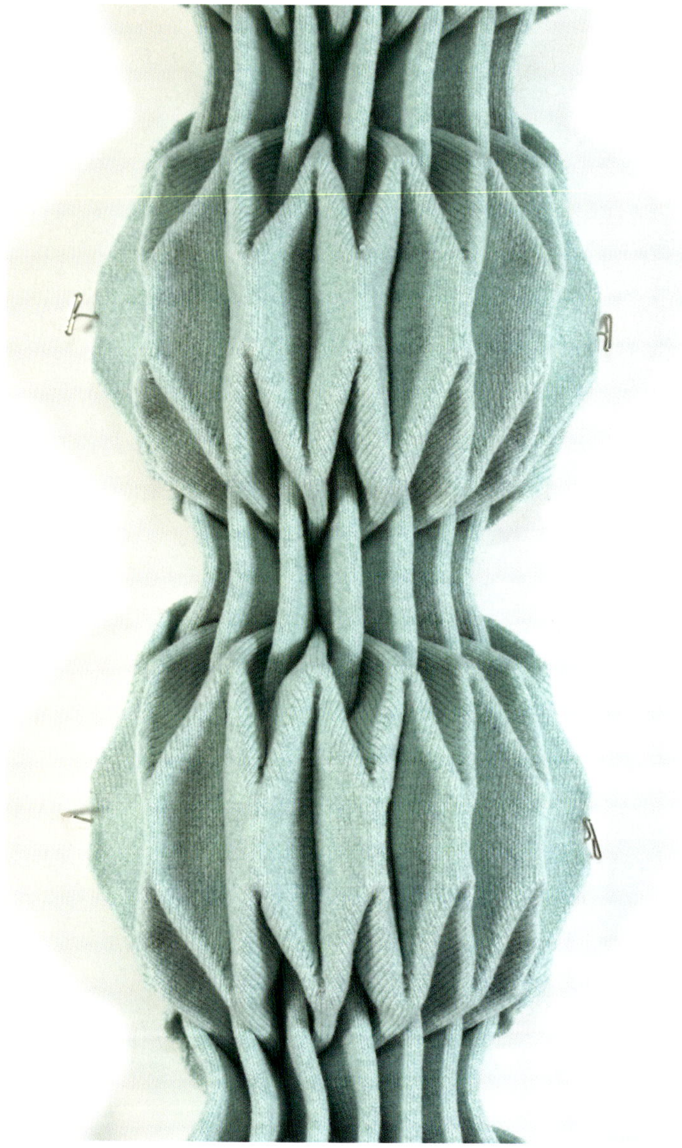

Pinned into place, this mirrored V-pleat sample creates an interesting geometric form. *Yarn: One end 2/36NM wool–cotton blend plated with elastomeric yarn.*

Again, altering the basic accordion folding areas within the herringbone variations, we can create X-pleats within the knit structure. Whilst this has no additional structural developments and is done by eliminating the number of rows knitted between the mirrored V-pleat, it creates yet another pattern and structure that can be explored to enhance the properties of three-dimensional knitting.

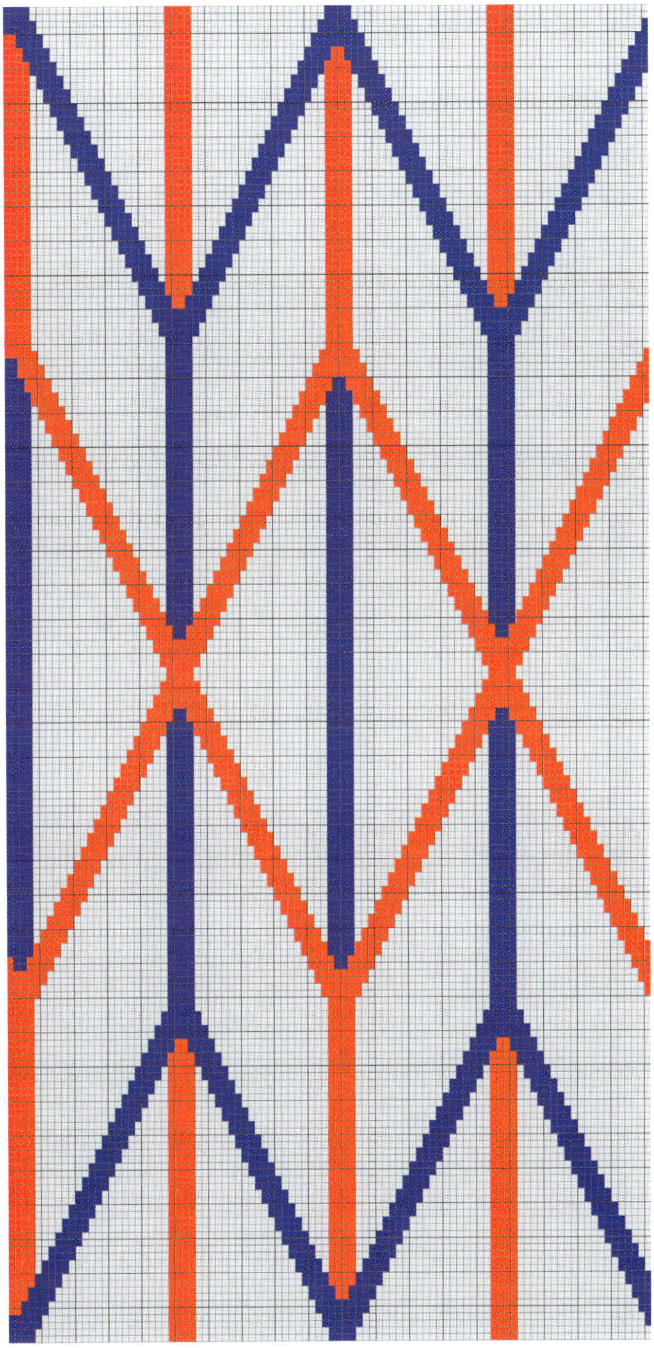

1 square = 1 stitch and 1 row

Stitches on the front bed

Stitches on the back bed

Double jersey

A very similar chart to the mirrored V-pleat fold but with the rows in between the V-pleats taken out.

The X-pleat when repeated creates a material that has a much more complicated fold structure than the typical herringbone fold, despite the folds being very similar. *Yarn: Two ends 2/60NE cotton plated with an elastomeric yarn.*

The versatility with the herringbone fold allows for simple and slight adjustments to alter the overall form and shape of the piece. I have designed and knitted a series of origami vases based on the herringbone pleat.

A close-up of one of the vases to show the inverse plating. Three yarn feeders were used to knit the inverse plating: one for the light green, one for the darker green and one for the thermoplastic. The thermoplastic feeder plated as a standard feeder compared to the other two feeders, which switched places throughout the pattern.

'The Flippables' collection, 2020. Herringbone-based vases were knitted on the Stoll ADF 14gg machine in cotton and thermoplastic Comfil yarn. The colour elements created through inverse plating meant that colour patterns could be incorporated on both the outside and the inside of the vases.

The V-Pleat on the Horizontal

Turning the V-pleat on its side can create more options to develop folding structures. Technically, there is no difference in structure between making the fold on the horizontal or the vertical apart from the direction of repeats that we might want to integrate.

Working the V-pleat on the vertical, as we have been doing, we are limited to the number of V-pleats that can be repeated on the horizontal due to the number of needles we have on the bed. However, we are not restricted to the number of repeats on the vertical.

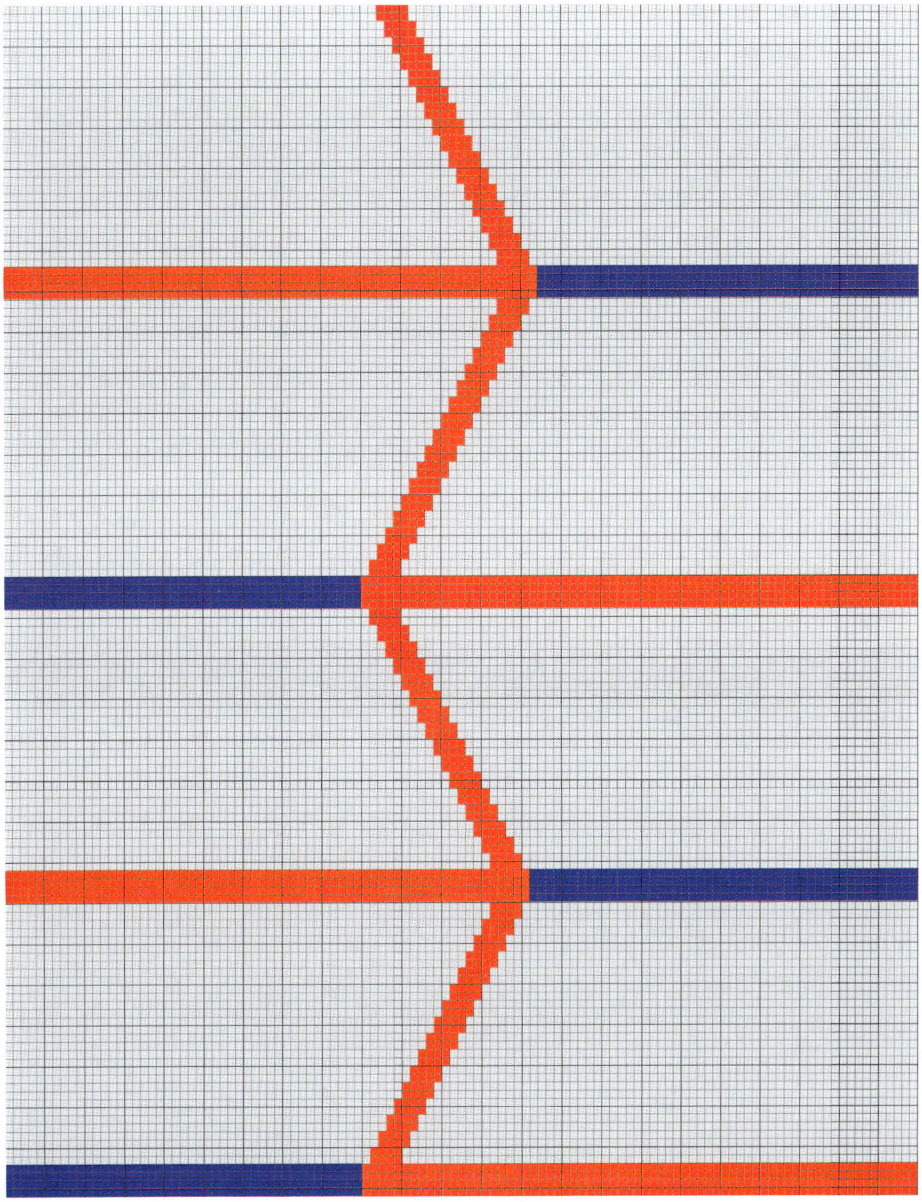

1 square = 1 stitch and 1 row

Stitches on the front bed

Stitches on the back bed

Double jersey

The V-pleat chart on the horizontal.

Repeating the folds into a longer form and joining the edges to create a folded vase. *Yarn: One end 2/28NM wool plated with an elastomeric yarn.*

The V-pleat, but knitted with its placement on the horizontal. We are able to then repeat the V-pleat as many times as needed. *Yarn: One end 2/28NM wool plated with an elastomeric yarn.*

This structure can very easily be used to create forms outside of the flat knit; for example, knitting a length that can then be joined, forming a tube. The folding properties give structure and additional form.

The scale of the V-pleat can also be an important element to consider. The areas outside the V can be reduced, effectively making the V the only fold within the sample. The example of this was knitted on a Stoll 12gg machine implementing a Jacquard, hence the two colours used.

On the other hand, the V-pleat can be elongated across almost the full width of the sample. This makes the pleat somewhat subtler in aesthetics.

Using the V-pleat across the width and knitting a relatively small piece, the knitted form can become playful and interactive.

This reversible piece was knitted as part of my master's degree research in 2019. Although knitted on a Stoll machine, the same fold placement would be easy to knit on a hand machine.

The elongated pleat, which becomes smaller in height but lengthened across almost the full width.

Additionally, a secondary pleat can be implemented to further the folding properties. In this instance the V-pleat is knitted on the opposite bed to bring an opposing fold into the structure. This will in turn bend the material back into the original direction.

Making a secondary V-pleat but on the opposite bed folds the pleat in the other direction. This adds further shape into the knitted length. The shapes that these combinations can create are endless and perfect for experimentation.

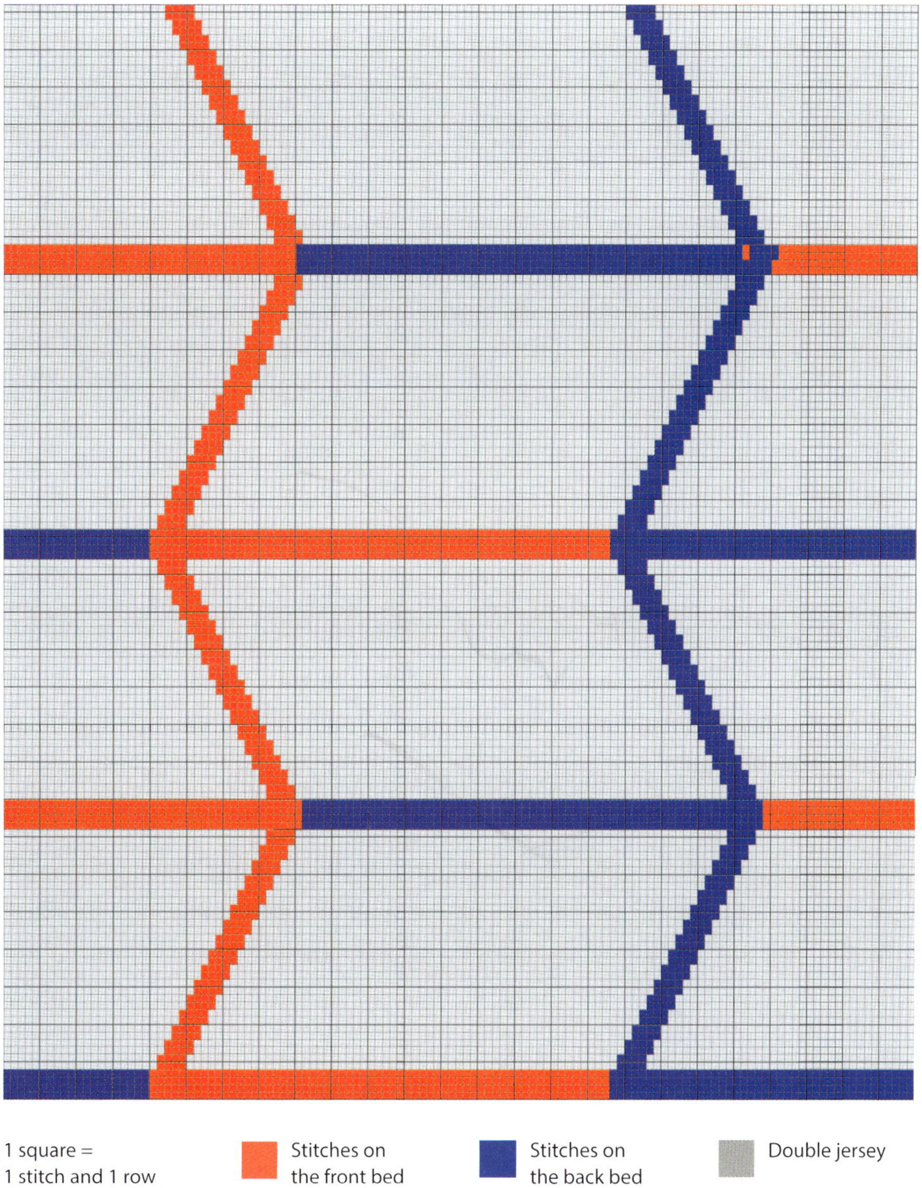

The fold skeleton with two V-pleats on different beds. The number of V-pleats across the bed is a little limited, but the length knitted is not, meaning that this process is perfect for building vessels and geometric forms.

COLOUR AND ORIGAMI FOLDS

Unfortunately, implementing colour into origami is tricky on domestic and Dubied machines as their colour and pattern functions are more suited to flat materials. Working a Jacquard into the folds is possible with a domestic machine but it would be advisable to use a 1×1 needle selection on the front bed. This is possible with Brother ribber carriages and some Knitmaster carriages, and also Passap machines. Where there are needles out of action for the folds, the yarns will float over them, but this will not affect the fold.

Implementing colour using a V-bed machine is even more limited, to horizontal stripes within the basic folding techniques. Otherwise, tucks with colour changes using the high and low butts could be a method to incorporate colour pattern into the material.

The colour elements in some of the samples in this chapter are due to inverse plating, whereby the two feeders used to knit and plate switch positions mid-row to reverse the colours. These samples were knitted on a Stoll ADF 14gg machine as part of my Master of Fine Arts course at the Swedish School of Textiles. This process is not possible on domestic or Dubied machines.

Other Folding Structures

To begin creating other tessellating and folding forms, we will continue with the X-pleat fold. This is a basis for the water-bomb tessellation. Generally, this fold is worked with adjacent chevron folds, plus vertical and horizontal folds building up a grid.

A simple starting place is to work an X-fold into the structure, then a horizontal fold across the whole working area at both the apex of the X and the base of the X. This will create a length that folds up into mini pyramid shapes. The size of this piece is determined by the number of needles that have been cast on. This is a basic single shape rather than a repeated fold over the entire working area. It is advisable to work over a smaller area to begin with and then scale up once you are comfortable.

All of the folds for this structure will be worked on the front bed despite it having both mountain and valley folds within the structure. This is a good example of the rules of folding that were covered earlier regarding the needle bed required and the direction of the fold. The X-fold needs to be a mountain fold, and as the angle is over 45 degrees it will be treated as a vertical fold, therefore all the stitches for the fold are transferred to the front bed. The horizontal folds are valley folds within the structure. The formation for horizontal folds is the opposite for vertical folds, meaning that a valley fold is also knitted on the front bed. This combination of valley folds on the horizontal yet mountain folds for the X-pleats means that all of the folds within this structure are made on the front bed.

A length of X-pleats worked one after the other creates a very moveable piece. *Yarn: Two ends 2/48NM merino wool plated with an elastomeric yarn.*

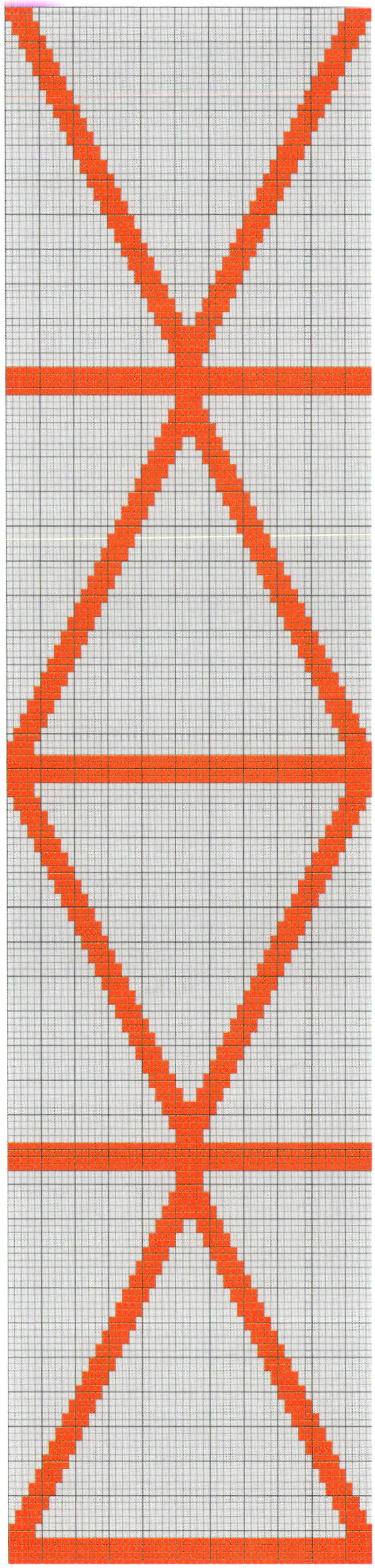

The chart for the length of the X-pleat piece. All folds are worked on the front bed despite having both mountain and valley folds implemented into the structure.

1 square = 1 stitch and 1 row

Stitches on the front bed

Stitches on the back bed

Double jersey

From this base, we can implement the X-fold further into a water-bomb tessellation. These structures will naturally have a more complicated fold skeleton to integrate, therefore make good charts of your knit structures and work from squared paper to remember your placement as you knit. Ensure that you work with the row counter and tick off each full section as you go. You will notice that once you get into the swing of the transfers and begin to understand the placement of the folds and the structure you are knitting, the process will become more intuitive and quicker to follow.

The front side of this fold pattern creates a tessellation of mountain X-folds that seem to interlock with each other. *Yarn: Two ends 2/48NM merino wool plated with an elastomeric yarn.*

The underside of the water-bomb tessellation showcases the fold skeleton more, with recesses instead of mountain folds.

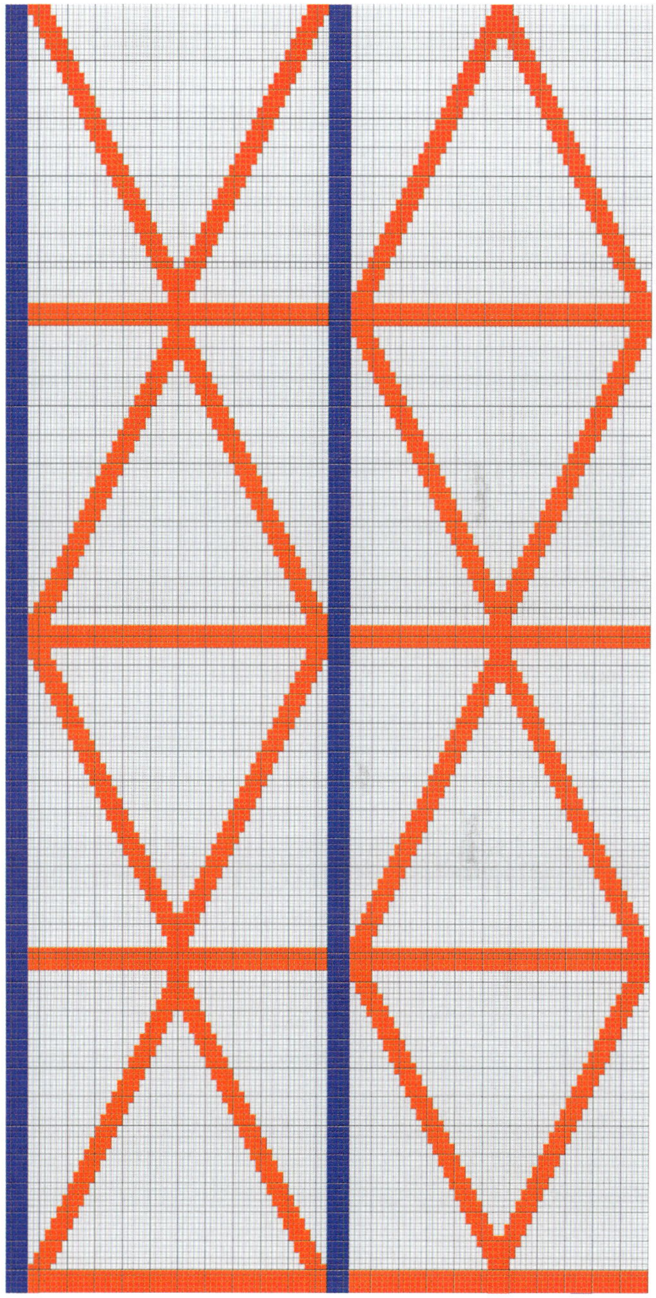

1 square = 1 stitch and 1 row

Stitches on the front bed

Stitches on the back bed

Double jersey

The previous X-fold is essentially repeated on the horizontal but with a vertical valley fold to space out the folds.

Like the original X-fold length, the majority of the folds are worked on the front bed. There are some vertical folds implemented on the back bed, however, these are stationary and once placed into the needle structure they do not move. On the whole, this will make the structure slightly easier to knit as you know that you are only moving needles on the front bed.

Each side of this fold is presented very differently and it is up to you, the knitter, to decide which is the side to show. I have decided to show the front side that has a tessellated pattern of interlocking mountain X-folds. The underside shows more the fold structure with the chevron folds accented by horizontal mountain folds. Both sides are linear and geometric, but the three-dimensional element is more effective on the front side with the mountain X-folds, compared to the underside which is flatter but has recesses that create the form.

The tessellation of the X-fold across the working area can build up to create a star effect with the fold. This pattern is most effective when we have calculated to make the plain sections square; however, if they are not, the fold is still made well. *Yarn: One end 2/36NM wool–cotton blend plated with an elastomeric yarn.*

The underside of the textile shows the fold structure, and where the plain squares are more visible.

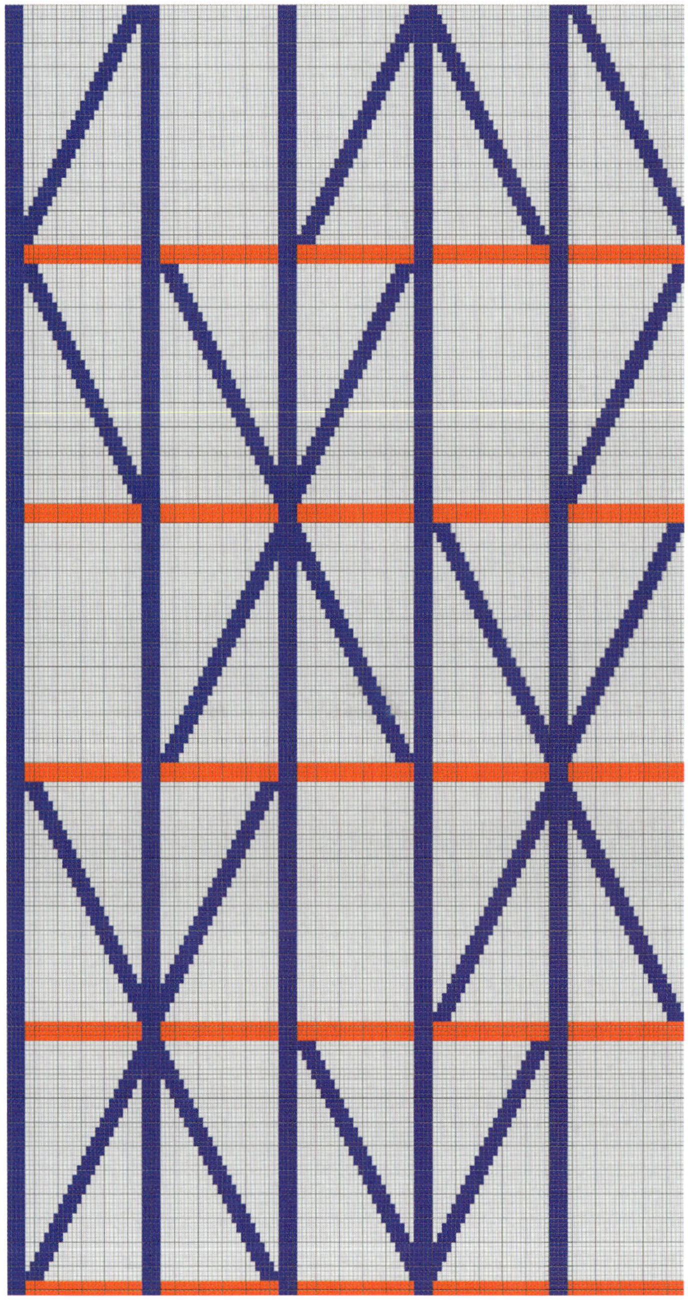

1 square = 1 stitch and 1 row

Stitches on the front bed | Stitches on the back bed | Double jersey

This is a much more complicated fold to follow as there is no simple repeat. Ensure you follow the chart slowly and mark off as you go.

There is a secondary water-bomb tessellation that is popular for origami makers due to the dimension that it can create. It is a squared base with X-pleats incorporated into the structure. Despite squares being a structural point of the pattern, the knitted material that is made with this fold does not have to replicate a square, therefore a tension piece and proper calculations do not need to be made first to ensure that the structure is successful. The diagonal fold has the same transfer rate as the previous herringbone folds: transferring one stitch every two rows on the diagonal.

Other folds to be worked into the knit could be simple folds from each side and corner of the basic rectangle or square. In these two samples, the folds alternate between mountain and valley, and join each corner to corner, and edge to edge: a very simple fold skeleton but one that is limited in terms of its development. The fold cannot be tessellated, and the material is also limited in the size it can be knitted up to. Despite all of this, these two forms are two of my favourites that I have developed using folds.

SCALING UP FOLDS

Once the basics of the folds have been knitted, it might be tempting to scale up the piece not only to increase the dimensions of the knit, but also to increase the size of the folds. On a domestic machine this would technically mean fewer transfers to work with, as the transfers are worked over a larger area. However, working at an increased scale may have negative impacts on the textile.

You will need to consider the weight of the material that is being made and how our friend gravity will have an impact. Even when working with a structural yarn core, such as a thermoplastic or a Lycra yarn to give density and support to the structure, the overall material may become too heavy for the supporting yarns to work their magic, and the folds and dimension may end up collapsing. There is a delicate balance between the crisp folds and the size that they can work with.

There is no rule to understand the support that the secondary yarn can give and the size that you can knit up to. My advice would be to test and trial if you are looking to knit larger shapes and sizes, but know that there will be a point when the weight is too much and gravity takes over.

Folds from each edge and each corner combine in the centre of the piece then enable it to fold up into a point. This is best worked when the sample is an exact square. Knitted on the Stoll ADF 14gg machine.

Similar to the previous sample, but integrating a couple of additional square folds which are parallel to the outer edge. Also knitted on the Stoll ADF 14gg machine.

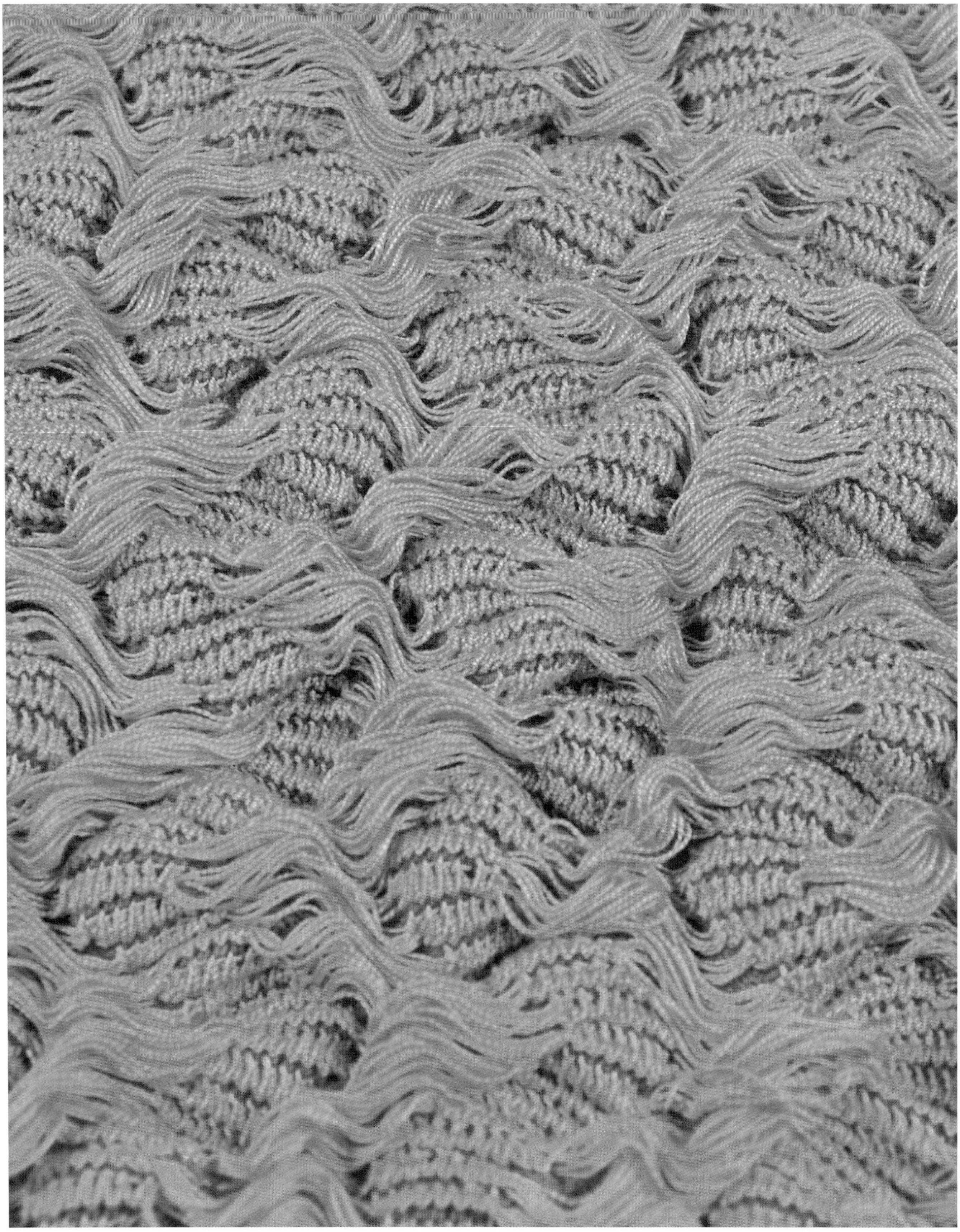

CHAPTER 5

TIPS AND TRICKS

This chapter is purely to give you some explanations, hints, tips and tricks not only to make your knitting easier, but also to problem-solve anything that may arise. Within this chapter we go through elements and methods that are included in many of the patterns to explain in more depth what they mean, the alterations you can make and how these could affect the knit.

PITCH AND HALF PITCH

Pitch and half pitch refer to the needle position when working with a double-bed machine, whether a domestic machine or a V-bed machine. Ribber attachments with domestic machines have a useful lever integrated into their racking system that allows you to rack into pitch from a half-pitch position. This important little lever means that the needles on either bed can either sit exactly opposite each other, or in a half-pitch position in which the needles are positioned in the spaces of the needles on the opposite bed.

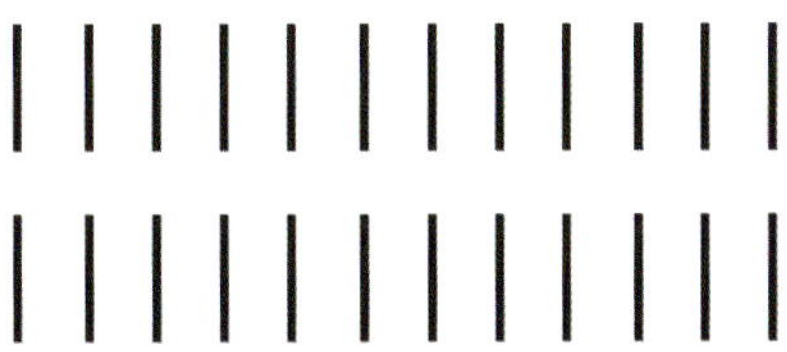

A diagram of needles in pitch position.

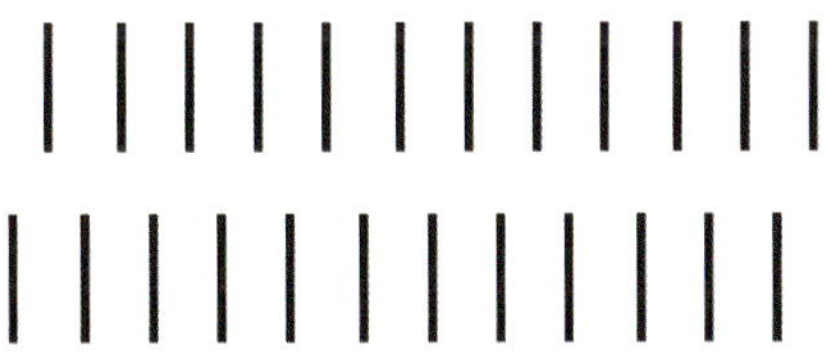

A diagram of needles in half-pitch position.

OPPOSITE: A ripple structure with floats.

The importance of this is in controlling whether the needles will clash or not when knitting (if working a double jersey) or whether the balance of stitches will sit evenly across a rib fabric. It is important to ensure that, if a double jersey is worked and needles interlock each other, the lever is placed into H or half pitch to ensure that the hooks of the needles do not get caught and tangled when the carriage is driven across.

If you are working a rib structure, or through Chapter 3: Transfers and Rib Structures, you can have the ribber attachment set in pitch position, as the needles will have their own space and will not be interlocking.

V-bed machines (such as Dubied, Universal, Stoll) are permanently set in half-pitch position. Therefore, all ribs will be made with needles in half-pitch position. If a structure that is not a rib structure is to be knitted on the V-bed with the half-pitch position, consideration may be needed for the needle placement.

The main difference, especially for ribs, regarding the pitch and half-pitch position, is that with pitch positions we can generally work with equal rib structures, such as a 2×2, 3×3, 4×4 or 16×16. There is an equal number of needles in work as there are out of work. This is because each needle will have its own space on either bed to move, as there is no needle in action directly opposite it.

Pitch position allows us to make even rib structures, with the same number of needles out of action as there are in action. In this example, four needles are working and four needles are out of work across both beds.

Working in the half pitch position, we can begin to work slightly different rib structures that are uneven. For example, a 2×1, 3×2, 4×3 or 16×15. This is due to needles each having their own space to work in, meaning that we don't need to be concerned about needle hooks becoming tangled.

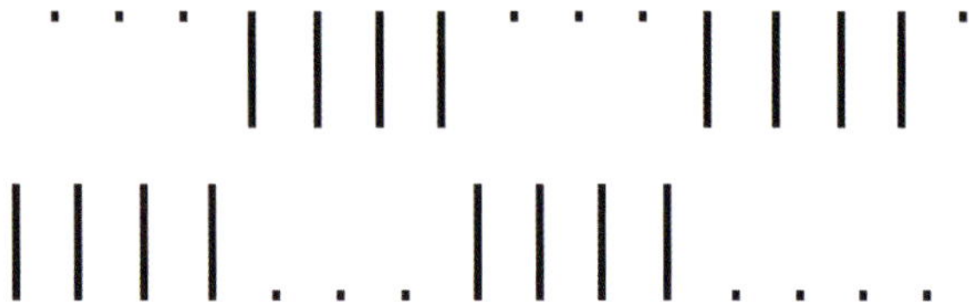

An uneven rib structure is made by using half-pitch position. In this example there are four working needles and three needles out of work across the two beds.

Step 3: Needles are racked two places into position and knitting can continue

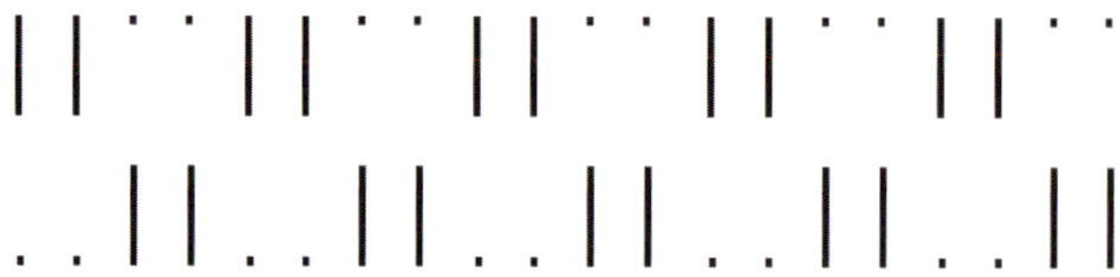

Step 2: Ribber attachment moved into pitch position (ribber shifts slightly to the left)

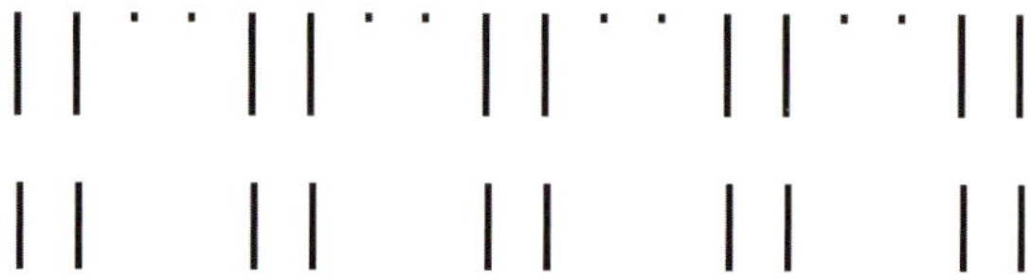

Step 1: The 2x2 rib needle set up is the position for the set up row and circular rows

The process for casting on and setting a rib structure.

CASTING ON WITH RIBS

Ribs are cast on out of the desired rib structure and with needles in an interlocking position. We are unable to cast on in the rib structure as we need interlocking needles to create stitches. In a 2×2 rib structure, there are two needles working and directly opposite them are two needles out of action. We are unable to create stitches over two empty adjacent needles, therefore the needles have to be interlocking for at least that first row and then the needles can be racked into place.

If we are working a rib structure that is greater than a 2×2, it is suggested to cast on the desired width with all needles (double jersey) and to then transfer the needles into the rib position after the two circular rows.

Additionally, you must cast on in the half-pitch position. Before racking, place the ribber attachment into the pitch position, and then rack into position. For my ribber, it will rack the needles half a position to the left, meaning that in order to get my needles into position based on the diagram, I will need to rack twice. Always double-check your needle placement before and after putting the ribber into pitch position.

V-bed machines will always stay in the half-pitch position, therefore this additional step of placing the bed into pitch position will not occur. Only rack to get the needles into the rib position.

Drawthread Cast-On

Casting onto the machine with a waste yarn is often recommended to ensure that the needles are all behaving and working, but to also create a tighter cast-on edge. Casting on the double bed can often result in a loose first row due to working needles on both beds.

1. To achieve the drawthread cast-on, bring all needles to be worked into the working position and cast on as you usually would, but using a waste yarn. This waste yarn is a yarn that will be discarded at the end so use something that is not precious to you, but it must be relatively strong and in the same weight yarn or lighter. I tend to use acrylic.
2. If you are racking to create the rib (2×1, 2×2 rib structures) you do not need to rack into position. You can leave the needle placement in the original cast-on position.
3. Once you have knitted a few rows to ensure all needles have cast on, disengage the front bed and knit three rows on the back bed only.
4. Re-engage the front bed and knit one full row with double jersey.

5. Now, remove the yarn from the carriage, or disengage the yarn feeder, and turn off the front bed. We will take the carriage across, intentionally dropping all the front-bed stitches. The rear-bed stitches will remain on the needles.
6. Once all the stitches are dropped, we will have elongated stitches as our last row. This is thanks to the three rows on the back bed that we knitted earlier on. These elongated stitches will make it easier to remove the waste yarn once the knit is off the machine.
7. Take the carriage back across to the original starting side to pick up the yarn feeder or insert the main yarn.
8. Now cast on with the main yarn to create that tight cast-on edge. It is recommended to drop the stitch size for the first row and the following circular rows. Domestic machines can go down to To, and V-bed machines a couple of points down.

Single-Bed Cast-On

If, like mine, your comb wires are often discarded around the studio in the excitement of taking a project off the machine, and are not immediately placed back in the comb, it is inevitable that a kink will appear which makes threading the comb a near impossibility, taking almost as long as the knitting itself. Thankfully, there is a solution. We can do a single-bed cast-on.

This is possible with both domestic machines and V-bed machines, and is currently my favoured cast-on method. Not because my wires have a large number of kinks in them, but more for time-saving. Casting on is my least favourite part of a knit, so if I can get it out of the way I have a clearer mind to focus on the structure I am making.

1. For the single-bed cast-on, turn off the front bed on the carriage completely. It is also possible to drop the front bed down to cast on if you prefer.
2. With the threaded comb, hold it against the needles on the rear bed so the wire is above the needles and each needle can easily pass through the gaps of the comb. With the carriage threaded up and at a large stitch size (approximately T8 on domestic machines, T17 and higher on V-bed machines), slowly take it across. The needles should move out between the gaps of the comb, pick up the yarn and take it back through the gaps of the comb. This means that, after that first row, the comb is caught by the stitches and can be dropped to its usual position and the weights added.
3. Knit a couple more rows with only the back bed, to even out the tension and move the comb out of the way of the stitches.
4. We can next bring into action the front bed and reduce the stitch size. Working a few rows of both beds (the front-bed needles will automatically pick up and make stitches over 2 rows) we are then making a full fabric.
5. Next work the drawthread cast-on as described above, after the steps of the initial cast-on with waste yarn.

PLATING

Plating with knit is the process of using two differently coloured yarns to knit at the same time. A plating feeder is needed in which the two yarns are placed in different positions: an A yarn and a B yarn. The A yarn is typically the main yarn and used for casting on and casting off. This yarn can be seen on the front-facing stitches of each of the samples. The B yarn sits behind the A yarn when being fed into the needles, therefore it is seen as the rear-facing stitches, or the purl stitches.

Stitch size when plating should be considered, as there will be twice as much yarn being fed into the needles than without plating, therefore ensure that you increase the stitch size accordingly. It is also suggested to cast on without the plating yarn if you are after a tight cast-on. Casting on with the plating yarn can cause issues including burst stitches and damaged needles if the stitch size is not altered considerably.

It is advisable to have the same needle placement at either end of the working area to help the plating yarn get into position at the back. For example if you have a front-bed needle working as the end needle on the left-hand side of the working area, generally you should also then have a front-bed needle working as the end needle on the right-hand side of the working area.

It can also help to have a needle or two working on the opposite bed on each edge if you have a large number of needles on either bed on each side. This should help the yarns to get into the correct position on the first stitch.

An example of having needles on the same bed on either side of the sample to help the plating yarn to get into the correct position behind the main yarn.

An example of a large area of needles on one bed and the edge stitches on the opposite bed. This can also help the plating yarn stay in the correct position in the stitch.

Exploring plating as a technique in itself, there are several ways that colour can be experimented with when working with the plating feeder. I have included the four basic methods below.

DOUBLE BED AND CHANGING COLOUR

To change colour with the double bed, using a V-bed you will often have two or more feeders that allow you to change colour quickly and easily. Working with a four-feeder machine, you can thread up four different colours and use them when desired. As long as an even number of rows has been knitted and all feeders are on the same side, select the feeder with the colour you want and work with that.

Similarly with a domestic machine, you can work with a colour changer on the left-hand side of the machine to change up to four colours. If you do not have a colour changer, it becomes a little more time-consuming as you will need to reinsert the yarn between the double bed with each change, but with perseverance it will work.

If an odd number of rows is to be knitted and to include a change of colour, this can be done by turning off all the cams on the carriage for both the front and the back bed and taking an empty course across the needles – a row with no yarn. Turning off the cams will ensure that no needles are selected when the carriage is driven over the needles, ensuring that no needles are dropped in the process.

Striping by changing the plating yarn every ten rows means that the front-facing stitch will stay the same colour throughout the knit, but the rear-facing stitch will change colour. When the material is relaxed, the main colour seen will be the front-facing stitch and the material will be one colour.

Striping with the main colour yet keeping the plating yarn the same throughout will create the opposite effect as before. The front-facing knit stitches will have a striped effect yet, once opened up, the plating effect will reveal one colour on the inside stitches.

Combining the last two methods, we can change both the plating and the main yarn at regular intervals. This in itself creates a striped effect on both the front-facing and rear-facing stitches. Whilst it can be a little chaotic, the colour play and the pattern it creates can make for some really sophisticated materials.

Lastly, a development from the last sample: we don't have to change the colour simultaneously, but can change the main yarn and the plating yarn at different intervals. This gives even more colour play and colour pairings. Within this sample, one yarn was changed every six rows to create blocks of twelve rows.

Working with V-bed machines, simply then pick up the yarn feeder (assuming there is a yarn feeder on the side you have taken the carriage across to) and continue knitting. If there is no yarn feeder, you will need to either take the feeder across or reinsert the yarn. Ensure the cams for the carriage are off so that no knitting will take place as you take the feeder across. You will notice that the yarn is now sitting on top of the stitches. If you take the carriage across to knit with this long float over the top, you will risk that yarn getting caught up. Therefore ensure that you hold the yarn down directly below the working needles or, better yet, break the yarn and reattach it to the new side that the carriage is on. Then continue knitting.

DRAWING UP YOUR OWN CHART

Before any knit design is worked on the machine, I tend to work all patterns out on squared paper or graph paper. This is not only to test the pattern, but also to work out the dimensions of the needles I need to cast on and work.

Each square on the paper might not necessarily represent one stitch, due to the size of the paper or the design, therefore always note the scale of each square along with actual notes of the stitches and rows within the sketched design.

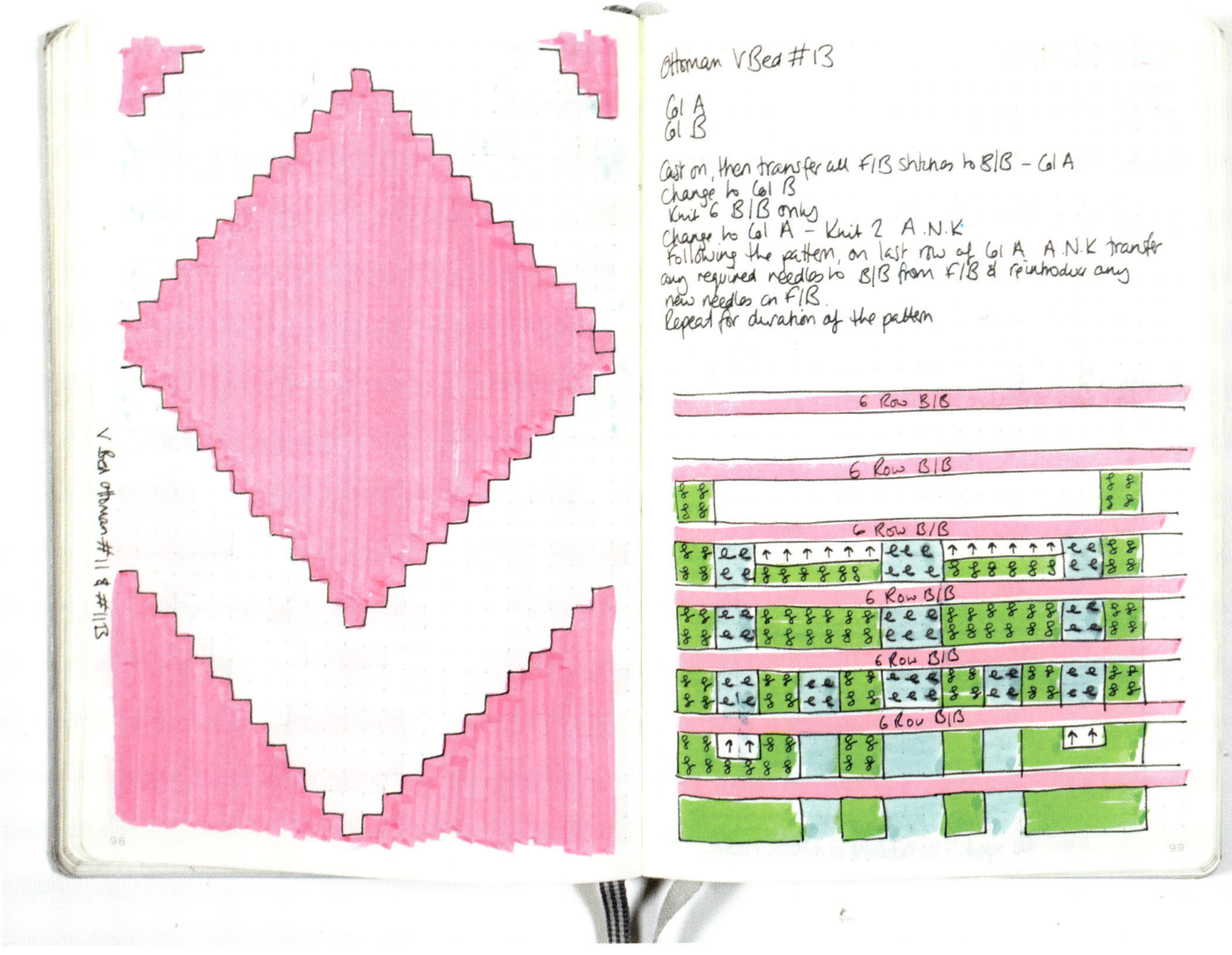

My notebook not only works as a place to write down techniques but also, as it has dotted-grid pages, I can draw up patterns to implement into the knit.

AFTERWORD

I really hope you have enjoyed discovering the endless possibilities of incorporating form and structure into your knits as much as I did whilst writing this book. Having been machine knitting since 2009, I sometimes feel that I have exhausted most techniques. However, writing this book allowed me to have a deep dive into areas and fall back in love with the domestic machine, and also to become humbled knowing that there really is an infinite number of techniques and methods to explore.

I truly hope that this book inspires you to do your own deep dive into a specific technique and to experiment to create weird yet wonderful knit samples and pieces. I have given away my secrets and knowledge from my specialist area, and hope this knowledge is used wisely. This book is only the start of the techniques and methods that can be incorporated into your knit, and should be used as a basis to delve further.

All samples within this book have been made from either deadstock yarn or donated yarn. The deadstock yarn has been from my own catalogue from previous projects and has been left over for many years. The donated yarn has come from The University of Central Lancashire, after it cleared out its vast yarn store. The only yarn purchased specifically for the project has been the elastomeric yarn used in Chapter 4: Pleats and Folds, to help create the density of the material.

OPPOSITE: Repeating herringbone folds in two different colours which have been placed in a staggered position to create an interesting material.

GLOSSARY

Count: A term used for the weight of the yarn.

Course: Industry term for a row of knit.

Decreasing: Making the knitting area smaller in width.

DesignaKnit: Software for designing knit patterns using electronic domestic machines.

Double jersey: Knitted material using all needles on both beds of the machine. Sometimes referred to as full rib.

Even rib structure: A rib structure with an equal number of needles working and out of action across both beds, such as 2×2 or 3×3.

Fine gauge: A machine with more needles to the inch (roughly 2.5cm) than a standard gauge. Fine gauge for a domestic machine is 7; for V-bed machines it is up to 14.

Fold skeleton: The fold pattern that is, or will be, implemented into the knit.

Forward working position (FWP): D Position on Silver Reed machines; E position on Brother machines.

Front-facing stitches: The knit side of the stitches on a single-jersey material.

Gauge: The number of needles per inch (roughly 2.5cm) on a machine. Abbreviated to 'gg'.

Half gauge: Knitting on every other needle.

Half pitch: A position of the ribber attachment on the domestic machine that places the needles in an interlocking position so they are not directly opposite each other.

Hold: Holding needles so they do not knit.

i-Plating: A technique used on industrial machines to switch the main and plating feeders within the knitted sample. This allows the user to create reversible colour patterns on single jersey with plating as the main colour method. Also called 'inverse plating'.

Increasing: Making the knit area larger in width.

Intarsia: A colourwork technique, normally worked with a block pattern.

Lifted stitches: The process of lifting an already-knitted stitch back up onto the needle bed.

Odd rib structure: A rib structure with a different number of needles working on either bed and out of action. Often 2×1 or 3×2.

Ottoman: A technique that builds up rolls and ripples.

Partial knit: Short rows, holding.

Pitch: A position of the ribber attachment on the domestic machine that places the needles directly opposite each other.

Plating: The process of using two colours together to create a colour effect, especially when working a needle placement on a double bed.

Ply: How many ends of yarn have been stranded together to create the weight of the yarn.

Punch card: A manual card device that allows you to incorporate pattern and texture into the knit on a domestic knitting machine.

Racking: The movement of a bed to shift the needle position when working on a double-bed machine.

Rear-facing stitches: The purl side of the material over a single jersey.

Ribber: A secondary bed that can be attached to a main bed on a domestic knitting machine.

Ripple: A technique to create a horizontal tube of knit.

ABBREVIATIONS AND SYMBOLS

Glossary contd

Roll: A technique to create a horizontal tube of knit.

Single jersey: Knitted material made using one bed of the machine.

Standard gauge: A mid-gauge machine. The most common gauge.

Take-down: The weight on the knit and the amount that the material is held downwards away from the needles.

Transfer: Moving stitches between needles or beds.

Upper working position (UWP): C Position on Silver Reed machines; D on Brother machines.

V-pleat: A pleat structure when working with folds and origami, which resembles a 'V'.

Working position (WP): B position on both Silver Reed and Brother machines.

Wrap: Wrapping the end needle with yarn when working with partial knit.

X-pleat: A pleat structure when working with folds and origami, which resembles an 'X'.

ABBREVIATIONS

COL: Carriage on the left

COR: Carriage on the right

LHS: Left-hand side

RHS: Right-hand side

FWP: Forward working position

UWP: Upper working position

WP: Working position

SYMBOLS

Needles out of action

Needles in action

→ Carriage moves to the right

← Carriage moves to the left

Carriage moves to the right / finishes on the right

Carriage moves to the left / finishes on the left

[ ] Brackets to show a repeat

Wrap the end needle on the right

Wrap the end needle on the left

Double jersey stitches

Front bed stitches

Back bed stitches

Transfer to the back bed

Transfer to the front bed

Transfer from a specific needle to the right of the opposite bed

Transfer from a specific needle to the left of the opposite bed

Transfer from a specific needle to the left of the same bed

Transfer from a specific needle to the right of the same bed

Left leaning 1×1 cable made on the back bed

Right leaning 1×1 cable made on the back bed

Left leaning 2×2 cable

YARN SUPPLIERS

Coatyarn
Thermoplastic yarn.
www.coatyarn.com/en

Comfil
Thermosetting yarns but large minimum orders.
www.comfil.biz

Copley, Marshall & Co.
Cotton yarns for fine gauges and heavier gauges.
www.copleymarshall.co.uk

Elton Vale
Fine-gauge cotton yarns, but can be plied.
www.eltonvaleyarns.co.uk

Fairfield Yarns
Deadstock yarns. Online but mainly in store in Heywood, Lancaster.
www.fairfieldyarns.co.uk

Jamieson's Of Shetland
Shetland wool for heavier gauges and hand knitting.
www.jamiesonsofshetland.co.uk

J C Rennie & co.
Wool yarns for machine and hand knitting, including greasy coned yarn.
www.knitrennie.com

The Yarn Store by Robert Todd
For natural cottons, cashmere blends and Cashwool merino.
www.theyarnstore.co.uk

Todd & Duncan
Cashmere and wool yarns for both fine gauge and heavier gauges.
www.todd-duncan.co.uk

Uppingham Yarns
Good for natural and synthetic yarn. Has shrinking thermosetting yarns.
www.wools.co.uk

Yeoman Yarns
Good for natural and synthetic yarns, elastomeric and Lycra yarns.
www.yeoman-yarns.co.uk

INDEX

First published in 2025 by
The Crowood Press Ltd
Ramsbury, Marlborough
Wiltshire SN8 2HR

enquiries@crowood.com
www.crowood.com

British Library Cataloguing-in-Publication Data
A catalogue record for this book is available from the British Library.

For product safety-related questions, contact:
productsafety@crowood.com

ISBN 978 0 7198 4547 5

The right of Victoria Salmon to be identified as author of this work has been asserted by her in accordance with the Copyright, Designs and Patents Act 1988.

Page 2: a close-up of the structure explored on page 103.

Page 4: a structure using transfers with smaller sections of double jersey creates an undulating and playful structure. The material has been plated for colour detail.

Page 190: different yarns can felt at different rates which then allow for further texture and form to be incorporated as a post knit process. These lifted stitches were knitted in a treated sport wool compared to the background which felted more as a standard wool.

Typeset by Emilia Kalyvides
Cover design by Sergey Tsvetkov
Printed and bound in India by Parksons Graphics Pvt Ltd

Acknowledgements

It is nearly impossible to put into words the thanks that are owed in relation to this book. I must start by giving my thanks to Manchester Metropolitan University for allowing me endless access to the Dubied machines on my days off over the summer and during teaching breaks. To all the students that I meet, teach and have taught, you give me endless inspiration and make me challenge my knowledge of knit to the extreme. You make me question and experiment, and this is something that keeps me fascinated and motivated.

To everyone who has given support along the way, whether words of encouragement, words of support or an ear that listened when this process consumed my whole mental capacity. There are far too many of you to mention individually, but please know that you all helped the project to become more achievable, and that your validation spurred me on during the times of doubt, imposter syndrome and overall exhaustion.

A huge thank you to my mum, who proofread, corrected all the grammatical mistakes and highlighted all the unfinished sentences. Thanks to you, the readers...!

To Lara, without whom half of the diagrams would not make sense. You became my go-to person when I needed to make sure that my instructions made sense, that a chart was correct, or just replying to a text about a sample or idea. You really helped me more than you even know.

The biggest thanks to Gilly for putting up with me taking over the living-room floor and also turning the flat into a full-on photo studio. For providing me with sustenance, keeping me fed and watered and for generally putting up with me throughout the whole process. You say 'Never again', but never say never!

And finally, I cannot forget the Useless Studio Assistant. For demanding long walks in the fresh air, insisting on time away from the screen to play and for being that companion who stayed nearby whilst the day turned into night. Yes, you did steal and try to chew a good few of the samples, but your continuous affection during the last couple of months of writing certainly made the process more enjoyable. You're not so useless after all.

The author:
www.anotherknittedthing.com
@anotherknittedthing

OTHER MACHINE KNITTING TITLES FROM CROWOOD

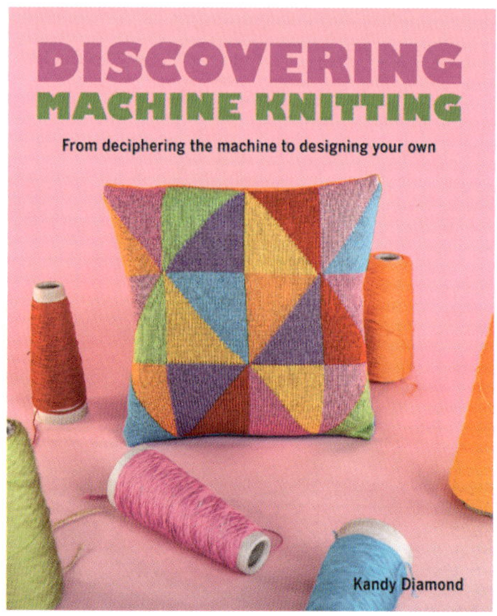